# ON THE HO CHI MINH TRAIL

## BY THE SAME AUTHOR

Trần Trung Tín
Paintings and Poems from Vietnam
(Asia Ink, 2002)

Vietnam Zippos
American Soldiers' Engravings and Stories 1965–1973
(Chicago, 2007)

Mekong Diaries
Việt Cộng Drawings & Stories 1964–1975
(Chicago, 2008)

Vietnam Posters
Collection of David Heather
(Prestel, 2009)

SHERRY BUCHANAN

# ON THE HO CHI MINH TRAIL

*The Blood Road,*
*The Women Who Defended It,*
*The Legacy.*

ASIA INK, London

Published by Asia Ink
1 Alma Terrace
London W8 6QY
sales@asiainkbooks.com
www.asiainkbooks.com

Distributed by the University of Chicago Press
https://press.uchicago.edu/ucp/books/book/
distributed/O/bo68375353.html

First published 2021



Design: Asia Ink
Copy editor: Carenza Parker
Proofreader: Helen Cumberbatch
Maps: Peter Bull Art Studio
Production: Nicola Denny

A catalogue record for this book is available from the British Library.

ISBN-13: 978-1-9163463-0-7 (cloth)
ISBN-13: 978-1-9163463-1-4 (e-book)

Printed in Italy by Graphicom.

*Cover Image:* Dramatic landscape with lonely fisherman and
tree reflection on the fog lake. Dalat, Lâm Đồng, Vietnam.
Photo monochrome version by Khanh Bui.

*to William*

Phan Hoài Phi, *On the Ho Chi Minh Trail,* oil on canvas, 1995.

*Opposite*: On the Trail through southern Laos.
*Overleaf:* On the Trail through the north of Vietnam.

Nguyễn Văn Trúc, *Carrying Ammunition*, watercolor, 1971.

# *PREFACE*

The Ho Chi Minh Trail lives on as an epic military road, one of the great logistical achievements of the twentieth century. It began as a web of paths through the Trường Sơn Mountains, which form the border between Vietnam and Laos. Its purpose was to support the communist insurgency in South Vietnam—the National Liberation Front (NLF) or Việt Cộng to the United States and South Vietnam—and bring about the reunification of North and South Vietnam, after the general elections promised by the 1954 Geneva Accords at the end of the First Indochina War or French War (1946–1954) did not happen.

When the United States bombed North Vietnam in 1965, the Trail expanded to support the North Vietnamese People's Army's general offensives against South Vietnam. By the end of the Vietnam or American War (1965–1975), the Trail was a 10,000-mile-long network of mountainous paths, tracks, paved roads, bridges, waterways, lakes, and pipelines, built by the People's Army's Engineer Corps, Group 559, that later became the Trail High Command.

The Trail was a living organism—messy, moving, always shifting, in places invisible beneath a canopy of dense forest. It was not one passage but many, destroyed and refashioned in response to the sheer tonnage of explosives dropped on it by US and South Vietnamese forces. It was the single most important strategic target in stemming the flow of military supplies and armor from Hanoi to the south. It needed to be disabled if the United States was to win. And the US Air Force, Marines, and Navy dedicated enormous resources in their attempts to destroy it.

The Vietnamese call the Trail the Trường Sơn Road. Trường Sơn is the Vietnamese name of the Annamite mountain range that marks the border between Vietnam and Laos. To the Vietnamese, the road is a symbol of tenacity. Following each attack, it grew more complex, shifting west, crossing the border into Laos and Cambodia.

What is only beginning to be understood in the West is that many who enlisted and were drafted to build and defend the Trail were women and teenage girls. They overcame intractable monsoon rains, forbidding jungle terrain, and a ferocious air war deployed by the US Air Force, the US Seventh Fleet, and the South Vietnamese Air Force, to build and defend the logistical backbone that allowed North Vietnam to prevail.

During the war the Ho Chi Minh Trail achieved legendary status. I had seen it on the television evening news, filmed from the open hatch of a B-52, the sounds of rock 'n' roll coming from the cockpit. "Millions of men and women" had marched along the Trail roads, "one million tons of weapons transported." The news featured broadcasts from the "front" by rugged male correspondents clothed in battle fatigues. Night after night they delivered vivid accounts of skirmishes, deadly bombings, and US progress in overcoming the pernicious Việt Cộng and North Vietnamese, deemed to be carriers of a virulent strain of communism that threatened the liberty of our allies in Southeast Asia. There was urgency to the bombings. If Southeast Asia fell, who knew what would happen next?

Vietnam was a country few Americans were aware of or had visited. In the sixties there were not many US citizens of Vietnamese descent. That has changed of course; still, despite our deep involvement in Vietnam in the sixties and seventies, the place seems far away. So much of what Americans learned during the war came from small flickering images on television screens like the one my friends and I watched at Smith College. The battles, the explosions, the pyrotechnics of huts ablaze, and bodies singed by napalm: my fellow students and I looked on with horror.

The images grew worse: the Mỹ Lai Massacre became public knowledge in November 1969. We consumed pictures of the unspeakable slaughter of civilian women, children, and the elderly in that village. *Time*, *Look*, *Life*, and *Newsweek* magazines all published full-color photos of the women before they were killed by US troops.

What about women in the war? If one appeared on the evening news, she was almost always an American nurse, or a prostitute in Saigon, or a helpless victim like the inhabitants of Mỹ Lai, or the girl Phan Thị Kim Phúc running naked down a road, her back burning with napalm in an award-winning photograph by Nick Ut. Such images did nothing to inflect the mass message that the Vietnam conflict was primarily a man's war, pumped-up, vulgar, a telegenic dystopia accompanied by raucous rock 'n' roll, and peopled by disaffected American GIs and robotic Asian snipers lurking along the Trail who popped up from holes in the ground to do their worst.

US popular culture hasn't done much to balance that view. The withdrawal of US forces from the country in 1975 was followed by a spate of macho epics like *Apocalypse Now* that depicted the disintegration of moral feeling by American troops while, nearby, shadows in the forest signaled the lethal presence of enemy "gooks." How many Oscars were bestowed upon these cultural products? (*Full Metal Jacket*, directed by Stanley Kubrick, did feature, in a short but essential scene, the character of a female sniper, presented as both a menace and a victim, who begs the US GIs who have wounded her to kill her and put her out of her misery.)

What was rarely shown or discussed was how critical women were to the North's efforts. Beyond fulfilling women's usual roles in wartime as nurses and functionaries, female volunteers were singularly responsible for building and defending the Trail roads, bridges, and junctions while men fought on the southern battlefronts. To repeat, the Trail was a key strategic target for the United States. Destroy the Trail and you cut off the lifeblood of the North's military. As a consequence, casualties from the US bombing along the Trail included a high concentration of women and girls.

It would be reasonable to ask, why did I decide to explore the Ho Chi Minh Trail in the winter of 2014, forty years after the fighting had ceased? What did I hope to achieve? Several things: as a student who had followed the war at a distance, I felt a measure of responsibility for our actions. No—I didn't support the war. Like millions of Americans during the conflict, I came to feel it was hopeless and cruel. At the same time, the destructive tentacles of another war had profoundly affected me. My father was a Marine in the Korean War (1950–1953). When he came back with post-traumatic stress, my mother divorced him. I grew up without ever knowing him. As I got older, I couldn't shake the injustices of war within and without.

As a college student in the seventies, I had been convinced by the British philosopher Bertrand Russell's *War Crimes in Vietnam*, and by *The Winter Soldier Investigation: An Inquiry into American War Crimes* edited by the Vietnam Veterans Against the War and published by Beacon Press in 1972, that the killing of the majority of civilians was a consequence of US rules of engagement, not the actions of rogue soldiers. This was brought home to me years later when I was a journalist with the *International Herald Tribune*. Starting in 1991, I made a number of trips to Vietnam. While there in 1995, the Vietnamese government published its first estimate of war dead since the end of the war: 3.1 million. The estimates were shocking: two million civilians had lost their lives across the North and the South. Dismissed as communist propaganda, few in the US political establishment or media paid attention. Even if civilian casualties were half that, even if civilian casualties in North Vietnam were "only" the 30,000 in collateral damage that the US government admits to, I felt that the scale of the tragedy for the Vietnamese, and the US responsibility for its part, was and remains largely ignored.

The after-effects of the war could be seen everywhere: in the poverty, in the people's fear and mistrust, in the legacy of unexploded bombs and toxic chemicals, in the scores of memorials to the war dead, and in the presence of US veterans who had returned to face their own personal histories as combatants.

While visiting Vietnam, I saw artworks made by the North Vietnamese during the conflict that had torn the country apart between 1964 and 1975. There was something about these images that offered glimpses of redemption for the cruel war I had watched unfold on the nightly CBS News in a senior's dorm room at Smith over take-out pizza and Dunkin' Donuts.

Thousands of films and television series, tens of thousands of books and memoirs by American historians, journalists, photographers, and veterans, as well as accounts by the South Vietnamese diaspora, our allies, had illustrated and chronicled the Vietnam War and its legacy from our perspective. In contrast, little had been published in English from North Vietnamese historians, journalists, artists, and veterans—women and men—and few accounts that reflected independent or dissenting voices.

I shared my discoveries in *Trần Trung Tín: Paintings and Poems from Vietnam*, published in 2002, and *Mekong Diaries: Việt Cộng Drawings & Stories 1964–1975*, published in 2008.

Trần Trung Tín (1933–2008), a veteran of the French War, was painting the suffering of women, children, and men at a time when official war propaganda censored it.

While Tín portrayed inner states of being, the war artists showcased in *Mekong Diaries* developed an in-depth archive of life along the Trail. Employed in war propaganda, they were part of the cultural troops "embedded" with the North Vietnamese People's Army that included writers, poets, journalists, musicians, and photographers. Some of the artists were soldiers, others civilians. The activities they portrayed were mostly common to soldiers on both sides—the US Army had a similar artist program in 1965—as they tried to hold on to normal life: a soldier writing a letter home, musicians playing a violin duet for the fighters (their version of Raquel Welch entertaining the troops), friends smoking cigarettes in an underground bunker before the siege of the US Marine Combat Base at Khe Sanh, and scores of portraits of soldiers.

Fighters sent the portraits home to be displayed on the family altar if they were killed.

What struck me was that so many of these wartime paintings were populated by figures of women. Trần Trung Tín painted portraits of scarred women, of women nude, carrying a gun, holding a flower or a small bird, of mothers, symbol of life, drafted to kill, and of women, Buddhist or Catholic, praying to absent gods.

The official artists sent down the Trail recorded life behind the lines. Women transporting ammunition. Women digging tunnels. Women aiming weapons about to kill their mark. The more images I saw, the more women were revealed. I found them in photographs, too, tucked away in the archives. The teenagers in those snapshots would have been about the same age I was during the war. But while I was ambling around campus with an armload of textbooks, they were lifting hundred-pound bags of rice onto their shoulders and carrying the load miles down the Trail to feed soldiers in camp.

I wanted to meet these women face-to-face. I wanted them to step out of these images and speak to me as embodied selves. I wanted to hear how they had been actors during the war rather than victims. I was appalled that so little had been written about them. An important exception was the book *Even the Women Must Fight: Memories of War from North Vietnam*, a scholarly treatment by Karen Gottschang Turner with Phan Thanh Hao, published by John Wiley and Sons in 1998.

I learned that women ran the logistics. Women built the roads, the tunnels. They tended camp, they nursed the wounded, and they defended North Vietnam's territory against American bombings. Sixty thousand Youth Volunteers—many were women—between the ages of 17 and 24 defended the mountainous Trail; 1.7 million women who were married with children, and who had enlisted in or were drafted into the Three Responsibilities Campaign, defended the coastal Trail and the home front, while the men fought on the southern battlefronts.

In South Vietnam at the end of the Trail, the "Long-Haired Army" took up arms in the early sixties to defend their homes and villages against South Vietnamese government attacks, and later against US and South Vietnamese ground forces and bombings. The all-female militia was led by Nguyễn Thị Định (1920–1992), the first female general of the People's Army and an NLF deputy commander.

After the war, women veterans were at the forefront of the efforts to rebuild the country and to fight for the social justice they went into battle for.

I came to realize that it wasn't just the other side of the war I sought; it was another side, a gendered one.

The Trail had been a great feat of military engineering. Close to eight million tons of bombs were dropped on Vietnam, Laos, and Cambodia. How did they build it? How did they ferry armies and war material along more than 10,000 miles of roads, bridges, and river ways while under attack from the most extensive bombing campaign in modern history? And how did eight years of bombings fail to cut the Trail?

On the other hand, the Trail was a "blood road" of suffering and death. Heroic to the North Vietnamese and, to them, a symbol of the just war they had won against the foreign invader and their collaborators, it was shameful and painful to American veterans and South Vietnamese veterans and civilians. Emotions were still raw and I did not want to reopen old wounds. Veterans and their families, on all sides, had lost loved ones. I was apprehensive, knowing the sensitivities of reporting in Vietnam where times had changed but censorship was still very real.

I decided to journey down the Trail to collect stories from both sides of the front line, especially from the women who had built and defended the Trail. At the very least, I could help disseminate their stories. I knew their personal testimonies would confound the abstraction of war that makes it acceptable to those of us who live in more peaceful places.

### *My Traveling Companions*

The Trail network of tracks, paved roads, and highways presented challenges for the uninitiated. In Vietnam, the paved roads through the mountains were steep, narrow, and prone to landslides. There was heavy traffic on the coastal highways and a disregard of traffic rules and regulations. In Laos, the highways were uncrowded but the gravel roads that forded rivers, I was warned, were hazardous and needed an expert off-road driver and vehicle. For all those reasons, I directed my inquiry to Explore Indochina, specialists in off-road motorcycle tours based in Hanoi. Their email came back highly recommending **Hân Mai**: "We have a long history working with this guy and he speaks good English."

Hân, who was born in the north of Vietnam after the war, brought to the Trail an enthusiastic curiosity to discover his country's wartime past, a nose for great food, and exceptional driving skills. He multitasked effortlessly, managing his new restaurant by text, engaging Trail veterans along the way, and fording fast-flowing rivers.

**Nam Nguyen (Anandaroopa)**, a friend and colleague, was born in Saigon in the former South Vietnam. His mother told him they were going on vacation when they left the city on April 30, 1975, the day of the fall of Saigon. The clan settled in California where Nam grew up.

He returned to Vietnam in the early nineties to work for the first investment bank to set up in Ho Chi Minh City after the war, after graduating from the University of California, Berkeley and the Harvard John F. Kennedy School of Government.

He described the healing power of the war art in *Mekong Diaries,* which would later lead him to join me on the Trail journey:

"I was aware that my parents' generation might dismiss the war art as a whitewash of their own suffering. Given my background, this was not easy art to digest. But I came to see the collections by former enemy artists as a small step toward true reconciliation within the Vietnamese community. To swallow one's bitterness and anger enough to see beauty created by a former enemy is truly courageous—a balancing act of yin and yang."

Nam lives in Vermont with his husband while trying to exhaust his karmas by promoting LGBTQ rights and other social justice issues. He also teaches yoga and meditation.

**Trần Thị Huỳnh Nga** was my traveling companion in the south of Vietnam. Born in Saigon, she was widowed when her first husband, a fighter pilot for the South Vietnamese Air Force, was shot down over the Trail. She married the artist Trần Trung Tín after the war.

In the nineties, she launched the Blue Space Contemporary Art Center in Ho Chi Minh City. Through the work of her gallery, she contributed to the cultural rebirth of the city, promoted a new generation of young artists, championed cultural exchanges between former enemies—North and South, and Vietnam and the United States—and helped bring the collections of North Vietnamese war art to international audiences through publications, films, and exhibitions.

In the eighties, Nga held *Shaded Memories*, the first exhibition of Trần Trung Tín's works in Vietnam. Since then, she has organized exhibitions of his works in galleries and museums in Hong Kong, the United Kingdom, Japan, and the United States. She lives in Ho Chi Minh City.

HANOI
N
Route 15, where the road to war began.
LAOS
Thanh Hóa
Route 1A, the coastal Trail.
EAST SEA
PRC
Vinh
Vientiane
Route 15, the mountainous Trail.
Mekong River
Mụ Giạ Pass
Phong Nha-Kẻ Bàng National Park
Route 20, the way of the 1968 Tết Offensive.
Route 15 (West), the way of the 1972 Spring Offensive.
Đông Hà
Xepon
Khe Sanh
Route 23, the way of the 1972 Spring Offensive.
Salavan
THAILAND
Pakse
VIETNAM
Attapeu
Kon Tum
Pleiku
Route 14, the way of the 1975 Spring Offensive.
Mekong River
Buôn Ma Thuột
CAMBODIA
National Liberation Front Headquarters
Nha Trang
Phnom Penh
Dalat
Route 1A, the way of the 1975 Spring Offensive.
Tây Ninh
Sihanoukville
Phan Thiết
HO CHI MINH CITY
Mekong Delta
Gulf of Thailand
0
75 miles
0
150 km

## *A BRIEF HISTORY OF THE TRAILS, 1946–1975*

With 10,000 miles of Trail ways through Vietnam, Laos, and Cambodia, I had many roads to choose from. I connected my itinerary through Vietnam and Laos to the chronology of the war, following the Trail as it moved forward, in space and in time, battling against the US Air Force, Marines, and Navy. Close to eight million tons of bombs were deployed against it in Vietnam, Laos, and Cambodia, compared to 2.15 million tons dropped by Allied forces on Europe during World War II.[1]

The memoir of Đong Sĩ Nguyên (1923–2019)—*The Trans-Trường Sơn Route: A Memoir* (*Đường Xuyên Trường Sơn*), published by Thế Giới in 2005—who served as Trail Commander from 1967 until the end of the war, gave the historical context for my travels as did John Prados' seminal work, *The Blood Road: The Ho Chi Minh Trail and the Vietnam War*, published by John Wiley and Sons in 2000.

For estimates of the number of armed forces personnel and casualties, I relied mainly on Spencer C. Tucker's *Encyclopedia of the Vietnam War*, published by Oxford University Press in 2011.

### *1946–1954 The Indochina Trail*

The odyssey through the Trường Sơn Mountains began during the French War, I found out, when I was granted an audience in March 2006 with General Võ Nguyên Giáp (1911–2013).

Dressed in full military uniform and medals, at ninety-four years old the master military strategist of the French and American Wars greeted me with a firm handshake. He thanked me for publishing

*The author's Trail itinerary from Hanoi to Ho Chi Minh City.*

*Drawing Under Fire: War diary of a young Vietnamese artist,* a contemporaneous diary of the epic battle of Điện Biên Phủ, which won Vietnam's war of independence against French colonialism. I had discovered the rare handwritten diary at the end of the nineties while visiting its author, Phạm Thanh Tâm, in Ho Chi Minh City. Phạm Thanh Tâm (1933–2019) had been a war artist and veteran of Điện Biên Phủ and Khe Sanh, the momentous battle of the Vietnam War.

During that war, Giáp had built a transportation network through the rugged Trường Sơn Mountains, against impossible odds, to supply multiple fronts under enemy bombings over a theater of war that stretched 1,000 miles from north to south.

But, as Giáp explained to me, the Indochina Trail (1946–1954) through Laos was the precursor of the Trường Sơn Road–Ho Chi Minh Trail (1959–1975):

"Our push during the French War from Nghệ An Province down to Southern Laos along the Trường Sơn mountain range was the first step in opening what later would become the Ho Chi Minh Trail."

The Việt Minh forces—a communist-led national alliance created by Hồ Chí Minh in 1941—without any military aircraft, faced the French Far East Expeditionary Corps, majority financed by the United States and backed by considerable air power. In 1954, the Việt Minh won a decisive victory at Điện Biên Phủ.

The 1954 Geneva Accords temporarily divided the former French colony into two "regrouping zones," north and south of a provisional military demarcation line, pending unification after national elections.

## *The 1954 Geneva Accords*

The national elections to "bring about the unification of Vietnam," as outlined in Article 14a of the 1954 Geneva Accords, never happened.[2] The July 1956 deadline for the elections came and went.

The odds for peaceful unification had been slim from the start. Fearing a communist victory at the polls by the popular Hồ Chí Minh, who had brought independence to Vietnam, the United States had refused to sign the Final Declaration of the 1954 Geneva Accords but did commit to abide by the agreement. After July 1956, Vietnamese territory remained divided at the provisional military demarcation line, with a demilitarized zone which formed a buffer of between four and six miles in width, known as the DMZ.

North of the line, the communist Democratic Republic of Vietnam (DRV) or North Vietnam, with Hanoi as its capital, was led by President Hồ Chí Minh, the first president of the DRV and leader of the Việt Minh who had won the war against the French. North Vietnam was backed by the Soviet Union and Mao Zedong's People's Republic of China.

South of the line, the anti-communist Republic of Vietnam or South Vietnam, with Saigon—renamed Ho Chi Minh City after 1975—as its capital, was ruled by President Ngô Đình Diệm, an anti-communist Catholic aristocrat. The United States supported South Vietnam to contain the possible spread of communism in the region. The US Military Assistance Advisory Group (MAAG), based in Saigon since 1951, took over from the departing French forces to train the South Vietnamese Army.

US president Dwight D. Eisenhower's "domino theory" laid the foundation for the superpower's involvement in Vietnam. Successive US presidents John F. Kennedy and Lyndon B. Johnson later used the theory to justify increased economic and military assistance to non-communist South Vietnam and, eventually, the bombing of North Vietnam and the commitment of American armed forces.

By 1961, the United States was participating in combat against the Việt Cộng in South Vietnam, had set up secret fortified camps including a base at Khe Sanh to stop infiltration down the Trail, and was waging a limited secret war against North Vietnam.[3]

### *1959–1964 A New Trail is Born*

In 1959, three years after the deadline for holding elections had passed, Hồ Chí Minh and the Hanoi Politburo opened the Trường Sơn Road–Ho Chi Minh Trail to support the insurgency fighting for the unification promised in the Accords.

In January 1959, Hồ Chí Minh and the Politburo outlined their plans for unification at the 15th Central Executive Committee meeting of the Communist Party:

"We advocate national reunification by peaceful means ... However, the American imperialists, Ngô Đình Diệm, and the American minions, still deliberately invaded the South, deliberately prepared war to invade the North, in order to put the entire Vietnamese people under their yoke. As long as the United States and Diệm are in the South, the country will remain divided and the possibility of war will still exist."[4]

On May 19, 1959, the Politburo created an Army Engineering Corps, Group 559, of 500 officers and soldiers to supply the communist insurgents a thousand miles to the south. In June 1959, Group 559 launched its first modest mission to send fifty guns across the provisional demarcation line to the guerrillas in the Central Highlands.[5]

Southern Việt Minh, who had resettled in Hanoi after 1954, traveled down the Trail to set up the National Liberation Front of South Vietnam (NLF) or Việt Cộng in 1961, taking up the fight for unification promised in the Accords, against the Diệm regime.

From 1959 to 1965, fighters and cultural troops trekked on paths through the Trường Sơn Mountains. In the early years, they crossed the provisional demarcation line straight into enemy South Vietnam. After Hanoi forged alliances with the Laotian communists and Norodom Sihanouk, the Cambodian king, they took the shorter and less dangerous route through Laos and Cambodia to reach the new NLF headquarters in Tây Ninh Province. The sea route delivered the bulk of domestic, Soviet, and Chinese military material to the coast of South Vietnam, where it was unloaded clandestinely.

### *1965 The US Bombing of North Vietnam*

Between 1961 and 1964, North Vietnam increased its military aid to the Việt Cộng fighting for unification against the Diệm government. During that time, the United States and South Vietnam conducted a limited secret war against the Trail, on land and on sea, to pressure North Vietnam to stop helping the insurgency. In 1964, US president Lyndon B. Johnson, who was facing a presidential election that year, upped the ante.

On August 7, 1964, Congress voted overwhelmingly to pass a joint resolution, known as the Gulf of Tonkin resolution, giving the president full authority "to take all necessary measures to repel any armed attack against the forces of the United States and to prevent further aggression."[6]

To get the resolution through Congress, Johnson alleged North Vietnamese torpedo boats had attacked the US naval destroyer USS *Maddox* on August 4, 1964. In fact, the attack "didn't happen." Robert S. McNamara (1916–2009), the Secretary of Defense at the time, admitted as much forty years later in the documentary film *The Fog of War: Eleven Lessons from the Life of Robert S. McNamara*:

"It was just confusion. And events afterwards showed that our judgment—that we'd been attacked that day [August 4, 1964]—was wrong. It didn't happen ... President Johnson authorized bombing [of North Vietnam] in response to what he thought had been the second attack [on August 4] and hadn't occurred."[7]

Equally deceptive was the secret war the United States had been carrying out against North Vietnam. In the days leading up to the alleged attacks on August 2 and 4, 1964, South Vietnamese patrol boats had been conducting US-sanctioned bombardments against nearby North Vietnamese islands. Declassified documents suggest that the USS *Maddox* and *Turner Joy* were on patrol in the Gulf of Tonkin to support the US-backed South Vietnamese raids, and that they were engaged by North Vietnamese torpedo boats defending their territory against the earlier assaults.[8]

In November 1964, Johnson was reelected by a sixty percent majority in the popular vote, defeating the Republican hawk Barry Goldwater (1909–1998), who, during the campaign, had accused him of giving in to communist aggression.

On March 2, 1965, Johnson began bombing North Vietnam. He sent a limited number of US troops—3,500 Marines—to South Vietnam. North Vietnam was a small agrarian country, the United States was a superpower. Johnson hoped to pressure the Politburo to stop supporting the communist insurgency in the South and to bolster the confidence of the South Vietnamese government.

The bombing of the North severely disrupted the Trail overland. The US naval blockade of the South Vietnamese coast all but shut down the important sea supply route. But the US military actions against North Vietnam did not yield the results Johnson had hoped for. Hanoi denounced the false pretext used by Johnson to bomb North Vietnam, and accused the United States of aggression against its territory. Instead of backing down, Giáp convinced the Politburo to "urgently" build a new network of motorized Trail roads through the Trường Sơn Mountains through Laos and Cambodia to replace the blocked coastal Trail and sea routes. It was a huge undertaking that few military commands would have had the audacity to attempt unless they had no choice.

Hanoi was all the more dependent on the overland supply lines because it lacked a sizable air force to defend its territory, attack enemy positions, and deliver military supplies.

The Soviet Union began supplying North Vietnam with military aircraft in 1965, but the North Vietnamese fleet remained dwarfed throughout the war by the colossal size of the fleets of fighter-bombers of the US Air Force, Navy, and Marines. In the Christmas bombings of 1972, for example, about 140 B-52s were used in addition to other tactical aircraft—over 900 in all—compared to seventy-one Vietnam People's Air Force aircraft, including thirty-one MiGs.

## *The 1968 Tết Offensive*

Between 1965 and 1967, US military involvement escalated. By 1967, 500,000 US and 800,000 South Vietnamese forces backed by US air support were fighting the communist insurgency in South Vietnam. The United States built the high-tech McNamara Line and a string of combat bases south of the provisional demarcation line to stop infiltration from the Trail. The US bombings of North Vietnam that began in March 1965 intensified.

Faced with a superior foe, Hanoi waged a war of attrition to wear down Goliath, while ever alert to seize opportunities for a quick victory. Not many came. Eight months after the United States began its attacks against North Vietnam, Lê Duẩn, the hard-line Communist Party First Secretary, outlined the basis for victory at the 12th Plenum of the Party Central Committee in December 1965:

"The question of fighting and talking is not an entirely new issue. In our own nation's history, Nguyễn Trãi [the fifteenth-century Confucian scholar and military strategist] implemented the strategy of using weakness to fight strength and of fighting and talking in order to defeat the Ming dynasty's feudal army."[9]

Between 1965 and 1967, Group 559 expanded the construction of all-weather roads, for motorized transportation units, through the Trường Sơn Mountains. The Army Engineering Corps moved its Hanoi headquarters to the mountains to oversee the opening of east–west passes and north–south axes in Laos. Trail stations or *binh trạm* were built at regular intervals, linked by a communication network and defended by anti-aircraft defense units. They provided food, fuel, shelter, and security for troops on their way south. Communication centers, food depots, gasoline storage tanks, weapons and ammunition warehouses, truck and tank parks, hospitals, and bomb shelters were camouflaged in natural cave networks, man-made tunnels, and jungle surrounds. The women in the war drawings "protected" all this. They prepared food, repaired roads, transported ammunition and weapons between stations, drove the trucks, decommissioned live bombs, joined anti-aircraft defense units, nursed the wounded, and buried the dead.

Lê Duẩn, Hồ Chí Minh's designated successor, began pushing for an all-out North Vietnamese offensive against South Vietnam and sidelined Politburo moderates opposed to the idea. Seventy-seven-year-old Hồ Chí Minh, in failing health, was convalescing in Beijing and Giáp was recovering in Hungary when the Politburo took the decision to launch the first North Vietnamese offensive against South Vietnam.

On January 21, 1968, the People's Army attacked the US Combat Marine Base at Khe Sanh, built to stop infiltration against the Trail. Ten days later, the People's Army joined forces with the Việt Cộng to launch the Tết Offensive, a simultaneous attack against one hundred US and South Vietnamese military installations and headquarters in the cities and towns.

Neither side won a decisive military victory. The North Vietnamese and Việt Cộng suffered heavy casualties and did not gain the territory they had hoped for. The popular uprising that Lê Duẩn had predicted did not materialize.

But the Tết Offensive marked a psychological turning point in the United States that changed the course of the war. Americans, who had been told they were winning the war, were shocked by the People's Army attacks against South Vietnam, and by the mounting casualties among US and Allied soldiers and Vietnamese civilians.

On March 31, 1968, President Lyndon B. Johnson stunned the nation by announcing on national television that he would not run for reelection:

"I do not believe that I should devote an hour or day of my time ... to any duties other than the awesome duties of this office, the presidency of your country. Accordingly I shall not seek and I will not accept the nomination of my Party for another term as your president."[10]

The year 1968 was a time of anger in the United States. The divisive rift in evidence today dates from that time. Anti-war sentiment exploded in nationwide protests, demonstrations, and draft card hand-ins. On June 5, presidential candidate Robert F. Kennedy, the hope of the anti-war movement, was mortally shot shortly after midnight and died a day later in the early hours of the morning. In August, violent clashes erupted between anti-war protesters and the police at the Democratic National Convention in Chicago. By October, a Gallup poll showed a majority of Americans believed it had been a mistake to send US troops to Vietnam. Johnson suspended the bombing of North Vietnam, Hanoi's condition for peace talks to begin in Paris. A month later, Richard M. Nixon was elected US president on a campaign promise to achieve peace "with honor." The following year, in July 1969, Nixon announced his Vietnamization strategy to increase the training of South Vietnamese forces and their proportion of the fighting, and to begin the withdrawal of US troops from South Vietnam.

## *The 1972 Spring Offensive*

Between 1969 and 1971, the Trail continued to expand, facilitated by the US Marines' withdrawal from their combat base at Khe Sanh. Trail roads and parallel fuel pipelines were built in North Vietnam and Laos. Route 15, the main north–south axis in North Vietnam, was extended to the provisional demarcation line, and additional east–west roads were constructed to connect North Vietnam to Laos, strengthening the grid. In 1970, Group 559 was elevated to Trail High Command, adding infantry and artillery to existing logistics and anti-air defense units.

On the Allied side, Vietnamization opened up the possibility of sending ground forces to attack the Trail in neutral Laos and Cambodia to disrupt possible future North Vietnamese offensives. Between 1970 and 1971, South Vietnamese ground forces, backed by US air power, launched assaults against Trail stations in Laos and Cambodia that were off-limits to American troops. While

Vietnamization delivered some military victories, the 1971 Allied offensive against the Trail Command headquarters at Xepon in Laos ended in retreat. Covered Trail roads and parallel pipelines expanded south from Xepon to Salavan and Attapeu, giving the People's Army access to Kon Tum and the Central Highlands in South Vietnam.

After Hồ Chí Minh's death in 1969, Lê Duẩn was in charge. By the summer of 1971, with the promises of renewed Soviet military aid, the Politburo was ready to launch the 1972 Spring Offensive. People's Army divisions numbering between 200,000 and 300,000, three times the size of the deployment during the Tết Offensive, supported by tank units, attacked South Vietnam on three fronts.

In response to the offensive, the United States resumed the bombing of North Vietnam. The intensity of the attacks threatened the Trail like never before. North Vietnamese casualties were punishingly high. Shortages of rice, fuel, and ammunition reached crisis proportions. During the Christmas bombings alone, between December 18 and 29, the US military conducted massive bombing raids against North Vietnam, mostly Hanoi.

After six years of conflict, both sides were ready for compromise. In particular, US geopolitics had shifted. In February 1972, Nixon held a historic meeting with Mao Zedong, the communist leader of the People's Republic of China, and an ally of North Vietnam. The Nixon–Kissinger policy of *détente* replaced the domino theory that had led successive US administrations to support South Vietnam. South Vietnam was no longer considered a necessary buffer state against the spread of world communism.

The Paris Peace Accords were signed on January 27, 1973, more than four years after the talks began. Some claim the Christmas bombings may have helped bring about the deal, signed a month later, that led to an end to US involvement in the war. But the wording of the agreement was almost exactly the same as it was at the beginning of December, before the assault. All US ground troops had left South

Vietnam by March 1973. The air war by the US Air Force, Navy, and Marines, the Trail's "greatest obstacle," had come to an end.

### *The 1975 Spring Offensive*

The war between North and South Vietnam continued for two more years. The North Vietnamese People's Army, estimated at between 200,000 and 700,000, backed by tanks, faced the Republic of Vietnam Air Force (RVNAF) and ground forces one million strong.

The Trail expanded right into South Vietnamese territory. The Trail Commander, once concerned with rice and fuel shortages, faced a scarcity of cement and asphalt. The Trường Sơn soldiers built a paved highway to Lộc Ninh, within seventy-five miles of Saigon, in preparation for the 1975 Spring Offensive.

By 1975, six horizontal north–south roads connected twenty-one vertical east–west roads in North Vietnam, Laos, Cambodia, and South Vietnam. A web of parallel fuel pipelines and gas stations supplied trucks and tanks.

On April 30, 1975, the first North Vietnamese troops entered Saigon, the capital of South Vietnam. A nationwide election for reunification took place on July 2, 1976, merging North and South Vietnam into the Socialist Republic of Vietnam.

General Giáp wrote in his memoirs of the great human cost of the French War, and of the American one that came in its wake:

"Our nation had to pay a heavy price—more than a generation of its best youth—to erase colonialism, one of mankind's dark stains."[11]

It was a tragedy on an epic scale. One million North Vietnamese and Việt Cộng,[12] 254,256 South Vietnamese,[13] and 58,318 US combatants were killed.[14] Two million Vietnamese civilians across both sides lost their lives between 1954 and 1975.[15]

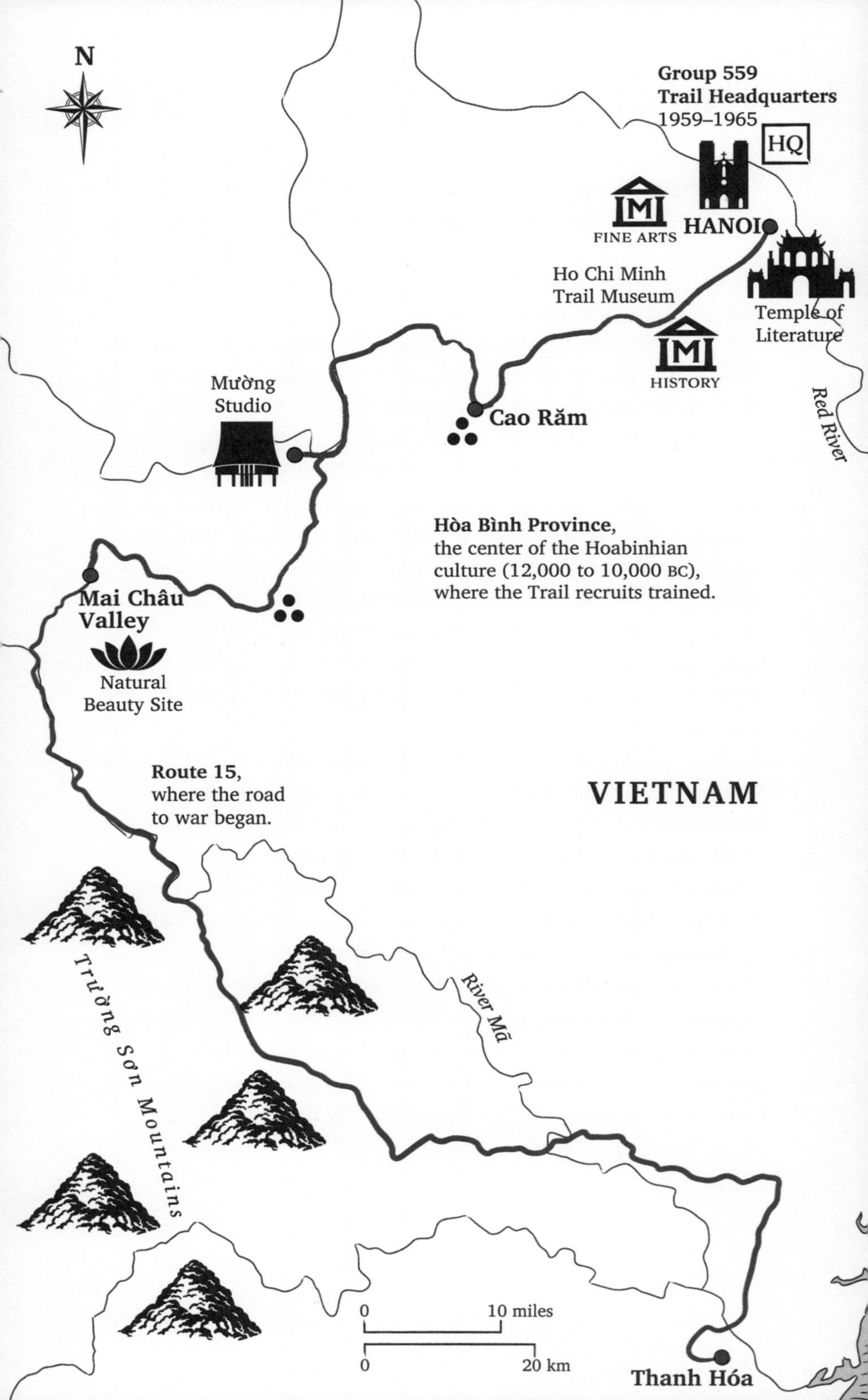
N
Group 559
Trail Headquarters
1959–1965
HQ
FINE ARTS
HANOI
Ho Chi Minh
Trail Museum
Temple of
Literature
HISTORY
Red River
Mường
Studio
Cao Răm
Hòa Bình Province,
the center of the Hoabinhian
culture (12,000 to 10,000 BC),
where the Trail recruits trained.
Mai Châu
Valley
Natural
Beauty Site
Route 15,
where the road
to war began.
VIETNAM
Trường Sơn Mountains
River Mã
0
10 miles
0
20 km
Thanh Hóa

Chapter 1

# *HANOI TO HÒA BÌNH*

*Over yellow-green tea with the artist who drew the women who defended the Trail.*

Before I started the Trail, I had arranged to meet one of the war artists who had made the trip in 1972, when bombings were at their most intense. As Trần Huy Oánh described it, the way they coped was to keep moving forward, waiting between strikes, at night, on covered roads or taking new undiscovered ways.

He greeted me at the door, a wool scarf wrapped around his neck for protection against the winter damp. The town house he lived in was tucked away behind the Hanoi College of Fine Arts he had once directed, the successor school to the École des Beaux-Arts d'Indochine. Offering me a seat, Trần Huy Oánh went to the open kitchen to make tea.

He waited for the water to boil. He carried the teapot over and served the yellow-green brew. He was widowed and lived alone.

"The tea is from Thái Nguyên," he said.

"Delicious," I replied, barely sipping the bitter elixir. I was not a fan, even though I knew it was the best tea Vietnam had to offer. There was a long pause, an eternity of silence that encompassed centuries of sizing up the foreigners who coveted their land.

"What is the purpose of your visit?" Trần Huy Oánh asked with the formality of first encounters.

"I was inspired to travel down the Trail by the war drawings," I explained.

"I have two hundred sketches from the Trail," he said.

A collection of that size was rare. The Trail journey was exhausting and harrowing. Few had the inclination to draw during the trek south. Those who did lost drawings to the jungle, the rivers, and the road.

I had come to check my Trail itinerary against his drawings. I had unraveled the secrets of the "blood road" by consulting People's Army maps, memoirs, and articles. But personal accounts and drawings connected the roads to the women and men who had built and defended them.

I unfolded the paper map that had been my companion during the months I was preparing for the trip. I had been a map-lover since my schooldays; I drew distant lands, mountains, roads, and waterways that held the promise of adventure. Institutional walls had inspired my desire in adulthood for freedom and discovery. A sense of over-belonging to one place created bigotry. Torn at the folds, it looked like a vintage map even though I was its only owner.

Trần Huy Oánh traced his itinerary on the map with his finger, connecting me to the places I would visit where he had been before: the spectacular Phong Nha Caves at the heart of the Trường Sơn Mountains, a choke point on the Trail during the 1968 Tết Offensive and 1972 Spring Offensive; to Xepon in Laos, the hub of the Laotian Trail and the Trail Command headquarters in 1968; to Salavan, the Bolaven Plateau, and Attapeu, important stations on the Laotian Trail; to Kon Tum in the Central Highlands of the former South Vietnam, the target of the 1972 and 1975 Spring Offensives. From Kon Tum, the artist followed the Sihanouk Trail through Cambodia to Kraceh, the last station on the Trail, to take up his post as director of the arts and propaganda section. I, instead, had planned to follow the Trail built for the final 1975 Spring Offensive through the south of Vietnam.

Trần Huy Oánh remembered:

"The roads were extremely dangerous. Route 1A was bombed so often we took a month to travel three hundred miles to Đồng Hới. We reached one point, turned back, and tried again the next day.

A year earlier, I had done the same trip by bicycle in a week. Our main advantage was that the bombing schedules were fixed. So we timed our movements between them. The Americans couldn't bomb twenty-four hours a day! I had left Hanoi for Đồng Hới with my art students in a military convoy. By the time I arrived in Đồng Hới, I had eaten my entire rice belt! The People's Army fed us. For extras, I had a salary from the university. But there was nothing to buy anyway! When we reached the mountains, we traveled at night in truck convoys. I don't know how the drivers could see with the headlights turned off. They drove by feeling. Even in the moonlight, I couldn't see a thing. The planes dropped electronic sensors camouflaged as plants that detected our movements in the dark. In Laos, the roads were 'covered' with trellises made from leafy branches. When the Americans discovered one, the soldiers built another. I kept my travel kit as mementoes. Let me show you."

He fetched the cloth belt that had contained his ration of rice, a mosquito net, his floppy hat for the sun, and his French colonial pith helmet for the rain. He then showed me his Trail backpack in which he carried his "weapons."

"My only weapons were my paintbrushes, palette knife, watercolor set, water tin, and a poster of Hồ Chí Minh. Before leaving for the Trail, I had stayed up half the night to finish painting it," he explained.

"How did you carry the poster?"

I had seen the image in the collection of the British Museum. The backpack seemed too small for it, even folded.

"We cut it into pieces. We then pasted them back together and exhibited the poster at the Trail stations," he replied.

The message on the poster, "You are still marching with us, Uncle Hồ," was designed to encourage soldiers to keep fighting even after Hồ Chí Minh's death a year earlier. Uncle Hồ was the affectionate name given to the first president of the Democratic Republic of Vietnam, symbol of Vietnamese independence, and archrival of the United States during the war.

The Trail stations provided food and shelter to soldiers on their way south. Cultural troops organized revolutionary art exhibitions, plays, poetry readings, and concerts.

"Here we are with our bamboo walking sticks," he said, showing me a photograph of himself with his students. "I engraved place-names on my stick. But I lost it one night when we moved camp in an emergency. Pity. I miss that stick. It had all my memories on it."

"Did the Army issue the sticks?"

He laughed. I was careful to question my assumptions after that. There were no PX (Post Exchange) stores on the Trail.

"No, we made our own when we entered the bamboo forest. Let me show you my drawings," he said.

I followed him upstairs into a bright and airy studio. He leafed through the drawings he had kept for forty years: lyrical portraits of the women who defended the Trail, scenes of daily life at base camp, and landscapes of the Trường Sơn Mountains and of the high Laotian plateaus, "beautiful even in war."

The drawings brought back memories. Trần Huy Oánh was despondent at some and cracked jokes at others:

"A woman fighter after a B-52 attack in 1967 when I went to Vĩnh Linh by bicycle; bulldozing a mountain to build the road; a bomb crater; and tunnels near the Phong Nha Caves. In Laos, I sketched the 'hidden road,' trellises covered in foliage, caves near Xepon, beautiful butterflies, and the King of Cambodia's luxury hotel room in the jungle! When the King came through our camp, the soldiers built him a hut with bamboo panels. It was probably the first time in his life that the King had to make his own bed when he woke up the next morning!"

King Sihanouk, who had maintained Cambodian neutrality in the early years of the war, became an ally of Hanoi after the secret US bombing of Cambodia in 1969 destabilized his government. Deposed in a coup in 1970, he had been living in exile in China.

After the 1973 Paris Peace Accords were signed, he flew to North Vietnam and traveled down the Laotian Trail to Cambodia.

Trần Huy Oánh continued:

"A drawing of the Sekong River in Laos, where we killed a crocodile. We had meat for a week! A waterfall in the Bolaven Plateau; a coffee plantation. I loved coffee. It kept me going. The capture of the US and South Vietnamese military base at Đắk Tô in April 1972. They had no time to bury the dead; a [captured] American tank; trees near Kon Tum, after the Americans sprayed Agent Orange."

The black landscape depicted a scorched earth populated by cindered trees, forlorn and lifeless. American planes sprayed the toxic "rainbow herbicide" to detect truck convoys and infantry and artillery troops on the move.

Trần Huy Oánh looked at me.

"I have a question for you. Do these drawings make you angry?"

"No. I find your personal drawings moving. They show the human side of war: young women and men living, fighting, and dying. And you kept drawing, no matter how tired, hungry, or scared you were."

As I reached over to decipher the markings on the American tank, I spilled tea on my notebook. The ink mark spread on the page, making my notes illegible.

"Wait a second," said Trần Huy Oánh.

He opened the drawing cabinet, took out the hairdryer he used to dry his ink paintings with, and blow-dried my notebook pages to stop further smudging.

Back in my hotel room, I opened the window onto Hanoi's rooftops. I checked my emails. The dank night air made me shiver. So did the message from a Trail veteran I would be meeting the following day. It was sent through a mutual friend and read as follows:

"When Kim Chi journeyed down the Trail to liberate the South, she was young. She thought it was a wonderful time. But now she regrets her lost youth and the lost youth of the soldiers. She would like to talk about this when she meets you."

Kim Chi was a film star whom I had met twenty years earlier during one of my trips to Vietnam. She had made the Trail journey in 1964, before the United States began bombing it.

The email today was surprising: veterans of the Trail journey did not openly question the war's legacy. Over one million soldiers perished, 300,000 were missing. Vietnam is proud of its victories. The bravery and endurance of the young men and women who had defended the Trail are celebrated while dissenting views are censored.

The next morning, I headed for the breakfast room. I wanted coffee badly. My traveling companion Nam Nguyen joined me. He had arrived late the previous evening after a month at an ashram in Bihar, India. He described the visits as soul-cleansing exercises. We spent the morning on last-minute preparations for the trip. We walked through the narrow streets of Old Hanoi. I bought a pair of running shoes—hot pink was the only available color in my size—and a Samsung phone with a local SIM card and an easy-to-find orange case. We went to Hanoi's gold district to exchange dollars for *kip*, the Laotian currency, hoping to get a good rate on the black market. The shop owner disappeared with the money for over an hour.

"Do you think she's skipped town?" I asked Nam.

When she eventually returned with stacks of Laotian banknotes, the black market rate was no better than that offered in the official currency exchange shop next to the hotel.

Hanoi was cold and gray as we went to meet Kim Chi that afternoon. I dressed warmly. Hanoi houses were unheated during the short winter months. We took a taxi to the West Lake. The cab dropped us at the entry of a lane too narrow for cars. Away from the wide boulevards, the city was a labyrinth of alleyways inside the medieval citadel built against invaders. Narrow town houses alternated with courtyards and gardens protected by wrought-iron gates. Jumbled and tangled electrical wires hung overhead, ever in danger of collapsing on passers-by—or so I feared. We walked down the lane dodging mopeds and them dodging us. The pleasant neighborhood was landscaped with palm trees.

"A dog spa! Do you believe that?" Nam remarked, incredulous. "This is the new Vietnam!"

During an earlier visit, we had stayed next to a dog abattoir. Urban dogs with economic development had become pampered pets.

Kim Chi welcomed us into her house. Elegant and trim, she wore a wool cap, green scarf, and tailored wool blazer. She appeared youthful and vivacious with the same smile as the young woman in the Trail photographs displayed on the piano. Kim Chi had hiked 600 miles on Trường Sơn mountain paths to the Việt Cộng headquarters. She had volunteered to join the cultural troops going south in 1964. She enlisted out of patriotism, adventure, and love.

The email mentioned that she was ill, and I had expected to find an ailing elderly lady.

"It's so nice to see you again. I kept the embroidered fan you gave me," I said.

The fan was a cherished memento from my previous visit.

"You gave me perfume," replied Kim Chi.

I realized too late that this time I was empty-handed. Kim Chi showed us into an American-style open dining room and kitchen. A picture window the length of the room faced onto the alley. A teapot with a crackle glaze was centered on the table.

"Please sit. Let's have tea. Then we can talk," she said.

Tea-sharing was an inescapable ritual, the way for a host to assess a guest's character and manners.

Kim Chi poured the tea. She settled back in her chair.

"Drink," she said.

More bitter tea. I would have to get used to it. I added sugar, tons of it, and took a sip. Kim Chi lifted her cup to drink. I waited for her to speak first. She took another sip. I glanced at the photographs on the piano: Kim Chi with General Võ Nguyên Giáp, Kim Chi at a film awards ceremony, and a young Kim Chi at the end of the Trail with Nguyễn Thị Định, the venerated NLF female leader.

The long silence made me uncomfortable but I tried not to show it. Impatience was a sign of rudeness, and weakness. A balance between silence and speech was a virtue in Confucian societies. We exchanged smiles. I must have passed the test. The connection was made. Trust was re-established. Our talk could begin.

"Please. Start. I gather you are interested in what life was like on the Trail," Kim Chi said, by way of encouragement.

"Yes, I am."

Kim Chi had followed in the family tradition when she joined the National Liberation Front, or Việt Cộng, battling for unification in South Vietnam. She came from a revolutionary southern family. Her father had fought for independence from French colonial rule.

"My father died fighting against the French. He was a lawyer and political leader in the district of Rạch Giá, in the south of Vietnam. After his death in 1953, we moved to the North for protection. The South Vietnamese government was targeting the families of Resistance fighters. We traveled north on a Russian boat and settled in Hanoi. I was sent to study in China [our ally]. I was eleven years old. I've forgotten all my Chinese," she said, with a girlish giggle.

Her crystal-clear laughter made you feel happy to be alive.

"You were sent to China on your own at the age of eleven?" I asked, incredulous.

"Yes. I went to a boarding school. We were about two thousand students in my school."

From her boarding school years, Kim Chi developed a sympathy for the poor and oppressed in her native South.

"In school, I was told that South Vietnam was poor. I was educated to think that the South Vietnamese government was bad for the people. I felt I should liberate the South. So, I joined the fight for Liberation. I wanted to contribute, do my part. My innocence felt that's what I should do. I was sad for the people in the South where my family came from. I grew up with these feelings and emotions."

There was more to why she made the perilous Trail journey to "liberate" the South. She continued:

"After I left boarding school in China in 1958, I returned to Hanoi. In 1959, I was accepted into the first class of the newly established Vietnam Film School, graduated in 1962, and began working for the Vietnam Film Studio as an actress. When the North sent people to liberate the South, my boyfriend, who was a filmmaker, was asked to go.

—I might die. Let's break up, he said to me.

—No. If you go, I go. Why don't we get married?

So we did. I applied but they still didn't want to let me make the journey because I was very thin, and they thought I might not survive. In the end, Tố Hữu, the deputy chairman of the Union of Literature and Arts Association, made the decision. I told him:

—You went to war, how come I can't go? Is it because I'm a woman? People don't only go to war with their feet, but with their heart and head.

—Let her go and let her see if she can do it, Tố Hữu replied."

Kim Chi enlisted. The draft for women was introduced later, after the bombing of North Vietnam began.

The romantic twist made me smile. Sentimental propaganda about the Trail was often based on true love stories. Kim Chi's husband Nguyễn Hồng Sến (1933–1995) was a well-known film director. His documentary about North Vietnam's large-scale irrigation project in the Red River Delta—*Nước về Bắc Hưng Hải* or *Water Returns to Bắc Hưng Hải*—had won the Gold Medal at the Moscow International Film Festival in 1959.

Kim Chi described their strenuous Trail journey with ease and grace:

"We left Hanoi in April 1964. We trained in Hòa Bình for six months. It was tough. I hiked up and down mountains carrying fifty-five pounds on my back. At the end of the training, with my husband and ten others from the film industry, I left by car for the Bến Hải River—the temporary line between North and South Vietnam. From there we walked on mountain trails. The journey was difficult. No pen and paper can describe it. Guides chopped a path through the jungle. We didn't know where we were going. Everything was secret. A scout took us to a midpoint between stations, where a new guide showed us the way to the next station. We walked from dawn to sunset. At night we stopped at a camp. When the dormitories were too crowded, we slept outside in hammocks. In the morning, I cooked rice for the team. On the road, the smoke might give us away [to enemy spies]. I carried a belt with enough rice for a week, and a heavy bag with a spare set of clothes, a hammock and, very important, toilet paper! I had a written dispensation saying the men should carry my bag. But my husband was sick most of the time so I ended up carrying his stuff. The mountains were so steep, you had to slide down on your behind. The leeches were terrible. I was bleeding all the time. They crawled into every part of my body. They dropped in my rice, but I was so hungry I ate it anyway."

"What did you film?"

I was curious to know what the arts and propaganda department back in Hanoi was looking for in the mountainous jungle.

"We filmed the ethnic people to gather information. They were so innocent, they went half-naked in public. They were curious to see what I looked like because I was tall and light-skinned. At one stop, the villagers asked why I bathed in the river fully clothed.

—Because I'm embarrassed, I replied.

There was an outburst of laughter, and one woman said:

—Show it off! Young women go bare-breasted, only old ladies cover up!"

"How long did the trip take?" I asked.

"We walked for months. But we were lucky because we reached the [Việt Cộng] headquarters before the Americans started bombing. At the end of the journey, my husband and I were separated. He stayed at headquarters where he joined a battlefield film crew. I was sent to the liberated zones where I acted in plays. We didn't see each other for ten years. I moved twelve times, whenever the American or South Vietnamese forces discovered our camp."

"Were you afraid?"

"Who is not afraid of death? We accepted it."

She paused.

"Do you want to see some photographs?" she asked.

A young Kim Chi with her husband looked like a couple enjoying an idyllic weekend away. In another, a guerrilla checkered scarf around her neck, she posed stylishly with militia women, one with a gun slung over her shoulder.

"Do you have any regrets?"

"When I was young, I thought defending my country was beautiful. I believed the Americans were the devil. Now that I'm older, I ask myself, what did I contribute to?"

I was shocked by her candor. Kim Chi was being mildly critical of a system that did not tolerate criticism.

"After liberation in 1975, I saw many things. I was sad when people were sent to the [reeducation] camps. The economy was terrible. Properties were seized. My whole family on my mother's side left for Utah."

In this culture of silence, Kim Chi talked openly about the camps. At the end of the war, defeated South Vietnamese military personnel, police and intelligence officers, and people from "reactionary parties" were interned. Many did not return.

Nam gave me a worried look. Was Kim Chi safe if we continued?

Were we? Kim Chi kept talking, unconcerned. There was more.

"Have you been to visit your family who left for the United States?" I asked, hoping to switch to a lighter topic.

"I saw them when I traveled there. They love me. They understand the situation. They support me. Without freedom, there is nothing."

What did she mean? It was my turn to look at Nam.

"What did you think of the United States?" I continued, interested to hear her impressions of the country she had been told as a child was the devil.

"It was nice. We were invited to Washington to talk about rights in Vietnam. But when I returned to Hanoi, the state media launched a smear campaign about the visit. They created difficulties for me and criticized my trip. Then a week ago, the security police came to visit me at home. Six plainclothes policemen showed up at my door," she said.

The room was cool but I began to sweat. The Trail veteran was an activist protesting against social injustice, poverty, and corrupt officials. She believed the socialist ideals she had fought for were being betrayed. Local authorities had been evicting farmers with little or no compensation and selling the land at inflated prices to developers. The evictions were creating hardship. (The state owned the land and extended land-usage rights at will, in return for rent, to farmers.)

Kim Chi continued:

"I gave the police chocolates and served tea. I told them:

—You came to my house because you were told to come. That's your right to come here. But you should listen to this. I will tell you what my purpose is. People have lost their property. They are destitute. The rich are stealing from the poor. They [some officials and developers] are taking farmers' land, forcing them to leave and destroying their houses. People are demonstrating, shouting: 'Give me back my land.' Desperate farmers are committing suicide.

How can you be a human being and turn a blind eye to other people's suffering?

"I cried so many times. I couldn't eat. I couldn't sleep. When the Film Association proposed me for a medal, I wrote a letter to the Prime Minister saying: 'I do not want an award in my house from someone who brings poverty to the country.' My nephew posted the letter on Facebook. Now I have thousands of friends!"

Facebook had become a forum for critical views censored by the state-controlled media.

"In a few days, we are holding a demonstration," she added.

Protests were rare in the one-party state.

"Why now?" I asked.

"Protests always happened. But with the internet, people are speaking out and joining forces. Before social media, we thought we couldn't do anything," she replied.

"Do you have permission for the demonstration?"

"No, but if we ask permission, they will refuse it."

"Aren't you afraid to go to jail?"

"No, I have to live that way. I have to do what I have to do."

"Do you have hope for the future?"

"Of course, more and more people understand. I'm not afraid. If we do good and they kill us, then our spirit will not die."

I wondered what she thought of the rapprochement between former enemies. As a sign of the new friendship, the United States, after removing the trade embargo against Vietnam in 1995, had lifted its ban on arms sales to Vietnam in 2016.

For Kim Chi, pragmatism and emotion went hand in hand.

"We were enemies in the past. That was fifty years ago. This is the future. The enemy of our enemy [China] is our friend. I trust the United States more than I trust China. The United States has the rule of law. The United States has freedom. The United States has become our friend now, because it's also in their interest."

Patriotic veterans were especially critical of a controversial law

War artist's hammock.

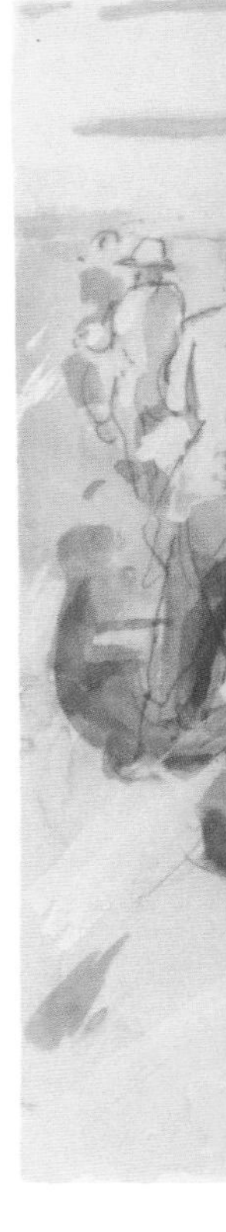

*"My only weapons were my paintbrushes ..."*
Trần Huy Oánh

Huỳnh Phương Đông, *Peace (Hòa Bình)*, pastel, 1975.

Lê Lam, *Untitled*, watercolor, no date.

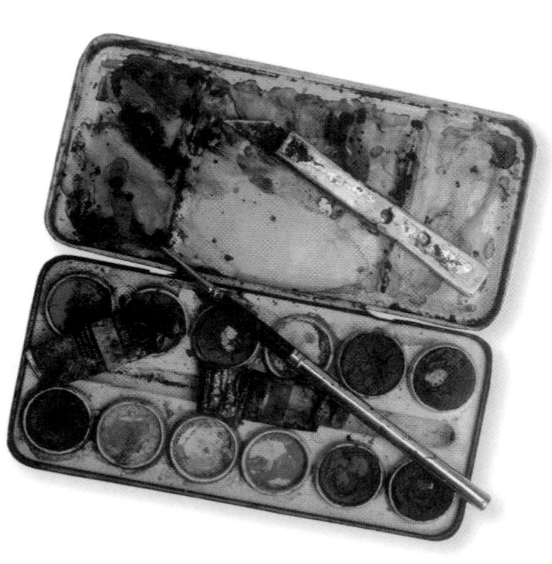

War artist's watercolor set and paintbrushes.

on special economic zones that allowed the government to lease land for ninety-nine years to any foreign bidder, including China. After nationwide protests in 2018, the law was postponed.

There are no eternal friends or eternal enemies, only eternal interests.

At that moment, Kim Chi's cell phone rang. I wasn't prepared for what happened next.

"Sorry. Do you mind if I take this call?" she asked.

"Of course not."

"Please wait a moment. I have to send the news out immediately. The writer Nguyễn Quang Lập was arrested today at two p.m."

"Where?"

"At his home in Ho Chi Minh City," she said, as she texted the details of his arrest.

The award-winning author was detained and charged for abusing "freedom of speech ... to infringe upon the interest of the state," a crime that carried a possible three-year jail sentence. (Nguyễn Quang Lập was later released from jail, but activists, writers, journalists, and others continue to be arrested on the Orwellian charge.)

Nam turned to me. He was rattled:

"I can't believe this! We have to walk out of here. They may not want to arrest a seventy-two-year-old veteran. It doesn't look good. But two Americans? The new American ambassador will only be sworn in this Thursday. We don't want to be his first cases!"

Kim Chi finished texting.

"Let's have some food," she suggested.

I checked the time on my cell phone. We had been talking for two hours but given the range of emotions I had gone through—happiness at reconnecting, admiration at her courage, and anxiety about what would happen next—it had felt like an eternity.

Kim Chi, with gaiety and calm, announced she had prepared a delicious meal of chicken stew with mushrooms, green vegetables, and a special rice dish.

"Tonight is the full moon," she said. "I made red sticky rice. The color comes from *gấc,* a kind of small jackfruit that is red inside. In Vietnam, they say if you have a big heart you cook a good meal!"

"Then you have a very big heart," I replied, after taking my first bite.

Night had fallen. Our gracious hostess accompanied us to the main road where a taxi was waiting. Kim Chi took me by the arm to walk down the alley. She was limping slightly.

On November 4, 2018, Kim Chi resigned from the Communist Party, following the dismissal of a prominent party member found to have printed books diverging from the party's political line. Several other party members also left.

When announcing her decision, the Trail veteran who had developed an empathy for the poor and oppressed during her school years in China wrote on her Facebook page:

"I wish that other party members who still have a conscience and passion for the people and country would also leave."

*Hồ Chí Minh and the Hanoi Politburo decided in May 1959 to support the Việt Cộng insurgency in South Vietnam "to liberate the South, defend the North, and reunify the country." Guerrilla fighters trekked on mountain paths through Laos to Việt Cộng strongholds in South Vietnam. It was the beginning of the Ho Chi Minh Trail through the Trường Sơn Mountains. The secret missions through the beautiful mountains inspired countless romantic songs, poems, and films.*

*Before setting off on their journey south, they trained in the military camp in Hòa Bình Province where Kim Chi had "hiked up and down mountains carrying fifty-five pounds."*

At 7 a.m. the next morning, I checked my emails and ordered a *cà phê đen* in the hotel breakfast room. The dark syrupy coffee had the bittersweet taste of my new home. Morning coffee was the best time of the day. Everything was possible.

I took out my paper map. I planned to go to Hòa Bình Province, at the start of Route 15, where the road to war began. It was an easy day's drive from Hanoi. On the way, I was curious to stop at Mường Studio, a contemporary art and heritage center, to learn more about the history of the area. Art in war—creation in destruction—had brought me to the Trail. Visiting Mường Studio was a good way to commence the trip.

Before our departure for Hòa Bình later that morning, I had a couple of hours to explore places in the city where the story of the Trail began. I left a note for Nam and took a taxi to Hanoi's French quarter. The birth of the revolutionary road had taken place in the unlikely setting of former colonial splendor. Leaving the narrow streets of Old Hanoi, past the Cathedral, the cab traveled along the wide boulevards of the French colonial neighborhood near the West Lake, bordered by grand shady trees and houses in sumptuous ocher. We reached 83 Lý Nam Đế, an address close to the Ministry of Defense, where the Hanoi headquarters of Group 559 had once been. The modest engineering unit of 500 officers and soldiers was created in 1959 to organize transportation to the communist insurgency in South Vietnam.

Contrary to popular imagination, there had been no grand plan to build a vast military supply network to conquer South Vietnam. The land Trail began as a single path across the Trường Sơn Mountains to reach guerrilla strongholds in the Central Highlands of South Vietnam. The limited mission was to deliver all of fifty guns, sixty or so miles south of the Demilitarized Zone.

Leaving the grand boulevards behind, the taxi continued to the warehouse at Bốt Lũ, 63 Kim Giang in Thanh Trì District, where the guns of the first expedition had reportedly been stockpiled. Google Maps figured out that the street was now in Thanh Xuân not Thanh Trì District, and estimated that it would take half an hour to travel the five miles to the site through Hanoi's heavy early-morning traffic.

The gunrunning to the South that had escalated into one of the major conflicts of the twentieth century had originated, I discovered, in a simple storeroom on the banks of the Tô Lịch River. Veterans wanted the building classified as a "cultural relic" to prevent it from being demolished. The quiet neighborhood a few miles from the city center was scheduled for redevelopment, with luxury high-rises and shopping malls, landscaped gardens and lakes, spas, bike paths, and jogging lanes.

The operation, according to the official story, had taken place in total secrecy. Secondhand guns "captured from the French" and "socialist" guns stripped of their mark of origin were sent by truck to a military base north of the provisional demarcation line and the Bến Hải River. An advance survey team had mapped a path across "a rugged mountainous terrain infested with malaria … The rivers were deep and the climate was harsh. The high peaks were shrouded in mist." Recruits disguised as mountain villagers carried the guns in rattan woven baskets strapped to their backs. They avoided villages in low-lying valleys infiltrated by enemy spies. They scaled the high peaks of the Trường Sơn Mountains and crossed Route 9 into enemy territory at a remote outpost to avoid patrols. They floated the weapons wrapped in waterproof material on rafts made out of banana leaves across deep rivers to deliver their cargo to the guerrilla stronghold in the Central Highlands.[16]

According to the National Archives Center in Hanoi, by war's end, sixteen years later in 1975, the single mountainous path had expanded into a grid of over 10,000 miles of roads, river ways, and pipelines through North and South Vietnam, Laos, and Cambodia:

"Six north–south roads were connected by twenty-one east–west roads. The north–south road network was four thousand miles long, the east–west network, three thousand miles long. An additional three thousand miles of bypass roads included five hundred miles of underground tunnels, one thousand miles of gravel roads, and over one hundred miles of paved roads. Communication lines stretched for eighteen hundred miles, fuel pipelines for over one thousand miles, and river ways for hundreds of miles."[17]

⛩

I made it back to the hotel in time to greet Hân Mai, our traveling companion and driver, who arrived on the dot of 10 a.m., clean-cut, and wearing a linen blazer. He was decisive and friendly.

Our triumvirate sat down in the lobby to plan our first day together. I had mapped out a tentative itinerary from Hanoi to Ho Chi Minh City that followed the chronological expansion of the Trail between 1959 and 1975.

"Where do we start?" asked Nam.

"Hòa Bình. Where the fighters trained before getting their marching orders to go south," I said.

"Where's the camp?" asked Nam.

"It's not there anymore, but Phan Cẩm Thượng has invited us to visit Mường Studio, the artist colony where he lives," I replied.

Nam and I had first met the artist in the early nineties when we were in Hanoi to research and collect war drawings.

"New art on the Trail. I like that. That's how it all began. Maybe they give painting lessons there," Nam wondered.

Nam had always fantasized about becoming an artist.

"We can spend the night in the Mai Châu Valley," said Hân.

"It's not far," I replied, pointing to the valley on my map.

"I have no sense of direction. I trust the two of you," said Nam.

Hân glanced politely at my paper map.

"I have a GPS in the car," he said.

Parked outside the hotel was the 4x4 that would take us for most of the 2,000-mile journey to Ho Chi Minh City, and to the "elusive" Việt Cộng headquarters, the "mini-Pentagon" that US analysts had believed was hidden in the jungle. When US and South Vietnamese Air Forces attacked the Việt Cộng camp in 1967 in the largest airborne operation of the war, they were surprised to discover thatched huts instead of the concrete bunkers they had imagined.

We left for the Trail at a snail's pace through Hanoi's chaotic traffic. Hân attached his cell phone to the front window screen, switched to video mode "to record memories of your trip."

Nam settled in the back seat to meditate with his wrist mala. He had told me that the prayer beads and the meditation they inspired helped him come to terms with the divisive past that had split his family into northern and southern sympathizers.

It took an hour to get to the outskirts of the city. Hanoi was pulsating with sound, movement, and expectation. The city had emerged vibrant from the darkness of war. Mopeds, cars, and trucks competed for road space. Bicycles, boarded-up shop fronts, power outages, and arrest for talking to foreigners belonged to the past.

We crawled alongside the cement pillars of Hanoi's new Metro. Billboards advertising Cartier and Louis Vuitton competed with propaganda posters celebrating the fortieth anniversary of the end of the war. Somewhere, under the new concrete jumble of highways, lay the vestiges of the old French Colonial Route 6, the Trail recruits' wartime way to the training camp in Hòa Bình.

We picked up Phan Cẩm Thượng on our way out of Hanoi for the drive to Hòa Bình. He jumped into the back seat next to Nam. His wispy beard trimmed in the manner of Confucius and Hồ Chí Minh suited his persona of artist, writer, Buddhist scholar, and professor at the Hanoi College of Fine Arts.

As we crossed the city limits, Phan Cẩm Thượng announced that he had turned sixty. I wondered why he was so cheerful about it.

"There's a belief in Vietnam that your second life starts at sixty. So, I'm happy to report, I'm one again!" he said.

"To new beginnings!" I said.

We left behind the alluvial plain of the Red River, heavy with rice and people, and entered the empty silence of the karst mountains and caves of Hòa Bình. The Trail meandered through a millennial land with an archaeological and historical past—unknown to Americans. The region had given its name to the Hoabinhian culture that flourished across south China and Southeast Asia between 12,000 and 10,000 BC. In the twenties, a French archaeologist had discovered Stone Age objects, ceramic shards, and settlements here.

We traveled through limestone hills and arrived at Mường Studio, set on five acres of a mountain slope. The slippery terrain, muddy in the rainy season, thick jungle cover, and steep inclines simulated the rough conditions of the Trường Sơn Mountains. Kim Chi had been sent to this challenging location to practice mountaineering, carrying fifty-five pounds of rocks in her backpack, in preparation for her trek south.

I found a peaceful creative space where war had once prevailed. The place, landscaped with stone paths, clipped hedges, a pond, and a pine forest, was named after the Mường who farmed the fertile valleys of Hòa Bình. They were the descendants of a Bronze Age people known for their stupendous bronze gongs and drums decorated with intricate lozenge motifs. The Mường heritage museum was housed in a disused anti-aircraft defense bunker.

The compound of tribal dwellings and contemporary art installations was a haven for visiting artists. Looking down from the hill, a wood-and-stone sculpture of a Mường couple by the Hanoi-based artist George Burchett stood guard over their ancestral land.

Vũ Đức Hiếu, the potter and founder, welcomed us into his open-air studio. Glazes in aquatic greens and celadon gleamed, their luster as translucent as glass. The objects stood in silent homage to Hòa Bình's millennial ceramics tradition. An urn was firing in the kiln.

"The sand is very special here. It was a good reason to come to Hòa Bình!" said Hiếu, who had moved here from Hanoi.

On the restaurant terrace nearby, we sat down to a sumptuous lunch of river fish soup with star fruit, pickled white baby eggplant, fresh herb omelet, and tofu with chili and tomato sauce. An amber-colored rice wine made from apricots was served in shot glasses.

After lunch, we visited the bunker-turned-museum, full of hand-woven beaded textiles with red-and-black geometric designs, traditional looms, farm tools, and an oblong basket to catch the apparently gigantic fish that once swam in the mountain rivers. Impressive traditional Mường houses on stilts, coiffed with sweeping sloping roofs, nestled in the trees close by. Hiếu had bought dwellings in danger of demolition, dismantled, moved, and reassembled them here in the pine forest. Several generations lived together in an open-plan room—my idea of hell—divided by invisible walls into assigned spaces for elders, married couples, and children. Bronze gongs, handed down through generations, decorated the walls.

"Since you are traveling down the Trail, you might be interested in sketches from the Indochina Trail," said Phan Cẩm Thượng, as we left the Mường ancestral home.

He invited us to his house for some bitter tea and to view a collection of war sketches from the French War, showcased in a recently published book he had authored. His white-washed cottage was sparsely furnished, almost monastic, except for paintings and sketches that hung everywhere on the walls. We sat outside in the front garden. The peaceful setting invited contemplation.

Phan Cẩm Thượng shared my passion for art drawn under fire. The Trail in art as in war, I discovered, was a continuation of the Indochina Trail. He presented me with a handsome art book. The aroma of new paper and freshly printed ink was intoxicating. I opened the book with reverence. The featured artist had been the pioneer of Vietnamese war art. His teachings had inspired the artists who had led me here. The sketches by Tô Ngọc Vân (1906–1954) had survived in the custody of his son, hidden from view until publication. The painter, who graduated in 1931 from the École des Beaux-Arts d'Indochine, the art school established in Hanoi by the French, had been celebrated for sensuous paintings of young women in love. A photograph in the book showed a fashionable Tô Ngọc Vân in a tailored linen suit and tie, standing at ease, his hands in his pockets, a bright future before him. But Tô Ngọc Vân's urban world ended abruptly when war broke out. The French had returned to Vietnam to reclaim their colony at the end of World War II.

The artist left Hanoi to join Hồ Chí Minh's fight for independence in the Resistance Zone. He became director of the itinerant art school in the jungle and sketched along the Indochina Trail, living with the fighters. A master at conveying emotion, he captured the pathos of war as he had young love, in natural, flowing strokes.

As I leafed through the war sketches from the French War, I had a feeling of déjà vu. Women featured everywhere: women carrying rice, women transporting ammunition, women repairing roads, women caring for the wounded, and women marked by poverty working the farm while the men fought at the front.

Tô Ngọc Vân was killed by enemy fire at the very end of the war.

I closed the book. Phan Cẩm Thượng turned to me.

"Foreigners don't care about Vietnamese culture," he said. "They think we have nothing. All they are interested in are war and politics."

The light was fading. We promised our hosts that we would return to their peaceful haven. Back in the car, the road wound its way through the fantastical shapes of limestone hills. We stopped at the top of a high pass, where Route 15, the road to war, began. I looked down over the wide Mai Châu Valley, covered in the mist of time, mysterious and beckoning. Eyelets of light from the villages below winked through the foggy dusk. Green sugar cane and oranges for sale lined the road, touches of color in the gray landscape.

At the Mai Châu Lodge over catfish served with lemongrass, banana blossom salad, and water spinach, we talked about the new Vietnam, marked by the contradictions of prosperity and protest.

In my hotel room, I was greeted by the scent of white lilies, the flowers in Tô Ngọc Vân's *Young Woman with Lilies*. He had painted the portrait of the girl with flowers before he had stopped drawing love to record war. The West as the sole source of all things was an old habit of mind. Until this image, I had associated lilies with Western culture—with medieval symbols, Catholic altars, and French royal fleur-de-lys.

Lilies bloomed early this year. They grew in the high plateaus of the limestone mountains of the northern and central provinces of Vietnam. Legend had it that winged ghosts flew over the fragrant fields, the spirits of the lost souls of those who had died too young.

Before surrendering to sleep, I took out my paper map. Where did the recruits go after training in Hòa Bình? To the coastal Trail Route 1A and across the Dragon's Jaw Bridge at Thanh Hóa. The bridge was a strategic point for troops traveling by land, and for military supplies going by sea.

As Kim Chi described it, the road had been long and arduous but relatively safe. That all changed in 1965 when the United States began a sustained bombing campaign against the Trail in North Vietnam, and launched a naval blockade against the sea route.

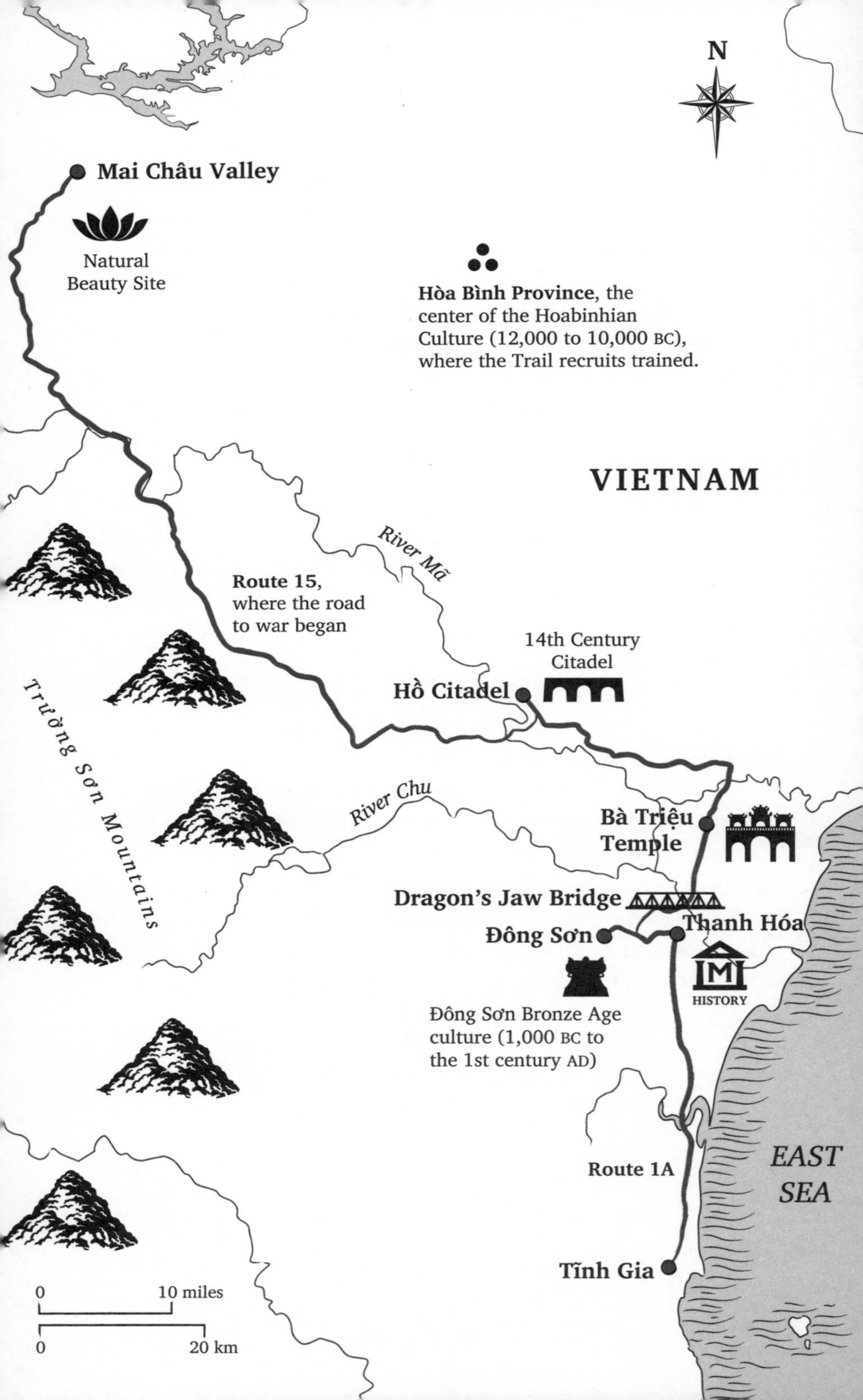
N
Mai Châu Valley
Natural
Beauty Site
Hòa Bình Province, the
center of the Hoabinhian
Culture (12,000 to 10,000 BC),
where the Trail recruits trained.
VIETNAM
River Mã
Route 15,
where the road
to war began
14th Century
Citadel
Hồ Citadel
Trường Sơn Mountains
River Chu
Bà Triệu
Temple
Dragon's Jaw Bridge
Thanh Hóa
Đông Sơn
HISTORY
Đông Sơn Bronze Age
culture (1,000 BC to
the 1st century AD)
EAST
SEA
Route 1A
Tĩnh Gia
0
10 miles
0
20 km

Chapter 2

# *HÒA BÌNH TO THANH HÓA*

*Where the road to war began, the Temple of Lady Triệu, and the defender of the Dragon's Jaw Bridge.*

*When the United States began bombing North Vietnam, the coastal Trail Route 1A was its main target.*

*The Trail Commander Đồng Sĩ Nguyên wrote in his memoir:*

*"Our air defenses [had been] too thin ... We strengthened our regimental air-defense units ... We combined artillery, infantry, and militia units to defend key points and bridges [along Route 1A] ... and fortified our coastal defenses."*[18]

*Of all the bridges along Route 1A, the Dragon's Jaw Bridge, in the city of Thanh Hóa, was legendary for its defiance of the air war waged against it. The bridge was "infamous" in Washington, where US planners became obsessed with obliterating it. Targeted in more than 800 sorties over seven years, it was eventually destroyed in 1972 by laser-guided bombs. Eleven American pilots were shot down and captured. Vietnamese casualties on the ground, both combatants and civilians, remain unknown.*

I was on my way to Thanh Hóa and the Dragon's Jaw Bridge to meet its defender, Lieutenant Colonel Ngô Thị Tuyển, a decorated hero of the People's Armed Forces. At seventeen, she had carried ammunition double her body weight to urgently supply the gunners defending the bridge against the first attacks by American fighter-bombers.

I was apprehensive. Would Ngô Thị Tuyển be welcoming or refuse to see me? She had served with the Youth Volunteer Corps (*Thanh Niên Xung Phong*), mostly women with some men, aged between seventeen and twenty-four, who built, repaired, and defended the Trail network. The social and military corps first established by Hồ Chí Minh in 1951 was reactivated during the Vietnam War. Their story of bravery and suffering was unprecedented in the history of modern warfare.

The morning mist lifted on a pond of pink lotuses in bloom and of dry rice fields the color of clay.

"Why don't we stay here?" asked Nam, when we all met for an early breakfast.

"Tempting," I replied.

But Hân had no time for dreams of bucolic retreats away from it all.

"Have you decided where we are going today?" he asked.

"Thanh Hóa, to meet Ngô Thị Tuyển," I responded.

"That's my city," said Hân.

"Lucky," I replied, relieved.

I didn't have an address for Ngô Thị Tuyển, and wasn't sure how to find her.

"Do you know where she lives?"

"No, but everybody knows her. It should be easy," Hân replied. "We should stop at Lady Triệu's temple on the way. She's also a national heroine."

Bà Triệu, or Lady Triệu, had fought the Chinese occupation in the third century AD, following in the tradition of the Trưng sisters who had rebelled against the Chinese two centuries earlier (40–43 AD).

"Sounds good," I said.

"Where should we stay tonight?" asked Nam.

"Tĩnh Gia, where I live," Hân suggested. "It's only twenty minutes south of Thanh Hóa. I'm inviting you for dinner tonight at my new restaurant. And I've texted my mother-in-law to ask her to join us. She served on the Trail."

We accepted his invitation, delighted at the opportunity to sample more Vietnamese cuisine, and to meet his family. By 7:30 a.m. we had left the Mai Châu Valley for the drive to Thanh Hóa. Route 15 passed through dried rice fields and villages of wooden stilt houses. At a remote junction, we began our climb into the foothills of the Trường Sơn Mountains. A soft mist blurred the ragged outlines of the limestone peaks. The white waters of a torrent sang in the wilderness. The road meandered, suspended between Earth and sky. We advanced, miniature figures in our anachronistic vehicle, as if in a Chinese ink painting of hills, streams, and waterfalls. I noticed slopes covered entirely in bamboo. The artist Trần Huy Oánh had carved his lucky walking stick from thickets like these, the cane he was heartsick at having lost.

The past filled the silent mountains. As we advanced on the road to war, the specters of the women and men in the drawings peopled the empty landscape around me. Floppy hats or helmets covering their heads, wearing canvas boots or Ho Chi Minh sandals, armed with an AK-47 rifle, a bamboo walking stick, a rice belt tied around their waist, they walked or rode in trucks to the coastal cities of Thanh Hóa and Vinh, where they rested before the trek south.

We reached a village of stilt houses, among terraced rice paddies in curved mirrored patterns. I felt oddly at home as I recognized scenes from the war drawings. Bright red patches waved in the light breeze. Gold-starred red flags of the Democratic Socialist Republic, flying on bamboo poles and garden fences, celebrated the seventieth anniversary of the People's Army. Spring onions, lettuces, and beans grew in well-tended vegetable gardens. Oval-shaped slices of manioc were laid out to dry, stretched out on the tarmac like white carpet runners. A small boy was teaching himself how to ride a bicycle in the middle of the road. Hanoi artists on their way to war had sketched the mountain people and landscapes, moved by their beauty and novelty, until they stopped drawing, defeated by the long marches, the blood-sucking leeches, the malaria fits that killed, and the hunger, the fear, the waves of napalm, and bombs, and the unburied bloated corpses by the roadside devoured by vultures and covered in maggots. Few had the stomach to depict the gore.

"It's a peaceful and simple life here," said Hân, drawing me out of my reverie.

"Are you thinking of early retirement?" I asked.

Hân was thirty-five.

"No, too boring! I grew up in the countryside. My father was a teacher in a remote village. I was impatient to discover the wider world. I love the open road," he replied.

He had been hooked on adventure ever since.

As we reached the bottom of a pass, we left the silence of the mountains behind us. The crowded plains, the lifeblood of the Viets, were suddenly upon me. Trucks, buses, cars, mopeds, bicycles, water buffaloes, and flocks of white ducks from nearby rice fields competed for the road. The stilt houses gave way to a jumble of orange, green, and blue cement houses, concrete blocks that jarred the eye. After the lush green of the misty mountains, in the plain the rice fields lay fallow. The roads appeared as bare bones lying across gray fields. We were traveling in winter, during the dry season when the military convoys left on the Trail for the southern battlefronts to avoid the monsoon rains, the floods, and the mudslides that buried roads and washed away bridges.

### *The Hồ Citadel*

We followed the road along a lazy river. Spiky green shoots of sugar cane stretched along its banks. The river was quiet.

"Where are the boats?" I asked.

"Too shallow for transportation," Hân replied.

We left the main road and drove down a track across a flat plain. At the end, a grand archway suddenly appeared before me.

"Where are we?" I asked.

"The Hồ Citadel," said Hân.

It was the southern gate of the mighty Hồ fortress built against Chinese invaders in the fourteenth century. The ruined citadel imposed its majesty on the alluvial plains. The scale was breathtaking. So were the engineering and construction skills deployed to ward off foreign occupiers. I measured the determination and mastery that centuries later built the Trail network of roads. The capital city had covered twenty square miles in its glory days. The gateway, at thirty feet high, was imposing. The walls, built of massive limestone blocks were as impressive as those of medieval European fortresses. Each block weighed between ten and twenty tons.

History here was about resistance to the Chinese, the neighbor to the north. The occupation that lasted over a thousand years (from 111 BC to 939 AD) was remembered in history books as the First, Second, and Third Periods of Chinese Domination. A few centuries later, the mighty fortifications notwithstanding, the armies of the Ming Empire invaded again. Emperor Hồ's realm became a province of the Ming Empire for twenty years during the Fourth, and final, Period of Chinese Domination. Blamed for having lost to the Chinese, Hồ was partially redeemed for having improved literacy. His dual legacy was on display in a makeshift museum at the Northern Gate. Terracotta tiles engraved with Sino-Vietnamese characters lay next to stone cannon balls, medieval weapons of war.

I climbed the crumbling fortress wall, up a mound covered in soft grass and purple flowers. From my vantage point on the ramparts, I was hoping to finally see the Trường Sơn Mountains I had caught sight of on the television evening news. But the cloud cover was relentless, thick and gray, hiding the mountain range of Vietnam's heroic suffering.

Leaving the Hồ Citadel behind, the road followed the River Mã that flows under the Dragon's Jaw Bridge at Thanh Hóa and into the East Sea. Gouged limestone hills littered the landscape, like the weird ruins of a lost civilization. The medieval stone blocks of the citadel had come from quarries like these. A deafening sound filled the air that was thick with dust. Workers, their mouths covered with bandit-like scarves, wielded power tools to cut the gigantic marble and limestone blocks that had once been carved by hand.

### *The Temple of Lady Triệu*

At the junction with Route 1A, we arrived at the handsome temple dedicated to the war heroine Lady Triệu. At nineteen, Lady Triệu had led an insurrection against the Chinese in the third century AD.

Vietnam had a long devotion to its warriors, both women and men, who had led the people to rise up against foreign invaders. Ancestor worship established a spiritual bond between the rulers and their subjects, between the past and the present, and had been encouraged by the imperial dynasties. Hồ Chí Minh and the communist leaders tapped into centuries of collective filial piety, and of resistance to foreign occupation, when they mobilized the country for the war for national salvation and unification against the Americans and the "puppet" regime in Saigon.

The temple was built of fine white stucco worn by monsoon rains. Ornate pavilions and pitched roves with scalloped terracotta tiles and extravagant eaves stretched up the densely forested hill. Sinuous dragons with bulging eyes, sharp canines, and menacing claws stared down at us as we climbed the steps to the shrine. Our guide assured me that they brought good luck, despite their fierce appearance.

We stepped into a luxuriant interior of dark tropical ironwood, gold leaf, and rich lacquer decorated with an elaborately carved gilded altarpiece, and sacred objects of silver, lacquer, and porcelain.

The air was heavy with the scent of burning incense. Auspicious cranes with gold wings and red beaks rested their claws on the backs of turtles, symbolizing longevity and friendship. Yellow silk parasols, pink gladioli, and red roses added to the ceremonial splendor. Gold-lacquered swords and a sacred bronze gong testified to Lady Triệu's power and glory. Above the swords a quote attributed to the virgin warrior, and known to all Vietnamese, was written in gold letters. I was surprised to learn that the revolutionary Lady Triệu had also been a feminist. She reportedly told her brother when he tried to dissuade her from fighting the Chinese:

"I want to ride the wind and the waves and slay the sharks in the East Sea. I want to reconquer our land and to drive out the enemy, I want to free our people from slavery, and, Brother, I will never bend my back to be anyone's concubine."

The quote was first recorded in a nineteenth-century history of Thanh Hóa written by a governor of the province. The author might have edited her words, which had been passed down through the generations, to suit the times of rebellion against French colonialism. But a Confucian governor would have had little reason to promote feminism. Multiple wives and concubines at the time were a sign of wealth, status, and authority.

Had a notion of gender equality existed in popular culture in pre-Confucian times and been reintroduced by war and communism? "Equality between man and woman" had been part of Hồ Chí Minh's manifesto when he created the Indochinese Communist Party in 1930.[19] He had been outraged by "the violence of colonization that becomes still more odious when it is exercised upon women ... and [the] unbelievably widespread and cruel [French] colonial sadism [against women]."[20]

During the Vietnam War, temples and other places of worship were closed. When they reopened, Lady Triệu became the patron saint of women veterans.

"Do people worship Lady Triệu now?" I asked the guide.

"Yes, women come here to ask for help. The temple is funded by the Women's Union in Thanh Hóa," she replied.

When the United States began bombing North Vietnam in 1965, the Women's Union launched the Three Responsibilities Campaign (*Ba đảm đang*), a kind of self-draft for married women with children at home. The campaign enlisted around 1.7 million women throughout North Vietnam. Women were expected to look after the family, fill the jobs vacated by men fighting at the front, and take up arms to defend their homes, communities, and places of work, against American planes.

When I met her in her studio in Ho Chi Minh City after the Trail journey, this is how Phùng Chí Thu, a sculptor who worked for Radio Hanoi during the war, remembered the campaign:

"I had to go to work, take care of my baby, take my rifle, climb onto the rooftop, and shoot at the planes. I also had to help the injured. Once, a body was cut in many different parts and I had to pick them up. When I got home, I took a bath. I couldn't breastfeed my baby because I felt so disgusted."

We reached the inner sanctum that sheltered the gold statue of the virgin warrior. The early feminist sat in the demure pose of Confucian saints. Not so in folk legend. A handsome Lady Triệu, six feet tall, rode into battle on a war elephant, wearing a golden tunic, her ample three-foot-long breasts flung over her shoulders. Her guerrilla army scored victory after victory against the Chinese occupiers, and more and more people joined her rebellion. The Chinese finally sent one of their top generals, Lu Yin, to put an end to the armed insurrection.

"Was she killed in battle?" I asked the guide.

"No. The Chinese general told his troops to fight naked, forcing Lady Triệu to flee in disgust. Her small army lost. She took her own life rather than surrender to the Chinese," she explained, citing one version of the story.

But that wasn't the end of Lady Triệu. Her spirit, according to popular legend, kept tormenting General Lu Yin in his dreams. Pestilence spread among his troops after her death. The general ordered craftsmen to carve hundreds of wooden penises and hang them on their doors to ward off her spirit.

### *The Dragon's Jaw Bridge*

At 4 p.m. we drove over the renowned Dragon's Jaw Bridge that we had come to Thanh Hóa to see. For all its notoriety, legendary or infamous, the Dragon's Jaw Bridge was not particularly long or especially wide. The structure that stretched across the silty River Mã followed a blueprint for an iron railway bridge designed by Gustave Eiffel, the French civil engineer who built the Eiffel Tower in Paris.

That afternoon, the bridge was quiet. High-school kids in blue-and-white school uniforms cycled across on their way home. The force used against it—more than 800 sorties—was disproportionate to its small size. Yet the bridge held for seven years until it was destroyed in 1972. During the first attacks against the bridge, Ngô Thị Tuyển and her platoon supplied rice and ammunition to the anti-aircraft defense units tasked with defending it.

Ngô Thị Tuyển lived in the center of Thanh Hóa. At a roundabout, Hân must have had a sixth sense and turned left down a quiet, tree-lined street.

"This lady looks about the right age," said Hân, as he stopped to ask directions.

The woman's gray hair was tied back into a bun and she appeared to be in her early sixties.

"My generation," I reminded myself, silently thanking Clairol.

"Do you know where Ngô Thị Tuyển lives?" Hân asked her, leaning out of the car window. The woman pointed at the attractive town house across the street. The upper-floor balconies and pagoda-shaped roof were trimmed in warm ocher tones.

Hân rang the doorbell. An elderly gentleman came to the door.

"I'm sorry, we don't have an appointment. We were hoping to meet Ngô Thị Tuyển."

He was instantly welcoming. I felt encouraged.

"I'm her husband," he said. "Ngô Thị Tuyển is out exercising. She'll be back soon and I'm sure she would be delighted to see you. She has already done two interviews today, one for the Army radio and one for television. Come in. I'll text her."

"Exercising?" I was impressed.

The pride of victory filled the room: a photograph of the Dragon's Jaw Bridge, the red-and-gold-starred national flag flying high over the Dragon's hill; honorary certificates; and a portrait of a handsome Ngô Thị Tuyển, with a broad smile, in a white military uniform with gold epaulets, gold buttons, and rows of multicolored medals.

Minutes later, Ngô Thị Tuyển made a grand entrance. Her smile and high energy made her appear taller than she really was. Dressed in a smart black pantsuit, her hair pulled back, she wore gold button earrings.

We sat down next to each other under the picture of the Dragon's Jaw Bridge. Ngô Thị Tuyển served the tea. I followed my usual technique. I took a sip and waited. I didn't have long to wait this time. Ngô Thị Tuyển didn't hang around. She was impatient to share her war stories with a foreigner who had traveled far to visit her.

"I enlisted into the Youth Volunteer Corps when I was seventeen, with my three sisters. Our parents were farmers. We didn't go to school, we worked in the fields. I'm now sixty-eight years old," she started.

"You look much younger," I said, which she did.

"How old are you?"

Knowing this question might come up, I had asked Nam to lie in translation, a bit. On my first visit to Vietnam, I'd been taken by surprise until someone explained the form of address varied with age and marital status. Communism had introduced *chí* or comrade, regardless of age and status, but traditional forms persisted.

Ngô Thị Tuyển relived the terrifying two-day assault against the bridge, her voice rising, her hands moving, pointing at imaginary planes. On April 3, 1965, American fighter-bombers launched their first attack. They dropped 120 750-pound bombs, and fired thirty-two air-to-ground missiles. During the second strike on April 4, sixty-nine fighter-bombers struck the bridge with 300 750-pound bombs. At the time, the entire North Vietnamese fighter strength was only fifty-six aircraft.[21]

Ngô Thị Tuyển remembered:

"I had begun my military training in January 1964. Our leaders suspected that the Americans might bomb the North. I was part of an all-woman transportation platoon when the American planes launched their first assaults against the bridge in 1965. They bombed for two days. During the attacks, my platoon shuttled rice, shells, and cartridges back and forth between the rear and our anti-air defense units. On the second day, our gunners were running out of bullets. A convoy arrived with ammunition. So, I loaded up with two boxes because I knew it was critical to resupply the front. Combined they weighed two hundred and sixteen pounds. I was only ninety-two pounds at the time. A photojournalist took my picture and published it in the newspaper."

"Weren't you afraid? So many bombs?" I asked.

"What am I afraid of? I was young. If you don't kill them, they kill you."

The fearlessness of youth served politicians and generals well.

The bridge was severely damaged but remained standing.

She showed me a copy of the newspaper photograph. She was smiling but the pain of her superhuman effort was etched on her young face. Her pose made me think of the graceful drawing of a woman balancing an ammunition box on her shoulder.

It was such a staggering load for a woman of her size, of any size, that I wondered if it had been a publicity stunt.

"Did you injure yourself?" I asked.

On Route 1A, at the Temple of Lady Triệu, Thanh Hóa Province.

"Not that time, but I did a few months later. Newspapers from socialist countries came to Thanh Hóa to write stories about me. A journalist asked me to show him how I did it because he didn't believe it was possible. So I loaded up with two sacks—one full of potatoes, the other one full of rice. The bags weighed two hundred and thirty pounds, heavier than the ammunition boxes. That's when I hurt my back. I held for ten minutes when suddenly I felt a stabbing pain. I was hospitalized. I've had three operations since."

I believed her now. Ngô Thi Tuyển was awarded the title "Heroine of the People's Armed Forces."

"Why do you think Vietnam won? You were so much weaker."

"We were home, they were far away from home."

Maybe it was as simple as that.

I thought it was a good time to raise the question that Americans who travel to Vietnam asked me.

"American visitors are surprised at the warm welcome they get when they come here," I said.

"We learned from Uncle Hồ that if the enemy fights with us then we fight with them. There are many Americans who are good people. Many protested against the war. We know how to separate. We have a long tradition, a long custom of knowing how to separate. When two US Navy pilots recently came to visit me, I welcomed them. They had come back to Thanh Hóa to see the bridge they had bombed. We put history aside and looked to the future," she answered.

The veterans from the other side had showed her respect. In spite of its victory, communist Vietnam had been treated as a pariah state after the end of the war, isolated, and sanctioned by the West.

During their visit, she offered the pilots a beer and the veterans toasted to friendship. The airmen who flew Phantom fighter jets presented her with a couple of copies of *Phantom in the River: The Flight of Linfield Two Zero One,* a book about their missions against the bridge, and the fateful day they were shot down and captured.[22]

She handed me a copy, with a marker at the page where she was mentioned.

"Please translate this for me when you get home," she said.

"Of course. Thank you for the book," I replied.

"Are you kidding? I bet you're not going to do that," said Nam.

"More and more Americans are coming here. They realize what they did was wrong," she continued, ignoring our aside.

"Why now?"

"They don't know the suffering."

She thought for a moment and added:

"They *know* the suffering but they can't *feel* the suffering. As you go further south toward the Demilitarized Zone, in Quảng Trị Province you will see a lot more suffering. So many cemeteries."

Empathy comes from feeling not knowing. Many feel emotionally removed from the tragedies that governments help to create. They prefer to believe the rhetoric about bringing freedom, democracy, and prosperity to foreign lands rather than question their government's responsibility for the deadly consequences of their military adventures.

Her bravado hid a personal tragedy. I asked her what she thought about war reparations, whether the vanquished should pay compensation to the victors.

"The Americans should pay war reparations for what they did," she said.

She wasn't joking.

"Please tell the Americans that they should resolve this Agent Orange issue. We couldn't have children," she explained.

Her willingness to forgive needed justice. But by war reparations, Ngô Thị Tuyển believed that Vietnamese veterans and civilians affected by Agent Orange should be compensated as American veterans had been. She did not seek more or wider reparations for possible US crimes of aggression—the bombardment and military blockades of ports, violations of the rule of proportionality, or war crimes against civilians. I felt a lot angrier than she did at the civilian deaths we had caused.

The United States was cleaning up dioxin storage sites at Da Nang and Biên Hòa Air Bases, but was doing little to assist those affected by the poison. The Vietnamese Red Cross estimated over one million Vietnamese were exposed to the dioxin. The "rainbow herbicide" has been blamed for infertility, birth defects, rare cancers, and other diseases. But the US government and manufacturers disputed the causal link, and did not accept liability.

"I continue to give to the country. I work as a volunteer security guard," she said.

"The neighborhood must feel safe under your watch."

There was one more thing she wanted to share.

"Hồ Chí Minh gave me a medal shortly before he died. It was the biggest moment of my life."

Ngô Thị Tuyển then turned toward Hân.

"Are you married?" she asked him.

"Yes," he replied.

"Oh," she said, disappointed. "I was thinking of my niece. Well, come back whenever you like."

It was time to take photographs to commemorate our meeting.

"I don't have time to put my uniform and medals on," said Ngô Thị Tuyển.

Not one to be defeated, she had another idea.

"First, take a picture of my portrait in my white military uniform," she said, pointing at the image on the wall in which she was wearing full military regalia. "Second, take a photograph of me now. Then Photoshop my face into the portrait."

"OK," I replied.

"What do you mean 'OK'?" asked Nam. "How are you going to do that? Don't you know how to say no?"

I looked at Nam, surprised. How could anybody say "no" to Ngô Thị Tuyển? Hân took the portrait off the wall and I took a photograph.

Then Ngô Thị Tuyển stood to attention, with a broad smile and the straight back of the seventeen-year-old girl of the Dragon's Jaw Bridge. She didn't need to wear her military uniform and medals. Her bearing expressed a life well lived in defense of her country and beliefs. I snapped the portrait of a heroic woman.

As we said goodbye, Ngô Thị Tuyển held me in a bear-like hug.

Back in the car, I opened *Phantom in the River* to the pages she had marked. I smiled. When the US Navy pilots had visited, Ngô Thị Tuyển had ordered them to wait while she changed into her military uniform to honor her fellow veterans.

Before leaving Thanh Hóa, we checked out the Thanh Hóa Museum that housed a collection of Bronze Age drums and artifacts. The fertile delta of the River Mã, bombed so many times, had been home to a sun-worshiping culture that produced stupendous bronze drums. The Đông Sơn culture was named after a village less than a mile from the Dragon's Jaw Bridge, where the first drum was found by a farmer in the twenties. The mysterious drums, decorated with a sun, oxen, frog, and bird motifs, were thought to have been used as symbols of power and wealth, musical instruments, even burial vessels for human skulls.

We headed down Route 1A to Tĩnh Gia. Hân had been orchestrating the food preparations by text throughout the day. There were roadworks everywhere. The coastal highway between Hanoi and Ho Chi Minh City was down to a single lane, unpaved, with potholes, and no markings. We were hemmed in by tightly packed houses, open-air cafés, and shops. Bright headlights suddenly flashed through the windscreen. Hân veered into the roadside ditch to avoid an oncoming truck. A car then headed straight for us, while another overtook us from behind on the outside. I closed my eyes. Hân didn't flinch. The car swerved into someone's front yard. I looked back at Nam. He was meditating in the back seat and hadn't reacted to the near collisions. The Zen attitude of my traveling companions was contagious. I settled back in my seat and unclenched my fist from the handle.

Tĩnh Gia was a stretch of houses, restaurants, and shops along Route 1A. The former fishing village had become a symbol of the country's prosperity: a nine-billion-dollar petrochemical complex was being built along the coastline. We turned on to a track that led to the beach. It was pitch-black. I listened to the sound of the crashing waves in an angry sea. High-rise hotels lined the ocean-front built in expectation of the new affluence the petrochemical plant would bring. The beach cafés were deserted in winter. A German shepherd guard dog barked mournfully. We pulled up in front of the traditional-style Ngọc Linh Villas.

"Welcome to Monkey Flat," a young girl said, handing me a drink as I stepped into the hotel reception.

"Monkey Flat?"

Maybe she was referring to the name of the exotic drink.

She escorted us to rooms that opened onto a courtyard where merrymakers were enjoying a Christmas party around an open fire. Orchids and tropical ferns sparkled with fairy lights. The hotel room decked out in bamboo furniture was soothing after our day on the road. A quick change and we drove back into town to have dinner at Hân's restaurant. The honeycomb interior with soft origami lighting was elegant and minimalist.

Hân's mother-in-law greeted me with a warm embrace. Her features untouched by the passage of time, her gray hair pulled back in a bun, dressed in a dark pantsuit, it was difficult to imagine that she was a veteran of a cruel conflict. Mai, her two-year-old granddaughter, nestled in her arms, the child's dark eyes curiously checking out the foreigner.

The toddler climbed out of her grandmother's embrace and came over to offer me a sweet.

"She likes foreigners," said Hân's mother-in-law.

I sipped a glass of perfectly chilled Chilean Chardonnay. Bringing up the war in these peaceful and comfortable surroundings felt slightly indecent.

"I'm surprised so many women served in the war," I started, by way of introduction.

"Yes, Hân told me you were interested in our story. I was in the war between 1971 and 1973. I 'volunteered' when I was seventeen. I was studying for the baccalaureate in high school and had to interrupt my studies."

US war propaganda had portrayed fanatic and malevolent female snipers enlisting to gun down American planes. As we continued talking, I realized Hân's mother-in-law was not one of them. She had not volunteered, she'd been drafted, as were most women between seventeen and twenty-four years old after 1965. The word "volunteer" was misleading: under communist rule, all citizens were volunteers and had a compulsory duty to serve the state.

"Who volunteered?" I asked.

"Most everybody my age volunteered."

"Was volunteering compulsory?"

"Yes. If you didn't want to go, you had to get a special permission. Or you had to pay."

She continued:

"When we joined, we were evaluated for our skills and given a mission. Women were usually drafted to serve in non-combat roles. Some, the strong ones, went into the Army. I was drafted into the Youth Volunteer Corps and sent to work on the Trail in the jungle. Even the older married women were self-drafted to look after the kids, organize food production, and defend their homes."

Young women without family obligations were posted on the Trail away from home; older married women usually remained at home to defend their farms, villages, and towns.

After the bombings of North Vietnam began, women in support

roles on the Trail, and those self-drafted at home, came under direct fire. They joined anti-aircraft defense teams out of necessity, not radical extremism, to make up for the shortage of men who were sent to the southern fronts. Equally, there was no gender barrier for those who wanted to join the military in combat roles, the "strong ones," as Hân's mother-in-law had put it.

Similarly during World War II, with men away fighting, unmarried British women between the ages of nineteen and twenty-four were drafted into support roles, but joined anti-aircraft crews when German planes began their raids against UK territory. Unlike Vietnamese women, though, they were technically barred from serving in battle.

Hân's mother-in-law continued:

"I dug underground shelters and trenches. The worst was transporting the dead bodies. It was terrible. I didn't recognize my companions. We wrapped the remains of the dead in plastic bags and buried them. If we recognized them, we wrote their name on the plastic bag."

She paused, shaking her head while she remembered.

"I don't like thinking about all the terrible things I saw. Once, a B-52 killed more than forty soldiers. Body parts were scattered all along the road. We couldn't identify anyone."

Her distress felt all the stronger for being so restrained. We sat in silence for a while until she regained her composure.

"We were hungry because the rice was sent to the front line. So there wasn't enough to go around at the rear. And the leeches in the forest. Bad. I don't usually talk about this. The young generations aren't interested."

"Were you afraid?"

"I wasn't afraid. But some of my friends who had been drafted with me were afraid, and they wanted to go home. So, they left the jungle and headed for home. The police went to fetch them and brought them back."

"Everybody was drafted, men and women," her husband, who had joined us, added. "Men between seventeen and forty were put on a list. They were sent to fight in South Vietnam. The women were usually drafted for the home front in North Vietnam."

Drafted at seventeen, he served with the Ministry of Information between 1971 and 1976 in Quảng Trị Province.

"What happened to the men who didn't want to fight?"

"If they didn't go, they felt lonely. If they were scared and ran away, they died. If there were three brothers, one could stay [to look after elderly parents]," he answered.

"When you look back, how do you feel?"

"War was tough. In the rainy season, we couldn't get rice. The supplies stopped coming. We ate wild spinach we found in the forest. I can't count how many times I was bombed. Everywhere, they bombed. And everywhere there were *bombis* (cluster bombs). I remember the kids going to school wearing helmets made out of rice stalks. I remember fear, leeches, viruses, disease, and dead people. After the war, the government gave me a little bit of land to grow rice."

"How did you feel toward Americans?"

"After 1972, we never saw Americans; we fought the South Vietnamese."

He looked straight ahead, lost in thought.

"The Vietnamese have a hard life."

He stated this as fact, without self-pity.

Mai, his granddaughter, was running around the room, laughing and playing hide-and-seek. She was enjoying being the center of attention. With her bowl haircut, she was as cute as could be. She offered me another sweet. She was wiser than her two years, determined and loved.

"What is important to me are my granddaughter and my daughter," said Hân's mother-in-law.

"How do you feel when you think about the war now?" I asked.

She was silent. A long time. Finally, she said:

"Some of my friends, they died. A family with eight children, all of them died. My sisters and I all survived. You don't know why some die and others live. I have a friend who was posted on the Trail in the mountains. Conditions there were a lot harder than where I was. When she came back, she was old and ugly. Nobody wanted her. She finally married but she has no children."

She remembered her lost friends. She remembered those who came back to difficult lives, bitter and disappointed. Some had been victims of sexual abuse during the war. Some didn't marry or bear children, and without enough education to secure jobs, some retreated into communities of Buddhist nuns or all-female collectives.

"Dinner is served," said Hân.

A feast awaited us.

The Trail and the war were so far away, they may never have happened.

After dinner, Hân drove us back to our hotel on the beach. Nam turned in for the night. I went to the pontoon opposite the hotel to watch the surf. During the 1972 Christmas bombings, B-52s had flown over this coastline from 2,500 miles away in the Pacific, from the island of Guam, to bomb Haiphong and Hanoi. The scale of war, of the logistics, and of the cost were difficult for civil society to grasp. What if the one trillion dollars that the war had cost had been used to build rather than destroy?

Back in my hotel room, all was quiet in the courtyard. The revelers had left. Hân's father-in-law had mentioned that he had only fought the South Vietnamese, not the Americans. I looked up the definition of 'civil war' in the Oxford English Dictionary online:

"A war between citizens of the same country."

Had North and South Vietnam, divided by a provisional demarcation line, been one or two separate countries after the 1954 Geneva Accords? Had the conflict been a civil war?

⛩

I unfolded my paper map. Where did the Trail go after Thanh Hóa? To the Trường Sơn Mountains.

After months of anticipation, I was excited to be going the following day to the heart of the mountains, to the Phong Nha Caves. The fortified choke point had been the departure for the 1968 Tết Offensive. It was also a place of outstanding beauty, known for a maze of caves, wide and deep, with spectacular stalactites and stalagmites, and clear underground rivers and pools.

On the way, I planned to visit the port city of Vinh, the People's Army's staging area; the Đồng Lộc T-Junction, another fortified wartime choke point that, after the war, became a popular shrine to fallen heroines; and the invincible Mụ Giạ Pass, the main supply route into Laos. I added Hồ Chí Minh's hometown near Vinh to my itinerary, after reading in a guidebook that the place "was of interest only to the Party faithful," which convinced me to find out more.

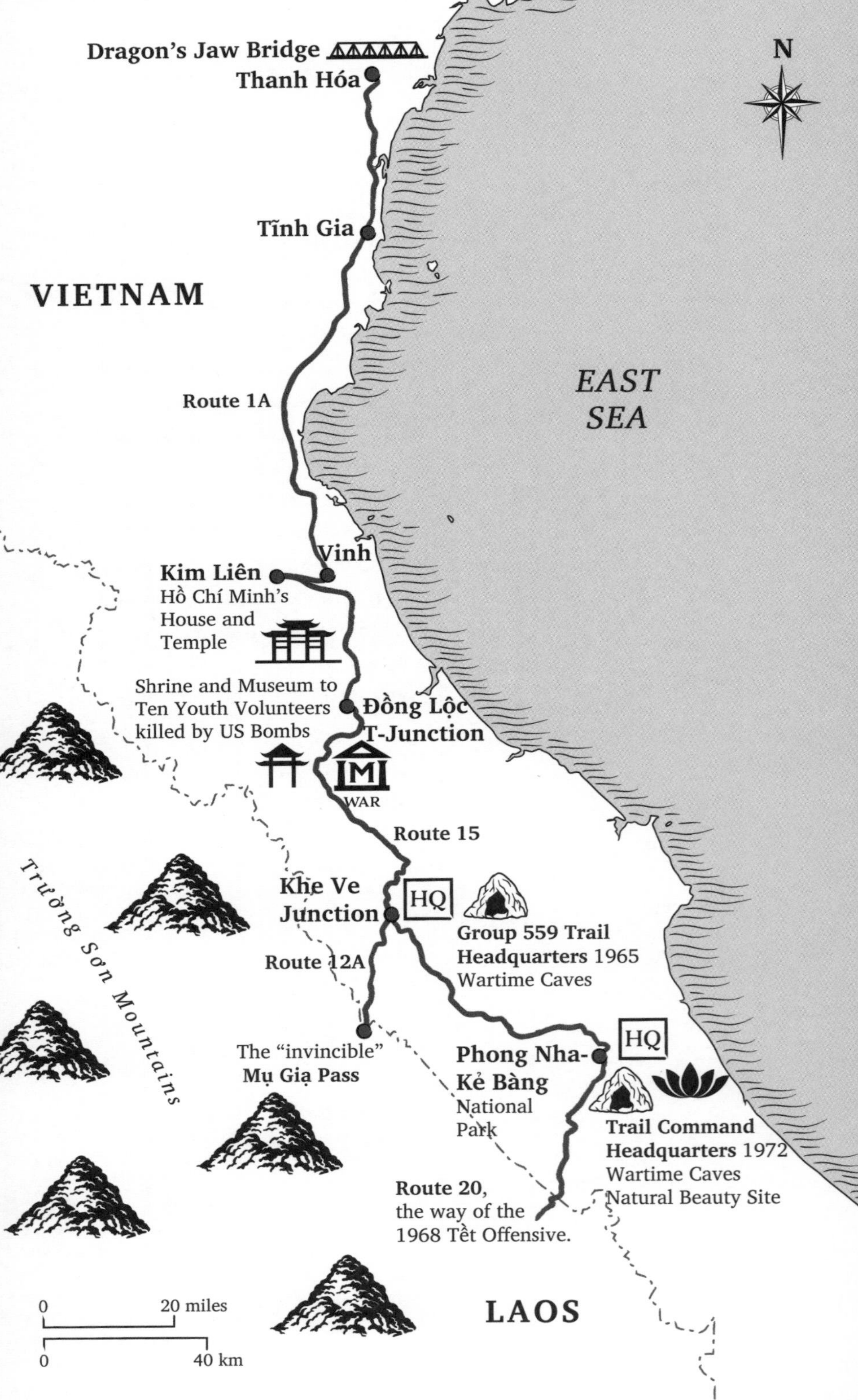

Dragon's Jaw Bridge
Thanh Hóa
N
Tĩnh Gia
VIETNAM
EAST SEA
Route 1A
Vinh
Kim Liên
Hồ Chí Minh's House and Temple
Shrine and Museum to Ten Youth Volunteers killed by US Bombs
Đồng Lộc T-Junction
M
WAR
Route 15
Khe Ve Junction
HQ
Group 559 Trail Headquarters 1965
Wartime Caves
Route 12A
Trường Sơn Mountains
The "invincible" Mụ Giạ Pass
Phong Nha-Kẻ Bàng
National Park
HQ
Trail Command Headquarters 1972
Wartime Caves
Natural Beauty Site
Route 20,
the way of the 1968 Tết Offensive.
LAOS
0
20 miles
0
40 km

Chapter 3

# *THANH HÓA TO THE PHONG NHA CAVES*

*Hồ Chí Minh's childhood home, the Trail through the Trường Sơn Mountains, and the invincible Mụ Giạ Pass.*

*The US bombing of North Vietnam compromised the coastal Trail; the naval blockade interdicted the sea route.*

*The Politburo took the momentous decision to construct all-weather roads suitable for motorized transport across the Trường Sơn Mountains into Laos.*

*The Trail Commander wrote in his memoir:*

*"[Our leaders believed they] had no choice. Almost a million US and South Vietnamese troops had been mobilized and the United States was planning to bomb 'the North back to the Stone Age' … By the end of December 1966, we had built one thousand kilometers of all-weather roads from the Mụ Giạ Pass south through Laos, and Route 20, the mountain pass which was not paved but ensured passage in the dry season."*[23]

*In 1965–1966, the Trail Command moved its Hanoi headquarters to the Khe Ve Junction to open the Mụ Giạ Pass. Trail stations were fortified with anti-aircraft defense units. In January 1967, the Trail Command moved again over the border into Laos to build new north–south Laotian roads.*

*This is how the Trail Commander described the dangers faced by the women and men building and defending the Trail roads:*

*"In January 1967, we moved headquarters to the Xiêng Phan forest in Laos. [Bombs and napalm followed us.] In this scenic, not to say*

*poetic, place, suddenly one morning the enemy aircraft was gliding through the sky. White rain clouds covered the forest canopy, fell to the ground, and dissolved into the streams ... The enemy was spraying toxic chemicals. The forest was contaminated all the way to Route 9. Except for elm trees, the whole forest was dry and dying, under the ever-blue sky ... Our command post was flooded in toxic rain. We did not understand the harmful effects at the time. Most of our soldiers were contaminated by this evil monster by drinking the water."*[24]

*By the summer of 1967, the Trail was ready for the 1968 Tết Offensive, the first assault of the war by People's Army units against South Vietnam.*

At 7 a.m. the next day, the three of us met over breakfast for an early morning war council. Nam arrived alert and smiling. I couldn't have hoped for a better traveling companion. He had the unique qualities of being a morning person who meditated during car rides on dangerous roads.

I stretched the map over two breakfast tables to show Nam our departure and arrival points: from Tĩnh Gia on Route 1A to the Phong Nha Caves.

"Will we be stopping at the caves?" asked Nam.

"Yep. The People's Army left from the caves to attack the US Marine Combat Base at Khe Sanh, during the 1968 Tết Offensive."

"We have a long road ahead today if we want to spend the night in Phong Nha. Or we should stop somewhere before we get to the mountains," said Hân.

I didn't realize this was a warning. I was too impatient to get to the Trường Sơn Mountains.

By 7.30 a.m., we were on the road. Route 1A was a monotonous stretch, heavy with traffic. We entered Nghệ An Province, a land that was so flat it could have been Holland with rice paddies.

Under colonial rule, Nghệ An had been a center of resistance against the French. During the Vietnam War, the thin strip between mountain and sea was saturated with bombs. The Youth Volunteers repaired and defended the road we traveled on and the bridges we crossed. As we drove through a land defended by so many women, I listened to a choir on the CD player singing: "All people will become brothers *(Alle Menschen werden Brüder),*" celebrating the triumph of universal brotherhood against war. Based on Friedrich Schiller's poem, the lyrics in Ludwig van Beethoven's "Ode to Joy" made no reference to "sisters" fighting for freedom as most—Western at least—historical and literary sources don't but should.

Near the Hoàng Mai Bridge, thirty-three Youth Volunteers, mainly women who filled in bomb craters, were "martyred" in the Hỏa Tiễn Cave: "not one body was intact" after the cave collapsed. Ten miles on from there, the bridge over the Giát River, bombed; eleven miles along, the bridge over the Bùng River, bombed; and twenty miles to the Cấm Bridge, bombed 800 times in 1965 and 1,200 times in 1966.

Cheerful houses rolled by in a patchwork of psychedelic rectangles painted bright orange, deep blue, and pale yellow. Elaborate stone balconies and intricate wrought-iron gates advertised wealth. The multitude of styles blended into an exuberant and quirky contemporary aesthetic. Wondrous roofs replicated the domes, cupolas, and steeples of churches, the frontage of Greek temples, and the eaves of pagodas.

Suddenly, the rain came down in vertical sheets. Winter was supposed to be the dry season, when troops moved south in preparation for the spring offensives. But a cyclone over the Philippines was bringing the unusually wet weather. I could only see a few feet ahead of the car. The Trường Sơn Mountains remained invisible, wrapped in a soft shroud of mist and cloud. Hân stared straight ahead to avoid oncoming traffic as Nam meditated in the back seat.

Vinh was a town of wide boulevards lined with glass towers. There was no visible trace of the past. Old Vinh and its port had been obliterated. We crossed the bridge over the Lam River that flowed timeless and languid, oblivious to its deadly past, carrying the tears of the hardened veteran, defender of the floating bridge, who had cried for his lost friends when he was interviewed on Vietnamese television. The bombed cityscapes of North Vietnam's coastal cities I had seen in photographs and drawings were no different to the scarred ruins of Coventry and Birmingham in England after the German bombings, and of Dresden in Germany and Mosul in Iraq after US and Allied aerial attacks. The fuel storage tank at Vinh had been destroyed in the first assaults. Vinh's floating pontoon over the Lam River, the Bến Thủy ferry, was hit during Operation Rolling Thunder. By the end of the 1972 round of bombings, not a house in Vinh was left standing.

We left the city, engulfed in the stubborn fog. The landscape, stripped of its radiant subtropical colors, was bleak. The wintry rice fields were gray.

"Can you usually see the Trường Sơn Mountains from here?" I asked, again.

"Yes," said Hân, mildly exasperated. "Wherever you are in Vietnam, you can see the mountains."

## *The Memorial to President Hồ Chí Minh*

A few miles from Vinh, we arrived in the market town of Kim Liên, Hồ Chí Minh's hometown. Hồ Chí Minh personified the "Red Menace" to his enemies who nicknamed the Trail after him. He had presided over the Trail's expansion with his old comrade, General Giáp, the Commander of the People's Army. He died in 1969, before his dream of a unified, communist Vietnam could be realized.

He was venerated in life and death as war heroes and heroines who had fought the Chinese had been before him. His belief in communism as the way to Vietnam's salvation, I suspected, lay in the abject poverty of his native province, and in the repressive colonial and feudal regimes he had witnessed. His province of Nghệ An, one of the poorest, was burdened with punitive taxation. The corvée introduced in 1901 was particularly odious. Male peasants were required to contribute thirty days of unpaid labor to public works.

The house where Hồ Chí Minh grew up attracted millions of visitors a year. Hân parked in the market square, at the entrance to the National Historic Museum and Park of Kim Liên.

Nam went up to the box office to buy tickets for the visit.

"Would you like to buy some flowers?" he asked me.

"Flowers? Why?"

"Say yes. It's for Uncle Hồ," Nam replied.

"OK, yes."

The lady behind the counter was not selling tickets to the site. She was selling flower bouquets, the customary temple offerings for ancestor and family altars.

Vietnam was officially an atheist state. I was intrigued that the communist hero was worshiped in a Confucian temple. The communist cult of Hồ Chí Minh had inspired hundreds of thousands to sacrifice their youth on the Trail roads. But the devotion of draftees and volunteers, women and men, to leader and country was rooted in the far more ancient belief in hero and ancestor worship.

Nam bought three bouquets of white and yellow chrysanthemums, one for each of us. A sacred Buddhist tree stood at the entrance to the temple grounds. Women in matching red hats took playful selfies in front of the Bodhi tree, enjoying a day out of the office.

I approached the graceful "atheist" temple. It was a mini replica of the elegant Confucian Temple of Literature in Hanoi, the classical model for Vietnamese temple architecture. Multiple pavilions and courtyards were set in immaculate landscaped gardens.

I followed a stone path across the first courtyard. The balustrades were sculpted with finials in the shape of a lotus flower, sacred in Buddhism. I came to a pavilion with white stucco walls, dark wood pillars, and pitched roofs decorated with dragons. Incense-burning vessels were engraved with the yin and yang symbol. Outdoor bonsai trees trimmed in domed shapes stood in octagonal ceramic pots, the auspicious shape in the *I Ching,* the ancient Taoist divination text.

Feng shui, the idea of harmony between the individual and their surroundings, had been introduced to traditional building under Chinese rule, along with Confucianism, Buddhism, and Taoism. Medieval cathedrals focused on the building, its scale, its aesthetic effect, and function, whose construction was intended to glorify the human triumph over nature, of good over evil. I felt intensity there, exaltation, rarely calmness except in cloister gardens. The temple scale compatible with nature, and the incorporation of courtyards, reflected the acceptance of the duality in all things. Where there was good there was bad. The aim was to find a balance between the two. I wandered through the silence, at one with my surroundings, across more distant courtyards and pavilions. I was seduced by the openness, the fluidity between inside and outside spaces, yin and yang, darkness and light, negative and positive. The harmonious space, the pungent yet delicate incense fragrance, and the tranquility conspired to induce a calm mind.

I arrived at the inner sanctum where popular heroes and deities were venerated. Taoist and Confucian temples like this one, or *đền,* housed statues of emperors, kings, warriors, and other popular heroes. Buddhist temples, or *chùa,* sheltered the deity. This was the "Memorial to President Hồ Chí Minh." Pilgrims lit incense sticks to welcome home the spirit of the father of the nation. The scent was intoxicating. Inside, visitors paid their respects to a bronze bust of Hồ Chí Minh, centered on the altar against a red curtain embroidered in gold with the emblems of the Communist Party. I half-expected raised fists and communist salutes. But pilgrims bowed their heads while raising joss sticks to their foreheads to pay their respects, following the same Buddhist rituals they carried out at family altars to honor their own ancestors.

Leaving the temple, I followed an enchanting way bordered by clipped box-tree hedges, bamboo thickets, banyan trees, and vegetable gardens. I wanted to see the house where Hồ Chí Minh had spent his teenage years. Hồ Chí Minh partly credited his youth in Nghệ An for the revolutionary path he followed later on in life, to free his "enslaved" people from colonial rule and feudalism.

I arrived at a single-story thatched abode. Although modest in appearance, the home was spacious compared to an ordinary village dwelling. Bamboo screens protected it from sun and rain. Doors opened on a courtyard. The house had been rebuilt in the traditional way. A wooden truss, beams, and pillars bore the weight of the roof. The rooms, three altogether, and partitioned by wood panels, were appointed with family altars. One was dedicated to Hoàng Thị Loan, Hồ Chí Minh's mother who died when he was eleven. A small field planted with sweet potatoes stretched out in front of the property.

The village authorities had used public funds to build the house for Hồ Chí Minh's father, the scholar Nguyễn Sinh Sắc (1862–1929), to honor him as "the first [from the village] to get a doctorate, second-class in the imperial examination, conferring on the village status and prestige," wrote William J. Duiker, the American biographer of Hồ Chí Minh. "A couple of acres of rice land were included with the house as well as a small garden, where Sắc planted sweet potatoes."[25]

Here, Hồ Chí Minh grew up between tradition and modernity. In this house, he had worshiped at the altars of his ancestors. He was also introduced by his father to Confucian scholar-reformers opposed to colonial rule. He discovered Marxist-Leninism, socialism, and later communism in Paris after a peripatetic world tour that included stops in London, Boston, and New York. Hồ Chí Minh's turn to the left came after the 1919 Versailles Conference, when the US president Woodrow Wilson ignored his request to press France, the colonial power, for "self-determination."

Living in Paris, he joined the French branch of the Second International in 1920, the precursor to the French Socialist Party.

Years later, in 1960, he wrote:

"The reason I joined the French socialists was that these ladies and gentlemen, as I called my comrades then, had shown sympathy toward me and toward the struggle of the oppressed people. But I understood neither what was a party, a trade union, nor what was socialism nor communism."[26]

Ultimately seduced by revolution as the only way to free his people, he became a member of the Intercolonial Union affiliated with the French Communist Party in 1922, left Paris for Moscow the following year where he was employed by the Communist International or Comintern—an organization that advocated world communism—and created the Indochinese Communist Party in 1930 while in exile in Hong Kong. His political manifesto called for "the overthrow of French imperialism and Vietnamese feudalism, independence, confiscation of banks, enterprises, and plantations, an eight-hour working day, democratic freedoms for the masses and education for all, and equality between man and woman."[27]

Yet, when Hồ Chí Minh proclaimed Vietnamese independence in Ba Đình Square in Hanoi on September 2, 1945, he did not quote from Karl Marx's *Das Kapital*. He quoted verbatim from the United States Declaration of Independence:

"All men are created equal; they are endowed by their Creator with certain unalienable Rights; among these are Life, Liberty, and the pursuit of Happiness."

Hồ Chí Minh's admiration, I suspect, was for the American Revolutionary War (1775–1783) against the British colonialists that led to American independence. He was drawing a parallel between the American War of Independence and the struggle of the Việt Minh—the communist-led nationalist alliance he created in 1941—against the French colonialists.

In 1946, before war with France broke out, Hồ Chí Minh appealed to US president Harry S. Truman to "interfere urgently in support of our independence."[28] But his letter and telegram remained unanswered. Instead, the United States financed the French War against him.

Had Truman supported him against the French colonialists, would Hồ Chí Minh have reneged communism in spite of years of affiliation with the communist movement? Could the Vietnam wars have been avoided?

On his visit back to Kim Liên in 1957, as the first president of the Democratic Republic of Vietnam, he noted with a touch of nostalgia for his lost childhood that "the sweet potato flowers [of my youth] are still beautiful."[29]

As I looked out on the small field in front of the house, I noticed that sweet potato plants still grew there, though they were not yet in flower.

## *The Đồng Lộc T-Junction*

We got back in the car to head south on Route 15 to the shrine at Đồng Lộc T-Junction, built in memory of Youth Volunteers who had died in the bombings. Shrines were as natural a part of Vietnam's landscape as trees, rivers, and mountains. We traveled along a narrow valley encased by hills, through the dense fog that had enveloped us since we left Hanoi. At the end of the valley we reached the shrine, set in a peaceful forest of pine, bamboo, and deciduous trees.

The junction critical to getting war material to the southern fronts during the 1968 Tết Offensive was defended by 16,000 troops. Between March and October of that year, American fighter planes dropped "forty-nine thousand bombs of all kinds"[30] to stop reinforcements and supplies from reaching the People's Army units fighting in South Vietnam. The sortie on July 24, 1968, the day the women were killed, went unreported in our press. Aerial bombings are so numerous in wars, only a fraction are reported by the media.

We walked up the steps to the altar that stood mournful in the gray rain. It was overflowing with bouquets of white roses, chrysanthemums, and lilies. People's Army officers in smart green uniforms, with gold epaulets and buttons, brought veneration wreaths. A plaque paid tribute to the women warriors—a squadron leader and her unit—who were killed when a bomb exploded at the opening of the cave where they had taken refuge.

The tombs of the martyred heroines lay behind the altar, hidden from view. Martyr, I thought, came from the French *martyre,* found on the graves of French Resistance guerrillas who had died fighting against the Nazi occupation of France. Vietnam's revolutionaries often compared their struggle against French colonialism to the French Resistance against the Nazis. They couldn't understand how they found themselves on the wrong side of history when they were battling against colonial oppression for the very ideals of freedom and liberty preached by the West.

Worshipers gave thanks to those who died too young while defending their country, with clasped hands, incense, and bows. Hân, Nam, and I followed. I tried to pray, but I couldn't remember the words of prayers I once knew.

"Tín's women with guns and flowers," said Nam, moved by the fate of the gentlewomen.

The artist Trần Trung Tín, who had lived and worked in Hanoi during the war, had painted *Girl, Gun, Flower* in protest at a conflict that sacrificed women on the altar of the war gods. As a teenager, he had fought in the war of independence against the French. His women, nude with hollowed imploring eyes, carried guns and flowers.

Nam continued:

"Remember when we sat in that hot room in Tín's house in Ho Chi Minh City and he pointed at the painting of a woman holding a flower, and shouted: 'No More War!' over and over?"

How could I forget it? I was researching a book on Tín's life and work. The heat: it was over a hundred degrees. The fan: there was no air con. And Tín's freedom from fear. Any anti-war sentiment, even in a small assembly of trusted friends, was dangerous and rare in a place that defined itself by its heroic victories. In the absence of a prayer, Tín's simple mantra, "No More War!" became mine.

During the war, Radio Hanoi regularly broadcast the news of the deaths of Youth Volunteers, especially if they were women, to fuel anger. But, if there was a propagandist intent to the memorial, I was unaffected by it. In this peaceful forest, war's only sad truth was that ten women had died too young.

We left the shrine and took refuge from the rain in the museum next door. The photo exhibition told the story of the thousands of women who had "protected" the Trail. A woman, barefoot, pushed a cart piled high with gravel to repair the road; another used a shovel to fill in a bomb crater; and a sentinel, a rifle as her only defense, stood on the lookout for planes.

A map showed the Trail roads 1A, 15, 12, 20, 21, and 16, which the women had built, repaired, and defended. They endured hunger, disease, and bombs. They lived at the Trail stations, in the jungle, and in caves. They built the roads, dug trenches and tunnels, cooked and foraged for food, repaired clothes, cared for the wounded, and buried the dead. They were the truck drivers who set out on precipitous roads over mountainous passes at night, headlights turned off. During the Tết Offensive, a forty-strong platoon hauled food, guns, and ammunition to the front, and took the gravely wounded to hospitals back up north. By 1972, 300 women drivers supplied the front. They were the bomb-disposal technicians. They filled in the bomb craters made by 1,000-ton bombs and they detonated live ammunition to keep the military convoys moving. And the "strong ones" joined the anti-aircraft defense teams who secured the Trail.

Some female units were so traumatized by the horrors they survived and witnessed that they experienced a kind of collective temporary insanity, as reported by the historian François Guillemot:

"Sometimes when the girls were gathered around to read a letter from the family, all it took was for one of them to break down and start whimpering, and then a chain reaction went through the whole squad or company, who then all began to scream, cry out loud, and so on, from one company to another. They wept, called out, ran, jumped, or even climbed trees, babbling on between words and fits of laughter for hours on end."[31]

The happy sound of schoolkids suddenly filled the silence of the museum.

"Are you here to visit the museum?" Nam asked, impressed that the children would come to a place of learning after school.

The boys, some wearing their blue-and-white school uniform, had arrived straight from class.

"No, we were passing by on our bikes. We saw you, so we came in."

Foreigners were a curiosity worth stopping for. The kid who emerged as the group leader wore a Qatar Airways T-shirt, while his friend had on an FBI baseball cap.

"Can we have our picture taken with you in front of Uncle Hồ?" asked the boy in the Qatar Airways T-shirt.

Nam volunteered to be the photographer.

I stood with the children in front of a sculpture of Uncle Hồ surrounded by Youth Volunteers. The boys and girls smiled for the camera and held up their hands in victory and peace signs. Victory and peace were indivisible. Nearby, an assortment of bombs found on site were artfully displayed.

"Have you visited the museum before?"

Shy silence.

"What do you know about the war?"

Shy silence.

"What do you think of the girls who died?"

Shy silence.

"Do you want to be heroes when you grow up?" Nam asked.

"Never," came the determined response of the kid in the FBI cap.

The message of heroic sacrifice was not lost on the boy. But he had no intention of being "sacrificed" in war. He looked forward to a bright future without war for himself and his friends. We waved goodbye as the children rode up the hill on their bikes.

We left the shrine and got back onto Route 15 to head west toward the Trường Sơn Mountains. We advanced through foothills covered in scrubby brush, past lakes, rivers, and villages, their thatched roofs drenched in the rainy mist that enveloped the area. Water-buffalo herds with their young crossed the road. We passed by acacia plantations that were part of a state reforestation plan after wide swathes of forests were destroyed by war and the poverty that came after.

And then it happened. The limestone peaks appeared out of the mist. I was at the heart of the Trường Sơn Mountains. The landscape depicted in the drawings expressed more than a geographical place, it reflected a state of mind, "the calm mind needed to survive such a cruel war."

The nanosecond did not disappoint. I sketched an outline of the legendary range in my notebook. The physical gesture connected me to the place. Pencil and paper suited strong emotions where the click of a camera didn't. More importantly, I didn't have a choice. The battery of my digital camera had died at the leopards-mating-in-the-moonlight moment that I had been planning for months.

### *The Mụ Giạ Pass*

In the late afternoon, we arrived at the Khe Ve Junction, at the crossroads of Route 15 and the Mụ Giạ Pass. The Trail Command moved here from Hanoi to "urgently" oversee the building of the pass and the expansion of the Trail into Laos, when the US bombing of North Vietnam had compromised the coastal route and sea lanes.

We still had a long road ahead, but I wanted to drive up the "invincible" pass that the women road builders—pictured in the photographs at the museum we had just left—had helped to build and defend. The French had opened the pass in the thirties, with a track, railway, and cable car to transfer copper from mines in Laos to the seaport of Vinh. But by the time of the Vietnam War, the rain forest had swallowed up the vestiges of previous constructions.

We started up the steep and windy pass. The road followed the Gianh River that snaked along the valley below. Few military commands would have dared to plan hundreds of miles of new roads through this mountainous jungle terrain; few women would have had the courage to build and defend roads through the inferno it became. Soon after the Youth Volunteers had finished building the pass, B-52 super bombers deployed their force against it.

The historian Jacob Van Staaveren described the first attacks:

"Twenty-nine bombers released their ordnance [on the pass] during their first mission on April 16, 1966. Each bomber carried twenty-four 1,000-pound bombs internally and twenty-four 750-pound bombs externally. All bombs were set for subsurface burst except thirty 1,000-pounders affixed with long-delay fuses."[32]

The newly paved road was wide. Sturdy stone walls had been built to stop landslides from the sheer slopes above. We followed convoys of high-tech trucks up the pass. Their headlights on full beam, they were on their way to Laos to load up with precious tropical woods.

We stopped at a rest area on the edge of a precipitous drop. In the declining light, a homestead on the banks of the Gianh River below receded in the thick jungle. Between vehicles, a bird sang a lament before nightfall. The deafening rumble of the next advancing truck drowned the melody. I imagined the sounds of war, the "sonic roar that tore eardrums," described in a Việt Cộng memoir,[33] the explosions of the 1,000-pound bombs dropped by B-52s, of iron bombs, of magnetic bombs that stuck to metal to blow up truck convoys, of cluster bombs targeting the road gangs to prevent them from repairing the roads, of people-sniffer bombs to detect body movements in the jungle, and of napalm and white phosphorous bombs used to destroy tree cover, that burned human flesh long after the initial exposure. From the ground came the crackling of over 300 anti-aircraft guns that defended the pass.[34] In the silence afterward, the women sang revolutionary songs while they risked their lives to keep the traffic moving through the pass.

In this landscape of jungle, thatched huts, and wild rivers, the odds appeared stacked in favor of the American planes. Yet despite frequent attacks, the US Air Force and Navy never put the pass out of operation for any sustained period of time.

An uplifting story emerged from the mayhem. A couple of US Air Force pilots who flew low over the Mụ Giạ Pass developed a tacit understanding with an enemy sentinel at the bottom of the pass. The pilots didn't target the sentinel who, in turn, didn't shoot at their aircraft. The aviators returned to the pass after the war to look for their friend and enemy. I didn't know the end of the tale. I hoped they had found each other and shared a few beers.

It was early evening. The light was dimming. We made a U-turn and headed back down the pass to the Khe Ve Junction and Route 15. I had forgotten that darkness comes quickly in the tropics. The moon that I had hoped would brighten the mountains was hidden. The thick fog, our faithful companion, had returned.

"Let's stop somewhere along the road for the night. We're not going to see a thing if we continue on to Phong Nha now," I said.

"There's nowhere to stop," Hân replied.

"Are you sure? There must be a hotel, homestay, something."

"No, there's nothing. I told you that this morning," said Hân.

"Yes, you did," I acknowledged.

"I'm not sleeping in the car," said Nam.

I did some deep breathing. Bad planning. I resigned myself to traveling down the heart of the mountain Trail in total darkness. We drove by the caves in Hóa Tiến where Station 12 had been, one of four in the area. The caves sheltered gasoline stores, ammunition and weapons depots, vehicle parks, even clinics. A drawing depicted a surgeon tending to a patient in a cave, wearing white coat, mask, and hat, as a nurse pedaled a bicycle to generate enough power to light up the improvised operating theater.

Suddenly, I felt the car lift up as if for takeoff. We were on a sharp incline I hadn't seen coming in the dark. The faint outline of a black stone stele on the side of the road appeared in the headlights, a memorial to the Youth Volunteers who had defended the Đá Đẽo Pass. The pass was a dangerous road sought out by motorcycle riders looking for thrills. Artist Trần Huy Oánh had recounted a dramatic wartime night drive:

"I almost lost my life. I was traveling in a truck at night with no headlights to avoid detection. The drivers were supposed to be trained to anticipate precipices, ravines, and road obstacles in the dark. But our driver was a kid. It was his first drive. He missed a bend in the road. We crashed head-on into a tree. The kid began to cry. He was so young. But he wasn't crying because he was almost killed. He was crying because he was afraid of his commander! Luckily, nobody was hurt."

Out of the darkness, we reached a junction flooded with electrical light. We drove over the River Son that the military convoys crossed on their advance south, while under attack from US fighter jets from the US Seventh Fleet positioned off the coast. We soon arrived at the Saigon Phong Nha Hotel in Sơn Trạch. The hotel overlooked the river, a mile from the entrance to the wondrous Phong Nha Caves. We made a beeline for the welcoming restaurant terrace, where we were served delicious noodles and river fish.

Annoyed at myself for having traveled down the mountainous Trail in pitch-black conditions, I ordered some wine to calm down. Zen was one thing: I was in need of some Western self-medication.

Off Route 15, in the Phong Nha-Kẻ Bàng National Park, Quảng Bình Province.

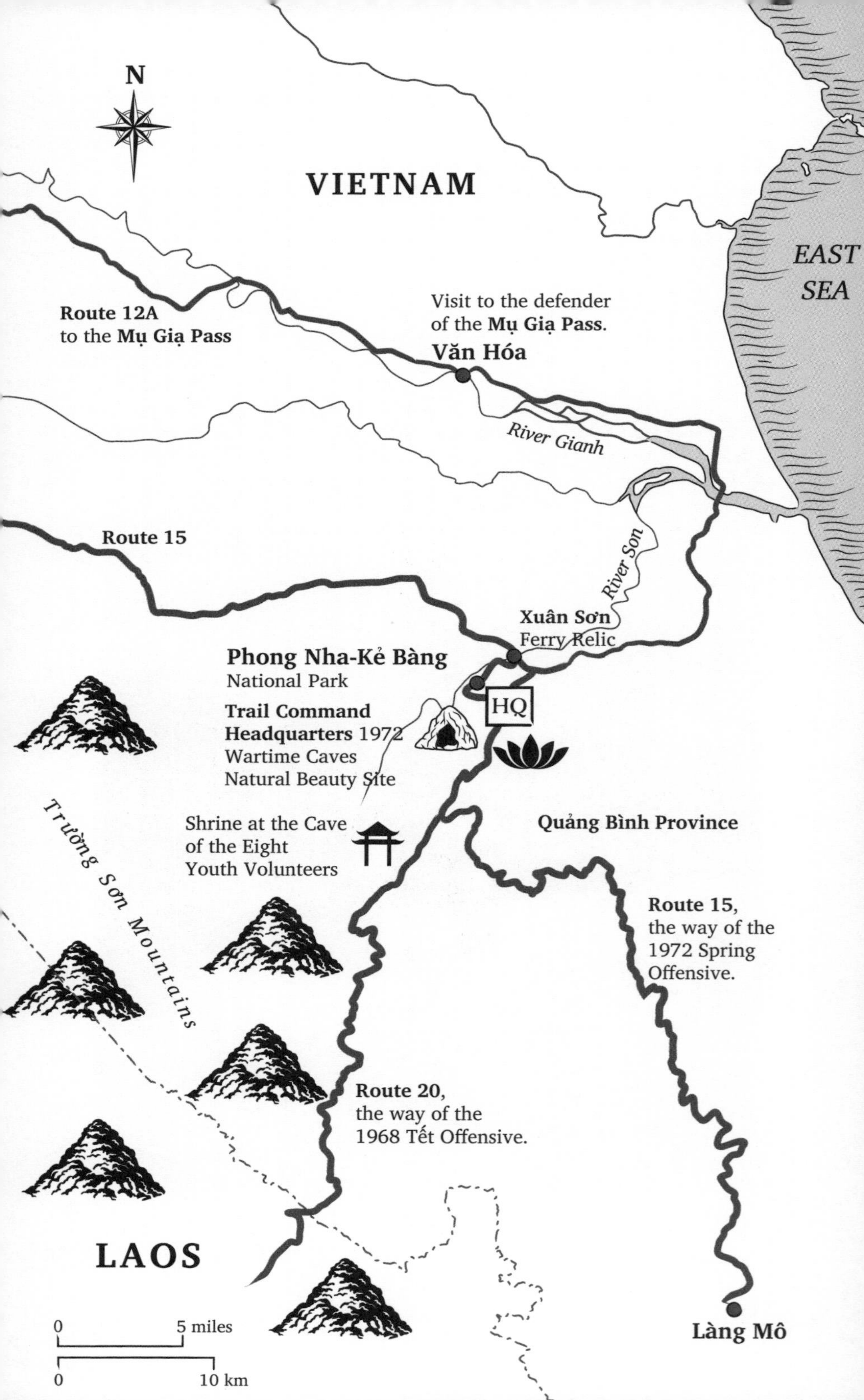

N
VIETNAM
EAST SEA
Route 12A
to the Mụ Giạ Pass
Visit to the defender
of the Mụ Giạ Pass.
Văn Hóa
River Gianh
Route 15
River Son
Xuân Sơn
Ferry Relic
Phong Nha-Kẻ Bàng
National Park
Trail Command
Headquarters 1972
Wartime Caves
Natural Beauty Site
HQ
Shrine at the Cave
of the Eight
Youth Volunteers
Quảng Bình Province
Trường Sơn Mountains
Route 15,
the way of the
1972 Spring
Offensive.
Route 20,
the way of the
1968 Tết Offensive.
LAOS
Làng Mô
0
5 miles
0
10 km

Chapter 4

# AT THE PHONG NHA CAVES

*A Trail headquarters, mountain shrines, and the defender of the Mụ Giạ Pass.*

*In the summer of 1967, the Politburo began planning the 1968 Tết Offensive. Infantry, artillery, and tank divisions massed at the Phong Nha Caves in preparation. The US Combat Marine Base at Khe Sanh in Quảng Trị Province in South Vietnam, built to stop infiltration from the Trail, was their first target.*

*Would the Trail be up to it? The People's Army numbered 120,000 troops—fighting on three simultaneous fronts in South Vietnam—compared to the 500 guerrilla fighters sent in 1959 to support the Việt Cộng. They faced 500,000 US and close to 800,000 South Vietnamese forces supported by the US Air Force, Navy, and Marines.*

*The Trail Commander was optimistic. He wrote in his memoir:*

*"I conducted a final inspection of the Mụ Giạ Pass and of Route 20. We chose Route 20 as the main direction for the crossing, as the road was quite good and closer to Route 9 [where secret Trail Command headquarters in Laos were built for the Campaign] … In December 1967, US bombings escalated dramatically, targeting Routes 12, 20, and 9. Enemy air strikes blocked the gateways. [Luckily,] nearly fifteen thousand tons of supplies had already been stored along Route 9 by November 1967 in preparation for the Route 9–Khe Sanh Campaign [the 1968 Tết Offensive]. These good results marked a new development in the direction, command, and operational organization of the Trường Sơn military transport."*[35]

Reconciling the charm of my surroundings with the violence of the past was eluding me. The following morning at the Saigon Phong Nha Hotel, I woke up to what could have been a tranquil ink painting of mountains and rivers in soft grays and greens. The silhouettes of miniature boats and figures were etched on the distant landscape. I was on the edge of the fantastical karst mountains, caves, and rivers at the heart of the Phong Nha-Kẻ Bàng National Park.

The River Son flowed gently by. Bright blue boats waited by the quay to take visitors upriver to the Phong Nha Caves. Their bows were painted with white eyes and black pupils rimmed with red to scare off aquatic monsters. We had our pick of the boats because it was the low season and there were no tourists. Hân and Nam negotiated a price with a cheerful boatman. The canopied river boat sped along the silky surface, the misty Trường Sơn Mountains ever present on the horizon. A church steeple rose on the northern bank of the river. The sound of the outboard motor was deafening. Hân, wearing only his linen jacket, huddled by the engine for warmth.

Ahead, a mountain appeared as an impregnable fortress blocking the way. The overhanging cliff towered a few hundred feet above the tranquil river. The boatman cut the motor. We drifted through the gaping mouth of a cave carved out of the limestone cliff. I imagined we had reached the River Styx, the border between the spirit world and the living world. I could hear high-pitched screeching from bat colonies hanging from the roof cave above my head. I put my cap on because I was afraid of bats getting tangled in my hair.

I disembarked on a beach. My feet sunk into the soft sand. Ocean sand, I thought. We transferred to a flat wooden boat. A woman sat at the front. She guided the boat through a narrow channel using a single paddle. We glided along the still, watery surface into an underworld of stalactites and grottoes.

The rhythmic circular motion of her paddle echoed in the subterranean chamber, breaking the silence. Droplets dripped from the stalactites and splashed in melodious pings. Designer lighting enhanced the rock formations. The stalactites were sculpted by centuries of erosion into the rounded shapes of giant corals and sea anemones. Tumbling petrified stone simulated frozen waterfalls. Beaches of golden and white sand nestled in the bends of the underground river. The dark underworld was made light with blond colors.

"Has anything been found in the caves?" I asked the river boatman, who had joined us in the grotto boat.

"There is a *lingam* from the Cham period up there. It was a place of worship," he said, pointing at a grotto as we went past.

The black stone pillar was an abstract representation of the Hindu god Shiva, destroyer of evil. The Indianized culture of the Champa kingdom had ruled southern and central Vietnam from the second to the seventeenth century AD, and built the coastal temples of Mỹ Sơn and Phan Rang. Champa trade ways through the mountains had reached all the way to southern Laos, where the Chams sourced the gold, silver, and spices that they exported to India and the Middle East from ports along Vietnam's present-day coastline. The old Cham trade routes—used by the French in colonial times and by the People's Army during the wars—extended as far as the city of Attapeu in southern Laos, which we would be visiting later on in the trip.

The boat turned back. We could have kept on going for hours. The web of underground rivers and caves stretched for hundreds of miles. Laughter and voices echoed through the cavernous chambers as we approached the beach where we had first landed.

Back on terra firma, we followed a sandy path bordered by the stone tentacles of giant stalactites until we arrived at a vaulted space. The cave was high enough above the river to escape flooding during the rainy season.

"Was the cave used during the war?" I asked the boatman.

"It was a hospital. Hundreds of wounded soldiers came here. The badly wounded were driven to Hanoi. The Americans discovered the hospital and tried to block the entrance to the cave. Munitions and weapons were also stored in the caves."

I followed him to an observatory platform at the mouth of the cave. I could see the bullet holes left by the low-flying fighter jets that strafed the main entrance. B-52s, flying at higher altitude, had targeted the rocky knoll above.

I exited the cave up steep steps carved out of the rock face that led to a mountain temple. A stone-sculpted mythical animal with a short, stubby horn guarded the shrine. The sacred half-dragon, half-mammal symbolized peace, good fortune, and mercy. The shrine's vantage point over the blue-green mountain and river invited remembrance. I lit the incense sticks, waited until the flames died down, and approached the altar. I was starting to feel at ease with the quiet rituals. Boxes of Choco Chips and cream puffs had been left as offerings. At the holy shrine to absent gods, I silently repeated Tín's mantra: "No More War!"

We returned to the boat and motored back down the wide river. I wondered aloud how the trucks had managed to get across.

"During the war, there was a floating pontoon," said the boatman.

This pontoon, the Xuân Sơn ferry, was a legend in the area. At 4 a.m. every morning, the pontoon was disassembled and floated upriver, where it was hidden in the caves. At 7 p.m. every evening, the floating bridge was moved back downstream and reassembled at the choke point to allow the truck convoys to cross the river under the cover of darkness.

I asked the boatman if his relatives had been in the war. Yes, he said. His grandmother, another woman of the war, had served on the Trail. He sent her a text asking if we could meet her. She answered back to say that she was sorry she couldn't see us because she was out shopping in town, in Đồng Hới. Her life had happily moved on.

At breakfast that morning, I had found an article online about a war heroine who had served on the Mụ Giạ Pass, the "invincible" mountain pass we had visited the previous day. The article gave her address as c/o Communist Party headquarters in a village close to the Phong Nha Caves. Nguyễn Thị Kim Huế was a Hero of the People's Armed Forces. She had served as a platoon commander in charge of sixteen women and men on the Mụ Giạ Pass between May 1965 and May 1967. Of the eighty in her company, sixty-two were women.

Encouraged by the welcome I had received from the defender of the Dragon's Jaw Bridge in Thanh Hóa, that afternoon after our visit to the caves, we traveled an hour and a half back up north to look for Nguyễn Thị Kim Huế. She lived along the same Route 12A she had built and protected.

Hân remembered to buy cakes and cookies for our hostess at a roadside shop. He came back to the car loaded down with several bags full.

"Twenty dollars' worth?" I asked.

It was an extraordinary amount to spend on cake.

"Older people like sweet things," he replied in explanation.

The modest house was elevated and set back from the main road. A turquoise wrought-iron gate with gold tips opened into a vegetable garden growing spring lettuces and beans. We walked up the hill to the house. The wooden shutters were closed. There was a padlock on the door. Nobody was home. Hân ran back down to see if the neighbor knew where Nguyễn Thị Kim Huế was. I stood on the front porch and looked at the outline of the splendid Trường Sơn Mountains on the horizon, where the young Nguyễn Thị Kim Huế had lived and worked. The distinctive limestone peaks were softly etched in blue against a pale sky. Nothing in the quiet skyline betrayed the cruelty that had pounded the mountains and caves.

A loud and assertive voice came from the neighbor's house.

"Wait, I'm coming," Nguyễn Thị Kim Huế shouted out.

A handsome woman, tall and slim, arrived to greet us. She took the padlock off the door, opened the shutters, and invited us in.

"Please sit down," she said.

On Route 15, the author in the Phong Nha Caves, Quảng Bình Province.

The dark wood furniture stood out against aquamarine walls. At the back of the living room, her bed was partially hidden by yellow gauze curtains that swung in the light breeze blowing through the open window. A Vietnamese flag hung on the wall next to a portrait of Hồ Chí Minh.

Nguyễn Thị Kim Huế was widowed and lived alone. Her three sons were married and worked in Hanoi. She lived comfortably enough on a pension of 150 dollars a month.

The house was cold. She poured the yellow-green tea. She handed me a framed photograph. Her identity, her life, and the beliefs she had fought for were contained in the picture. She had been a stunningly beautiful young woman when the photo of her with Hồ Chí Minh was taken. The image was her most cherished memento.

Nguyễn Thị Kim Huế talked excitedly about how she had been chosen to meet the aged leader several times for her skills as a marks woman and her bravery as a platoon commander:

"The first time I met Uncle Hồ was in 1966 at the Youth Volunteer Corps Academy in Hanoi where I had been sent for military training. He was impressed by what a good shot I was after I scored the top grade in the shooting tests. He told me: 'The daughters of Quảng Bình Province produce well, fight well, and do everything well.' I met him again later the same year when I was part of a delegation reporting on conditions at the front. I told him that we didn't get enough sugar, salt, and clothes. After that, individual sugar rations were increased by half a cup a month (2.5 *lạng* or 3.25 ounces). We were also issued with a second set of clothes.

"The last time I met Uncle Hồ was at the Presidential Palace in Hanoi in 1967. I had been invited with a Youth Volunteer delegation before we left for Moscow to attend the fiftieth anniversary of the revolution. We were served fish, rice, and tea. I remember that when Uncle Hồ held up his bowl, a grain of rice fell on the table. He picked it up, and said: 'Rice is very important. We have to appreciate it. You can't waste even a grain of rice,' and then he put it in his mouth."

I asked her about her life on the Mụ Giạ Pass. During her tour of duty, B-52s began bombarding the pass with 1,000-pounders. Nguyễn Thị Kim Huế didn't mention she was the first female commander of a "death platoon" who had been posted on the most dangerous stretch of road to decommission unexploded ordnance. She didn't mention she had been decorated with the highest military award by Uncle Hồ himself. Instead, she talked about how she tried to make an inhumane situation bearable, how to get enough food, how to forage for medicinal herbs, how to protect her team by digging bomb shelters, and how to give her friends a proper burial:

"The war was hard for women. We worked on building the road, and then on protecting it. After we finished building, we had to rebuild every day because there were so many bombs. We had problems with our periods, so we found leaves in the forest against the pain. We got sick with malaria. We didn't have enough rice because we gave our rice to the soldiers going to the South. There was a lot of traffic coming through. Their rice was either burnt when trucks burst into flames, or wet from the river crossings. So, I bartered for food with the villagers. We exchanged our old clothes for farm animals. Each one of us had a chicken, three shared a pig, and seven shared a cow.

"The Americans dropped all different kinds of bombs. They dropped antennas in the jungle that looked like trees and picked up movement, and the planes then bombed there. We had to go to the open road. So, we built individual bomb shelters into the rock face along the road. Bulldozers excavated large shelters for the trucks. You can still see some today. From the shelters, we watched to see where the bombs landed and how many didn't explode.

"The B-52s dropped many bombs. They destroyed entire mountains. Many died on the hill where the Central Command was."

She stopped talking, lost in her memories. When she continued, I felt I was listening in on her private thoughts:

"Lucky if you live, unlucky if you die. After each bombing, we counted how many people were lost. We tried hard to find everyone.

We didn't want to leave them in the forest. We prepared the bodies and put them in nylon bags. I didn't want to let anyone die naked. Then we sent the dead back to the rear."

She parted her hair on the side of her head to show me the scar where shrapnel had cut into it. She talked about the harrowing attack when she was wounded:

"The worst B-52 attacks were in 1966. In my platoon, out of sixteen, ten were killed. Many died when rocks fell on them. As the bombings continued, even though we were wounded, we stayed at the site and tried desperately to find them. We used shovels because I was afraid a digger would cut their bodies into pieces. After a few days, we sniffed the soil. There was no smell so we knew there were no more body parts to find. But we only recovered a few of our teammates."

The macabre details made me shiver.

The light was dimming, signaling the onset of early evening.

"Were you ever afraid?" I asked.

"No, I'm not afraid. Fear of what? You live once and you die once."

I flinched at her directness. I asked her the question I had put to Ngô Thị Tuyển, the defender of the Dragon's Jaw Bridge, this time head-on.

"Do you hate Americans?"

"No, why?" she asked, surprised. "When they fight us, yes. But not now. They are not our enemies anymore, no."

"Do you think the Americans should give war reparations?"

"No. Well, maybe, if it's for the state. There are many unexploded bombs in the country. But not for me, I'm old."

Nguyễn Thị Kim Huế, like the defender of the bridge, showed no animosity toward Americans as individuals, but she held the US government responsible for the live ordnance left behind.

"Now, our duty is to fight the Chinese," she added.

The millennial foe to the north had replaced the Western imperialists as the main threat.

Nguyễn Thị Kim Huế was hoping to move into a larger house.

"All I want is a room for my bedroom, a room for my living room, and a room to pray to Uncle Hồ," she said.

Nguyễn Thị Kim Huế followed us out to the porch to say goodbye. I asked if I could take a photograph to remember her by. She said, of course. She didn't smile. She stared at the Trường Sơn Mountains in the distance. I wondered what she was thinking.

We drove back to our hotel along the Trail coastal road, Route 1A. Nam and Hân turned in early. That evening, I sat on the hotel veranda overlooking the river that flowed gently by. The night was still. I could hear music from a nearby karaoke bar. During the war, this had been the time that the river filled up with the night shadows of pontoon boats, gliding from their hiding place in the caves to the place where the trucks waited on the riverbank to cross the water.

Once the pontoon was discovered, US Navy and Marine Corps attack aircraft dropped naval mines over the River Son to destroy it. The mines didn't explode when they hit the water; they lay underwater until they were triggered by the approach of a vessel.

A particularly intense bombardment in 1967 had prevented the floating pontoon from being set up; the convoys bringing supplies south for the Tết Offensive were immobilized. A local hero named Võ Thế Chơn sped through the minefield, a metal rod attached to his small boat, detonating the mines. Before he left on his mission, his friends, who did not expect him to survive, held a memorial service for him at an altar in the cave and came to say their goodbyes. Võ Thế Chơn cleared the minefield, opened the road, and miraculously lived to tell the tale.[36]

Women, too, from the area were drafted into mine-disposal teams. The teams were issued oil barrels with magnets attached to the bottom. They tied the contraption to a rope. A two-woman crew, stationed on either side of the river, dragged the rope along the river, combing it for mines. When the mines exploded on approach, the teams ran to take cover in nearby trenches.

⛩

The karaoke bar had closed for the night. In the silent stillness, I planned my itinerary for the following day. Soldiers, trucks, and tanks had left the Phong Nha Caves during the 1968 Tết Offensive, to attack the US Marine Combat Base at Khe Sanh. They crossed into Laos on the newly built Route 20, journeying south to the secret Trail headquarters dug inside a mountain.

To reach Khe Sanh, I had hoped to travel on the same Route 20, but we were restricted by the number of times we could go in and out of Vietnam in a car with Vietnamese license plates, so I settled for Route 15, built for the 1972 Spring Offensive.

Route 15 from the Phong Nha Caves to Khe Sanh was known for its high passes, streams, and thick rain forest. It was the romantic Trail of drawings, poems, and songs. It was the dramatic Trail of Vietnam's suffering. It was the heroic Trail of Vietnam's military victory. It was the pride of the Trail Command and the thousands of women Youth Volunteers who built the road, in a formidable battle against the jungle, the bombs, and the napalm. And it was the monstrous Trail of the US imagination that no matter how much our military bombed it, it grew stronger.

I planned to spend the following night in Khe Sanh, the site, in the words of Khe Sanh veteran Peter Brush, of "the longest, deadliest, and most controversial battles of the Vietnam War."

On Route 12A, Nguyễn Thị Kim Huế, the defender of the Mụ Giạ Pass.

Nguyễn Thị Kim Huế holding a bouquet of flowers with President Hồ Chí Minh at the National Congress of the Youth Volunteer Corps, Hanoi, July 1967.

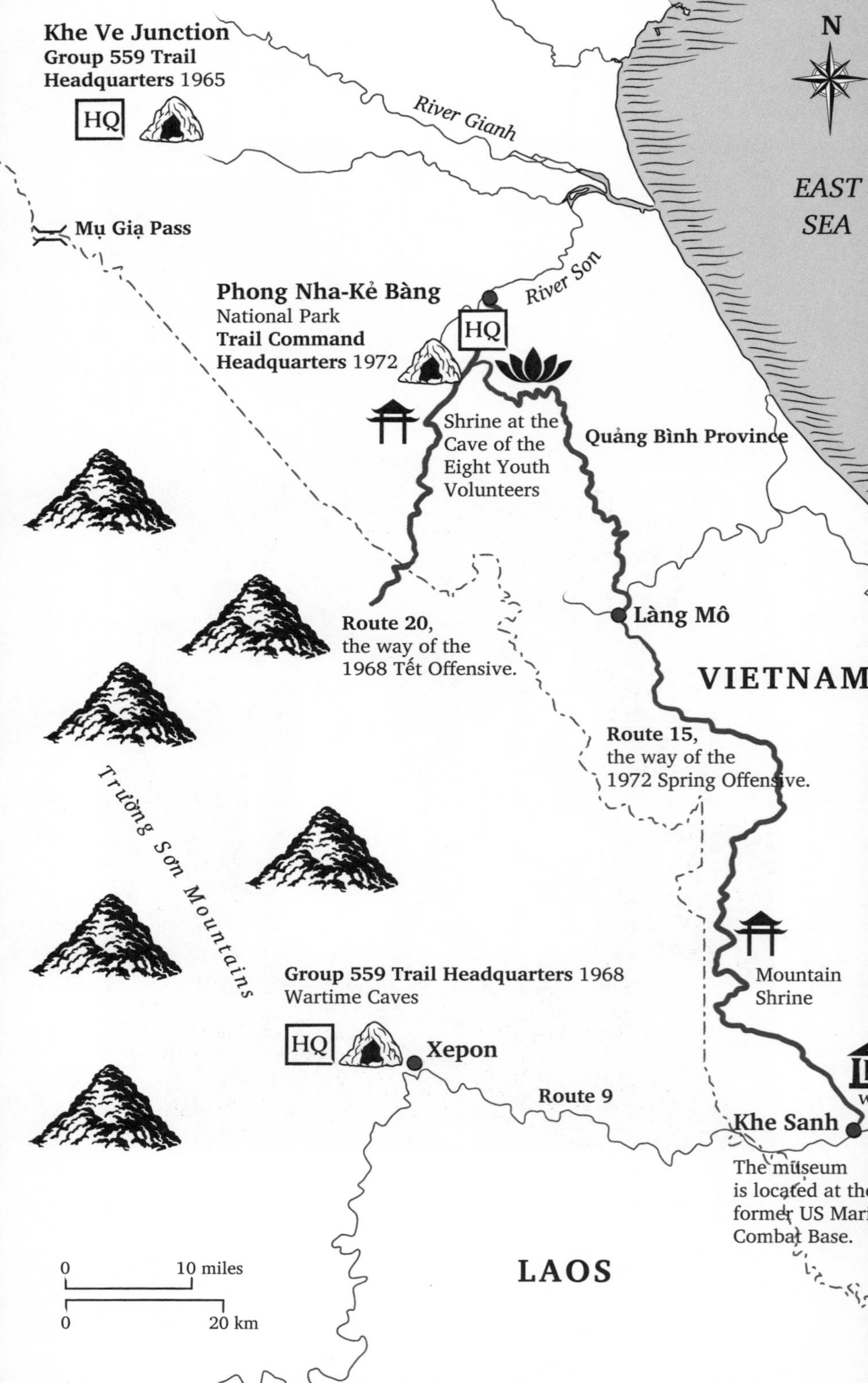
Khe Ve Junction
Group 559 Trail
Headquarters 1965
HQ
N
River Gianh
EAST
SEA
Mụ Giạ Pass
River Son
Phong Nha-Kẻ Bàng
National Park
Trail Command
Headquarters 1972
HQ
Shrine at the
Cave of the
Eight Youth
Volunteers
Quảng Bình Province
Làng Mô
Route 20,
the way of the
1968 Tết Offensive.
VIETNAM
Route 15,
the way of the
1972 Spring Offensive.
Trường Sơn Mountains
Mountain
Shrine
Group 559 Trail Headquarters 1968
Wartime Caves
HQ
Xepon
Route 9
Khe Sanh
The museum
is located at the
former US Mari
Combat Base.
LAOS
0
10 miles
0
20 km

Chapter 5

# *THE PHONG NHA CAVES TO KHE SANH*

*Wandering souls and the ways of the 1968 and 1972 Spring Offensives.*

The road wound gently down a green valley, along a limpid torrent, "mixed with the bones, sweat, and tears of Trail soldiers and Youth Volunteers ... More than eight thousand soldiers and sappers built the seventy-seven-mile road to the Laotian border. They leveled mountains and completed the road in record time."[37] This was the beautiful valley that the artist Trần Huy Oánh had depicted in his drawings. Construction on the road had begun in 1966 to ease traffic across the Mụ Giạ Pass.

We had left the hotel that morning to explore Route 20, the way of the Tết Offensive, before driving to Khe Sanh. We arrived at a mountain temple built against the rock face. The intimate shrine was dedicated to eight Youth Volunteers who had perished there while trapped in a cave.

"Do not use the incense burning at the temple to organize certain superstitious activities," read a sign at the shrine to fallen heroes.

"What does that mean?" I asked Nam.

"It's to discourage mediums from contacting the spirit world," he replied.

"Mediums?"

"People hire psychics to talk to their loved ones who died in the war," Nam explained.

Next to the temple was an underground cave. I stepped down into the dark grotto. The festive altar was decorated with gold and red lacquered dragons. The fragrance of cinnamon rose from joss sticks that pilgrims had left in a bronze incense burner. Custodians arranged white roses and yellow chrysanthemums. Office workers on a corporate outing, who had traveled by bus from Thanh Hóa, joined me in the grotto. They had brought gifts to provide the spirits with a happy afterlife. Angry spirits were feared should they return to seek revenge for their cruel and unjust death. Crisp 1,000-*đồng* banknotes were stacked up on the altar, along with boxes of crackers, bottles of mineral water, oranges, and bananas.

Trail marching songs played in an open-air visitor center next to the shrine. A short film told the story of the eight Youth Volunteers. They had taken refuge in a cave when B-52s carpet-bombed Route 20 on a day in November 1972. "One thousand tons" of rock collapsed and sealed the entrance. When the bombings stopped, the rescue teams heard cries. Mashed food was piped through a hole drilled in the rock. Tanks attached cables to clear away the rubble. But the cries stopped before the rescue teams could reach them.

I rang the temple gong, made from the casing of a US bomb.

Back in the car, we did a U-turn. We headed for Route 15. Destination: Khe Sanh. The road zigzagged up the steep mountain passes and down the deep gorges described in revolutionary poems and songs. The road builders had cut through rock face and the impassable rain forest of the Trường Sơn Mountains to build it, under attack from bombs, napalm, and toxic chemicals.

I was reminded of the poem "Bomb Crater Sky" dedicated to a road builder. The poet Lâm Thị Mỹ Dạ was inspired by a platoon leader and her all-female team while on assignment on the Trail. Revolutionary poets joined artists, musicians, dance and theater groups to entertain the troops stationed there. The platoon leader had confided in the poet that she had returned to the Trail, at the end of her tour of duty, to avenge the death of her family. She had found her grandparents, parents, and siblings all buried in a bomb crater when she had gone home to Thanh Hóa on leave.

She told the poet:

"I felt pain. Then, nothing at all. It was as if I had lost my soul. I stayed a few days with my cousin's family. When I had calmed down, I decided to return to the Trail. Now this was my home, my only home."[38]

On her next trip a few months later, Lâm Thị Mỹ Dạ looked for the women. The team had vanished. The poet found only bomb craters filled with rainwater where their camp had once been. She suspected the platoon leader and her team had joined so-called suicide teams. These teams lit torches to attract enemy planes onto themselves, away from the road. Few survived these missions. In their memory, she wrote "Bomb Crater Sky": [39]

*They say that you, a road builder*
*Had such love for our country*
*You rushed out and waved your torch*
*To call the bombs down on yourself*
*And save the road for the troops*

*As my unit passed on that worn road*
*The bomb crater reminded us of your story*
*Your grave is radiant with bright-colored stones*
*Piled high with love for you, a young girl*

*As I looked in the bomb crater where you died*
*The rain water became a patch of sky*
*Our country is kind*
*Water from the sky washes pain away*

*Now you lie down deep in the earth*
*As the sky lay down in that earthen crater*
*At night your soul sheds light*
*Like the dazzling stars*

*Did your soft white skin*
*Become a bank of white clouds?*

*By day I pass under a sun-flooded sky*
*And it is your sky*
*And that anxious, wakeful disc—*
*Is it the sun, or is it your heart*
*Lighting my way*
*As I walk down the long road?*

*The name of the road is your name*
*Your death is a young girl's patch of blue sky*
*My soul is lit by your life*

*And my friends, who never saw you—*
*Each has a different image of your face*

Soldiers on their way to the southern battlefronts relied on the road builders for safe passage. The artist Lê Quang Luân had served with an anti-aircraft defense unit in 1967 that traveled down Route 15, and crossed into Laos, transporting 12.7mm, 14.5mm, 37mm, and 57mm anti-aircraft guns. Most of his sketches were lost to monsoon rains. When I met him in his studio in Ho Chi Minh City, he talked about survivor's guilt and paid tribute to the women who had kept the roads open:

"The trucks carried the weapons and we sat on top. We were bombed all the time. We had no air support, none. People in my unit were dying all the time. Every day. In the end, we got used to it, we had to. Of the one hundred soldiers in my unit, ninety percent died. Only ten of us were left by the time we got to the southern battlefield. During the trip, I was injured. I thought I was going to die. I still don't know how I survived. I should have died.

"I am sad that so many of my friends died. Before I go to sleep, most nights, I remember them. And I remember the women at the Trail stations who helped us get through, and who died so young."

The trucks loaded with soldiers, ammunition, artillery, and rice advanced slowly under the cover of darkness. Some of the fighters, like Lê Quang Luân, rode in the back on top of the loads. Others walked. Malaria, cholera, physical exhaustion from hunger, and starvation were their natural companions.

The battle-hardened Trail Commander wrote in his memoir:

"I live in torment, tormented by the hunger of the soldiers."[40]

Discipline was harsh and enforced through Maoist-style group- and self-criticism sessions, which were conducted daily to correct mistakes and remedy weaknesses. Individual soldiers, assessed by their leaders and peers, were expected to "confess" their faults.

As we reached the top of a high pass, the challenging topography stretched before me. We stopped to look at the breathtaking view. Hân parked in a rest stop by a mountain cascade. As I stepped out of the car, I was enveloped by the sound of the wind and of melodious birdsong. I listened for the cries of gibbons I had been told lived in the forest. I didn't hear any. All around, waterfalls flowed into streams, torrents, and rivers that twisted and turned around the karst, above ground and underground, flowing through deep caves, as the water found its way to the East Sea.

Looking over the mountain range, I had the impression of floating above the Earth on a soft, undulating, endless sea without a shore; wave crests appeared as light-bluish peaks and ridges, and troughs as dark, hidden valleys. Hundreds of miles of steep slopes stretched south, covered in impenetrable jungle.

The succession of ridges must have been a daunting sight for those who made the journey, whether on foot or by truck. The artist and officer Huỳnh Phương Đông had imagined a mountain "as high as the waist of the sky" in the untitled farewell poem he wrote to his wife, on the day he left Hanoi in 1963 for his secret mission south.[41] They were reunited twelve years later, at the end of the war.

*Farewell my beloved*
*I will miss you endlessly*
*I think of the tiny lips Phương My [his daughter] kissed me with the other day*
*I think of Phương Đông [his son] lying still in his cradle*
*Oh my love, my children, my love, all is lost to me now*
*The time to go has come, all is torn apart*
*The river and the mountain do not say a word*
*The dark and silent night weigh heavily on my parting heart*
*Tomorrow in the quiet forest*
*Through wind and rain*
*Or on the mountain as high as the waist of the sky*
*Up steep paths or across valleys*
*Missing you, I will try harder for that joyful day*
*When our country is one again*
*And our happiness will burst through the sky.*

Back in the car, we negotiated hairpin turns, tracing serpentine loops on steep mountainsides. A team of invisible gardeners had clipped the sides of the road. Tall grasses rustled in the light wind. The patterned screens of tropical tree ferns overhung the road. Isolated high-canopy trees rose above the jungle along distant ridges in fanciful cutouts, shapes, and shadows, etched against the sky.

The landscape reminded me of a watercolor by Nguyễn Văn Trực, a Hanoi-based artist drafted to lead a propaganda team in a liberated zone close to Saigon. He had walked the length of the Trail to get there. He was so ill with malaria, it took him eight months. Despite his ordeal, he was entranced by the beautiful landscape and painted lush trees in pale greens and yellows, the silhouettes of soldiers with guns, waist-high in tall grasses. Thick vegetation had covered the hills until it was calcined by napalm and phosphorous bombs, "white as rice." Other drawings depicted desiccated trees drawn in the deep black of Chinese ink, so many crucifixes on this eastern Golgotha.

We stopped for lunch at the Khe Sanh boundary stone, a hundred miles from the former US Marine Combat Base that had been the cornerstone of the US defense line against the Trail, a five-hour drive at the slow pace of the night military convoys. I stepped out into the mountain air and perched on the Khe Sanh road marker to eat the sandwich Hân had bought in Phong Nha earlier that morning. The boundary stone was painted in the cheerful red and white of the those that lined the provincial roads of France. It was a familiar reference point in the alien, empty landscape, but I felt lost, destabilized. The silence was too quiet. The solitude was too lonely. The emptiness, too void. The road was deserted. Not a truck. Not a car. Not a moped. Not a human being walking along the road, carrying wood back from the forest. Not even a monkey crossing the road, looking for food in a hiker's backpack. The road had the "eerie quality" described by Sol Sanders when he flew at low altitude over the Trail in North Vietnam. The American journalist "had persuaded some Vietnamese ethnics flying for the Royal Lao Air Force to take him with them. The flight was surreal. They were bombing haphazardly, with an improvised explosive on their undercarriage, and machine-gunning. Although there was no doubt that we were flying over a heavily traveled road, I saw no sign of life during the entire time."[42]

The mountain was mesmerizing. The tall grasses sang in the wind. The place of remembrance and sorrow drew me into its embrace. A week earlier, in Hanoi, the artist Lương Xuân Đoàn had been reminiscing about his trip on the Trail after the war and his encounter with "wandering souls." We had met in a popular coffee shop near the West Lake. With his shoulder-length hair streaked with gray, a fetching mustache, and round glasses, the president of the Vietnam Fine Arts Association looked very much the bohemian scholar.

I was savoring a particularly rich and dark *cà phê đen*.

"Wandering souls?" I asked.

"When I went back to the Trail after the war, I was reminded of

Nguyễn Văn Trực, *Untitled*, watercolor, 1967.

*"The place of remembrance and sorrow*
*drew me into its embrace."*

*"The landscape reminded me of this watercolor by Nguyễn Văn Trực."*

On Route 15, sunset in the Phong Nha-Kẻ Bàng National Park, Quảng Bình Province.

what happened," said the painter. "Many women who repaired the Trail roads died there. During a storm, I saw the souls of five young women flying above. I stopped by a mountain temple and prayed for them."

Lương Xuân Đoàn crossed himself as he described his daytime vision. I asked him if he was Catholic. He said he wasn't. In this communist land, expressions of spiritual devotion were ever present.

"I got an emotional feeling. I felt the ghosts were next to me," he said.

"Be careful, next time they might keep you there," joked Đặng Anh Tuấn, an artist and friend who was having coffee with us.

Lương Xuân Đoàn continued:

"I wasn't fearful. I felt they protected me. Their bodies cannot be found. They cannot return home. Relatives are looking for the bodies. Families would like to find their loved ones. They cannot finish this task. When new roads are built, sometimes whole cemeteries are found."

In the urban surroundings of the café in Hanoi, the ghost story sounded romantic if implausible. But, as I walked along the road in the shadow of the mountain, I wondered. In *Century at Dusk*, Trần Trung Tín painted in remembrance of the ghostly figures of "wandering souls" standing side-by-side with the living. Gone without proper burial rituals, the dead become roaming spirits, doomed to a restless eternity. Neither the living nor the dead can find peace. Metaphorically, the "wandering souls" inhabited the landscape lest we forget the millions who died in Vietnam's wars.

The American military had seized on the belief during the war and launched an operation code-named "Wandering Soul." Helicopters broadcast "ghost" tape recordings of spooky sounds and voices urging enemy soldiers to desert. On one tape, a Ghost Father talks to his daughter and friends over funeral music:

"My friends, I have come back to let you know that I am dead ... I am in Hell. It was a senseless death. But when I realized the truth it was too late. Go home! Go home, friends! Hurry! If not you will end up like me."[43]

Back on the road, we reached a wide and verdant valley that followed a translucent river. The wind was blowing. It was misty and cool. Emerald-green weeds flowed on the riverbed. Sandy beaches stretched along the riverbank. I felt I was at sea level even though I was crossing a high mountain plateau. The sensation was deceptive and disorienting, as was everything else about the "eerie" yet beautiful mountains. The union between mountain and sea so striking in the landscape was at the heart of a romantic and bitter-sweet creation myth. The Vietnamese, according to legend, were the fruit of a love affair between the mountain fairy Âu Cơ and the sea dragon Lạc Long Quân. Âu Cơ bore an egg sack that hatched one hundred children. Despite their great love for each other, the lovers separated: Âu Cơ longed for the hills and Lạc Long Quân yearned for the ocean. Fifty of their children settled in the coastal plains by the sea and fifty in the mountains, or so the legend went.

We stopped at an observation point that looked down over the Long Đại River's fertile plain of rice fields. Làng Mô, along the banks of the river, was the first village we had seen since leaving the hotel that morning. The bend in the river, the gentle curvature of the fields, the fertility of the valley, and the protective shadow of the mountains made it a natural place to call home. During the war, writers penned poems about places like this where the soldiers felt at home. Artists portrayed "war mothers" in their drawings. Grandmothers in villages were chosen by Party officials to look after soldiers on their way to war to make them feel less homesick.

Beyond Làng Mô, the Trail followed the twists and turns of the Long Đại River. At the Khu Đăng Pass, we stopped at a concrete wall built against landslides. A weatherbeaten sign covered the full length of the wall. The inscription, dating from 2004, commemorated the forty-fifth anniversary of the Trail Command.

Had they ever considered giving up? When had the cost become too high? Or did they believe, as the Trail Commander wrote in his memoir, that they had no choice?

Lulled by the gentle valley of the Long Đại River, I thought the steep climbs had come to an end. But it was never the end. I surrendered to the tempo and rhythm of the road as we drove up another sharp incline. At the top of the pass another mountain shrine stood on a lonely hillside, in memory of Youth Volunteers from Thanh Hóa who "protected the Trail against the Americans between April 14, 1969 and December 31, 1972." A total of forty women and men had lost their lives here.

Down the road, a sign near a village pointed to a B-52 bomb site. I was curious to see the size of the craters the women filled in. We drove through the village in search of the bomb crater. Wood-burning fires flickered in preparation for making the evening meal. Satellite dishes connected the remote village to the world of soap operas and pop music. An attractive woman wrapped in a red sarong was taking an evening shower outside her home. Hân turned his head to glance at her and drove off the track into the neighbor's backyard. We left the village without having found the crater.

Back on the road, we crossed a motorcyclist with a People's Army pith helmet on his head.

"He's probably a teacher," said Hân, whose father had been a schoolteacher in the countryside. "Each ethnic minority village has a Vietnamese teacher in the local school. Nobody wants these jobs. But if you don't have connections or can't pay the bribes to get the good posts in the cities, you work in the remote villages. You get a higher pay for these mountain jobs. The salary can be as much as four hundred dollars a month. But you have to stay a minimum of five years. Some never leave. They marry a local and raise their families here. It's a peaceful life. No stress. But boring."

We stopped in a village of thatched houses brightened by pink, red, and purple sarongs hanging out to dry. The hill tribes had been conscripted by both sides as fighters, road builders, and laborers.

After the war, those on the losing side had been pushed back deeper into the inhospitable mountains where the land was poor and infertile. A band of barefoot children ran toward us, T-shirts torn, with runny noses. All we had was the peanut brittle that Hân had bought two days earlier at the Hồ Citadel. We distributed it as fairly as we could. But there wasn't enough to go around and fights broke out among the kids.

Shortly after we left the village, we began the long climb up the Sa Mù Pass. When we reached the top, we were engulfed in thick fog.

"Let's stop and wait for the fog to lift," I suggested.

"We have a long way to go," said Hân.

"It's dangerous," I replied.

"I know the road," said Hân, as he drove through the whiteout.

We descended into the unknown, hemmed in between hill and precipice. The incline was so steep that I braked with my legs to keep from falling forward into the dashboard. I hoped Hân had memorized the bends.

"Beautiful landscape," Hân said.

He was joking. We couldn't see a thing.

"Yep," I replied, trying to sound relaxed.

"Nam, are you awake for this?" I asked.

"Yes, the fog makes everything feel peaceful," Nam replied.

The balance between yin and yang in the car was working out well. One companion meditated, the other had nerves of steel, and I was hanging on.

As we came around a sharp turn, solitary figures appeared through the fog. The men were wearing Army uniforms.

"Stop," is all they said.

They looked in the car, shined a flashlight at us, and smiled.

"Now go."

What or who were they looking for on this deserted road?

On our way down from the Sa Mù Pass, the mountains softened into hills. Signs of life on the road indicated we were nearing the coastal plain. At the junction with Route 9, young women carried firewood in baskets strapped to their backs. We had crossed the "provisional demarcation line" into the former South Vietnam, which had been so wretchedly fought over, without even noticing it. The line had been defended by US combat bases that stretched from the romantic white sandy beaches of the East Sea to the dramatic jungle terrain of the Trường Sơn Mountains on the border with Laos, and by the McNamara Line, "the sophisticated electronic system, backed by gravel mines and troops at choke points … monitored from a computer center in Thailand … the start of the high-tech sensor warfare that continues to this day."[44]

Had the general elections promised by the Geneva Accords been held, would there have been a "line" or would there even have been a war?

I thought of how peaceful the once deadly Quảng Trị Province appeared in the evening light. I agreed with the artist Lương Xuân Đoàn. The "wandering souls" protected Trail travelers. As I visited the shrines and listened to the stories of the women who had defended the Trail, something unexpected had happened on this road to war: I became a pilgrim. I, who no longer said prayers and had forgotten the words, "prayed" at the mountain shrines for those who had died too young: from the North, the South, and from across the Pacific, fighting on opposing sides but united by youth, love, adventure, and patriotic beliefs.

Remembrance had no borders.

On Route 20, in the Cave of the Eight Youth Volunteers, Quảng Bình Province.

EAST SEA
N
Vĩnh Mốc
Martyrs' Cemetery Vĩnh Linh District
Vĩnh Mốc Tunnels
Bến Hải River
WAR
Trường Sơn National Martyrs' Cemetery
Route 15 (East)
THE FORMER DMZ
Martyrs' Cemetery Cam Tuyền Commune
Đông Hà
Route 9
Martyrs' Cemetery Route 9
Project RENEW
Quảng Trị City
Quảng Trị Province
19th-Century Citadel
Long
Relic
WAR
Former US Marine Combat Base
Thạch Hãn River
Khe Sanh
Thạch Hãn River
VIETNAM
Quảng Trị Province
LAOS
0
5 miles
0
10 km

Chapter 6

# *KHE SANH TO ĐÔNG HÀ*

*Going out with the bomb demolition teams in Quảng Trị Province.*

*The People's Army attacked the US Marine Combat Base at Khe Sanh in the early hours of January 21, 1968. On January 31, 1968, they joined forces with the Việt Cộng to launch simultaneous surprise attacks, on three fronts, against one hundred Allied headquarters and military bases in towns throughout South Vietnam.*

*The Trail Commander planned the North Quảng Trị Front from a cave dug deep inside a mountain over the border in Laos:*

*"I believe that our 'premises' [HQ] gave us the confidence [to carry out the Tết Offensive] ... After a rainy season of hard labor, the engineers had completed the construction of a tunnel two hundred meters (six hundred and fifty feet) long, dug deep into the mountain. Generators ensured continuous light. A telephone system communicated directly with the fighting units. It was difficult to imagine how our engineers were able to build the Command Center ... so close to Route 9, a road that was controlled and patrolled by the enemy."*[45]

*Both sides claimed victory at Khe Sanh. The North Vietnamese based their success on the withdrawal of the US Marines from the base several months later; the United States assessed their triumph according to a higher Killed in Action (KIA) ratio.*

*Khe Sanh and the Tết Offensive changed the course of the war.*

Khe Sanh Village was dark when we pulled into the main street that evening. In the winter of 1968, as dawn broke, the village had been engulfed in artillery fire. The People's Army pounded the US and South Vietnamese military headquarters located in the village.

Khe Sanh veteran Peter Brush described the onset of the surprise attack:

"During the darkness of January 20–21, the NVA [North Vietnamese Army] launched a series of coordinated attacks against American positions ... an NVA artillery barrage scored a hit on the main ammunition dump at Khe Sanh Combat Base, killing Lance Corp. Jerry Stenberg and other Marines. At about 6:40 a.m., the NVA ... attacked the Hướng Hóa District headquarters in Khe Sanh Village. This fighting was heavy ... The monumental Battle of Khe Sanh had begun."[46]

Khe Sanh Village fell to the communist forces later that day. The siege of the US Marine Combat Base lasted seventy-six more days.

I had come to Khe Sanh out of duty rather than desire. No Trail journey was complete without stopping here.

The coordinated surprise attacks by the North Vietnamese People's Army and Việt Cộng against the seats of US military power in South Vietnam shocked Americans who had believed they were winning the war. Television news reporters in battle helmets and bulletproof vests filmed the US Marines under siege in Khe Sanh, street fighting in the imperial city of Huế, and streams of refugees in Saigon, against a soundtrack of North Vietnamese artillery and Việt Cộng mortar fire. Anti-war protests grew louder around the country. Demonstrators picketed the White House shouting: "Hey, hey, LBJ, how many kids did you kill today?" Students in Boston turned in their draft cards. Massive anti-war protests broke out at the 1968 Democratic Convention in Chicago where police wearing gas masks fired tear gas and beat demonstrators with their nightsticks.

As the Tết Offensive was underway, on March 31, 1968, President Johnson declared he would not run for reelection, so that, in his words, he could focus on bringing peace to Vietnam. He suspended the bombing of North Vietnam, Hanoi's condition to come to the negotiating table, and peace talks between the warring sides began in Paris. The following year, in July 1969, Richard Nixon, the newly elected US president, put in place his strategy to end US involvement in Vietnam. But peace was six long years away.

The Battle of Khe Sanh had marked the beginning of a carnage. During the Tết Offensive alone, over 58,000 North Vietnamese and Việt Cộng, 21,000 South Vietnamese, and 24,000 American soldiers and other allies lost their lives; 14,300 South Vietnamese civilians were killed, thousands more wounded. Hundreds of thousands of refugees were displaced from their homes.[47]

We checked into our hotel. It was dismal and doubled as a brothel. Nam went down to the spa in the basement to book a massage after the long road trip.

"No problem," came the response, "but you will have to pay extra for the girl."

"Thanks, but no thanks," he said.

We ate in an empty dining room and turned in for an early night after a day on the road.

The sadness was in my room in a grim hotel in a border town, on the Trail, where a cruel battle in a cruel war had taken place.

So many Vietnamese friends had said to me:

"In the West you can't understand how cruel this war was."

So many had said to me:

"I hate war."

I checked my email. I opened a message from Nguyễn Thanh Bình, an artist celebrated for his muted paintings of ballet dancers and women in white traditional dress. He hadn't felt like talking about the war when we had met in his studio in Ho Chi Minh City.

"I'll email you something, a memory from my time on the Trail," he had said.

Now I read his message:

"Ngọc, my company commander from Haiphong, was a grumpy guy with a gruff nature. There wasn't a guy in the company who hadn't been cursed by him. And that included me. One day when we were out on patrol, we discovered a scout team that had been hit by a mortar. Two scouts had been killed. Ngọc ordered us to gather the body parts … The first guy was all broken up. We collected each piece … There was a pile nearby that looked like raw beef, red, slightly disgusting. When Ngọc caught sight of it, he said, 'Mother fuck, that's the other guy! Look! What the fuck! Time to hurry up! Time to get moving!' He took off his hat and handed it to me: 'Here! Put it in there!' Then he glared at me. I was horrified and scared. Fumbling, I took a fistful of meat and bone, and put it into the hat. The young man had been strong, but I gathered only enough to fill the hat, that was all."

Casualty numbers in war were abstract. How would we have felt in front of that? How many corpses and body parts had any one of us seen in a lifetime without the body bags or designer coffins to shield the macabre?

If I had to hit a low during the trip, Khe Sanh was it. Places have karma. And Khe Sanh's was bad. I played Aretha Franklin's "I Say a Little Prayer" on my iPad. I used to listen to the song when it was top of the charts in 1968, worrying about exams and my lonely existence in an all-girl Catholic boarding school. "My darling, believe me, for me there is no one but you … answer my prayer, babe …"

I shut my eyes and prayed for a dreamless sleep.

"Did you have a good night?" Nam asked over breakfast the following morning.

"Not bad," I said, deciding not to burden him with my angst.

"How was your room?" I asked.

"I found a used condom in my drawer," Nam replied.

"I guess it goes with the massage thing."

"That's not all. In the middle of the night, I heard a noise. I opened the cupboard door. It was a rat."

"Right. Let's finish drinking our coffee, pack our bags, and get out of here!"

We had scheduled a trip to a kindergarten funded by Judd Kinne, a US Marine veteran who had fought to the east of where we were along Route 9, near the "Rockpile," and elsewhere in Quảng Trị Province during the Tết Offensive.

"I wanted to go back to Vietnam and do something," Judd had told me. "Vietnam is finally getting over its trauma after fifty years of devastation. What we did to that country! And for what? [So that] the chairman of the Joint Chiefs of Staff could be shaking the hand of his counterpart in Hanoi! If you had told me in 1975 that we would have been best buddies, I wouldn't have believed it."

We drove along Route 9 and branched off onto a dirt road that led to Judd's kindergarten in a remote hamlet. Deep in the forest, wooden houses on stilts huddled together. Up the hill stood a welcoming schoolhouse in a pistachio green, built with bricks and mortar against the monsoon rains. The children ran out of the classroom, peeked at the foreign visitors, and ran back into the school.

I had met Judd over dinner on my stopover in Singapore, at the Mandarin Oriental Hotel overlooking Marina Bay's futuristic skyline. Trim, fit, and forthright with a natural commanding manner, the former Marine had married and settled in Asia after the war where he was a successful investment banker. Across from the hotel, giant stainless-steel petals shimmered on the bay's watery surface, light-years away from the fighting holes, machine-gun nests, and trenches of darkness.

During the conflict, Judd had been on the front line. As the 1st Platoon Commander with Kilo Company, 3rd Battalion 1st Marines, as he recalled he had little time for reflection:

"I was out in the bush. I didn't give it much thought, whether the war was morally wrong. We had to stay alive. You did wonder, though, when you would take a village and raze it, and then three months later you were back taking the same village again. And the body counts. They determined an operation's success, so units competed to get the highest number of 'killed in action'."

"What led you to build schools in Vietnam?" I asked.

"It was an encounter I had in 2006 with the war photographer David Douglas Duncan. He had served with the Marines and I had long admired the empathy his work showed for fighting men. I began collecting some of his war photographs. When I met him at his home near Valbonne in France, I bought his black paint Leica M3D which he used in Vietnam and at Khe Sanh, where he made a brief stay with the Marines under siege. After I sold the camera at auction in 2012 for a good bit of money, I thought, this is the time to do something in Vietnam, to honor David and my Marine Corps comrades. David was delighted with the idea of kindergartens near Khe Sanh, but was too frail to travel for the opening ceremony."

The photojournalist David Douglas Duncan (1916–2018) had been a combat photographer for the Marine Corps during World War II and a staff photographer for *Life* in the French, Korean, and Vietnam Wars. Before the end of the siege at Khe Sanh, he published poignant photographs of the Marines who were trapped there. His book *I Protest!* urged the US president and his inner circle of civilians with no experience of the battlefield to stop committing young men to suffering and death in an unwinnable war. He wrote:

"... I want to shout a loud and clear protest at what has happened at Khe Sanh, and in all of Vietnam ... on behalf of the men who will never get out, for whom help came too late."[48]

Judd thought to build schools close to the battlefields where he had lost friends under fire:

"My company had been set up for two days in Lam Xuan, a destroyed village located a few miles south of the Demilitarized Zone and close to the Cửa Việt river mouth on the East Sea. It was February 1, 1968, two days after the initial onslaught of the Tết Offensive. We had been receiving incoming artillery rounds from NVA guns across the Demilitarized Zone. Intelligence suggested they were preparing a big attack. We had been ordered by our battalion headquarters to remain in Lam Xuan that night. But along with my company and two other platoon commanders, we decided to move the men under cover of darkness a few hundred yards to the east, where we dug in the sand dunes. This was a fortunate decision! At around 2:30 a.m. the next morning, the enemy opened up on our old position in Lam Xuan with a huge barrage of artillery and mortar fire. Over three hundred NVA then launched a ground assault. But there were no Marines to be found in Lam Xuan! Had we stayed, we'd have had it!

"We then opened fire with our naval artillery and support guns. In the final minutes of the battle, our young artillery lieutenant was killed. He was the one who had helped to save us by pre-positioning the naval guns that stopped the NVA advance. He was a good friend, and I wanted to commemorate him and all the Marines lost in Quảng Trị Province by building schools near to Lam Xuan. But by 2013 it had become quite a prosperous farming area and the education authorities said they already had schools. We built the kindergartens for the Bru tribespeople a few miles from Khe Sanh, where they were badly needed."

One of the two kindergartens was this bright little school on the hill where we were. A bronze plaque on the wall was dedicated to "the American photojournalist David Douglas Duncan who first photographed Vietnam in 1953 and again in 1967–1968." The Leica he had used so passionately to draw attention to the suffering of war had provided much of the funding for the school.

I took off my shoes and positioned them next to the children's, which were all arranged in a perfectly straight line. As Nam and I stepped into the classroom, toddlers greeted us with a lively song-and-dance performance. A young talent belted out a festive tune. Tiny performers executed steps from a lotus dance, while an absent-minded kid looked on, unsure of what he was supposed to do. The children, between three and four years old, then counted to ten, recited the letters of the alphabet, and showed us their drawings of rainbows and stars.

With our suitcases in the back of the car, I was ready to leave Khe Sanh and skip the visit to the US Marine Base. I suggested that we press on to Đông Hà, where I had arranged to meet another American veteran who had come back to Vietnam "to do something."

Judd had warned me that there was nothing much to see at the old Marine Combat Base. Three months after the end of the siege, the Marines had received orders to raze the base at Khe Sanh, "so that the Vietnamese couldn't say they had a victory there," he explained. Why the Marines were ordered to abandon a combat base built to stop infiltration from the Trail, which had withstood a long and bloody siege, is still disputed today.

"We have to visit the base. That's why we're here," said Nam.

"Yes, you have to go," said Hân, seconding Nam.

The wind was howling on the plateau where the airfield of the US Marine Combat Base and airstrip had once been. A rusty old tank stood alone, profiled against the hills like a prehistoric beast. Nearby, a small museum full of weapons, maps with red arrows, and battle photographs glorified the People's Army victory.

Nguyễn Viết Minh, the museum's engaging deputy director who was fluent in American English, took us around the galleries. Vietnamese press photographs showed People's Army soldiers firing big guns and attacking with tanks. US press photographs showed Marines hunkered down in their hooches with inglorious captions that read: "US Marines shutting themselves in their bunkers for fear of their own shadows." "Preparing stretchers and body bags." "Praying for deliverance from Hellish Khe Sanh." And, "Making a panicky withdrawal."

But Nguyễn Viết Minh's appraisal of the Battle of Khe Sanh was evenhanded compared to the exhibits on display:

"I agree that both sides paid a heavy price. How heavy, I don't know. The number of our war dead remains secret. But the Tết Offensive turned the war in another direction. There was a lot of US television coverage. The American people were shocked. There were anti-war protests, Lyndon Johnson didn't run for reelection, and the commander of the US forces, General Westmoreland, had to retire."

Nguyễn Viết Minh turned to Nam.

"We need the contributions of the Việt Kiều. We welcome them back. There is a Vietnamese adage that says: 'We fight with those who are leaving, not with those who come back.' Goodbye brother," he said, in a gesture of friendship toward a former enemy.

"Goodbye brother," Nam answered.

Nam was overwhelmed by emotion.

"Did you hear that? He called me 'brother.' It's the first time anyone from the North has called me 'brother,'" he said.

The Việt Kiều—or overseas Vietnamese—who left South Vietnam after the war had for a time been considered traitors and collaborators by the new Vietnamese state.

We walked through a field white with flowers where the wartime landscape had been black and desolate. We stood in silence to honor those on our side who had fought and died here.

Where did the People's Army go after Khe Sanh? To attack the US combat bases in Đông Hà and Quảng Trị City where I had arranged to meet Chuck Searcy, an American veteran who had come back to Vietnam to clean up the unexploded ordnance left behind.

The South Vietnamese towns in Quảng Trị Province had been shelled by People's Army artillery attacking them, and bombed by American planes defending them. US planes had dropped more

Near the junction of Routes 15 and 9, a tank relic on the airfield of the US Marine Combat Base, Khe Sanh, Quảng Trị Province.

ordnance on Quảng Trị Province, an ally, than on Germany, an enemy, during World War II.

"Quảng Trị Province is where you will see the suffering," said Ngô Thị Tuyển, the defender of the Dragon's Jaw Bridge.

I was about to discover what she meant.

We left the museum and traveled the short distance along Route 9 to Đông Hà. In the evening light, we arrived on the banks of the Cửa Việt River. The riverfront, once a war zone patrolled by US Marines, was pleasantly landscaped. In the park was a statue of Lê Duẩn, the Politburo hawk who had launched the 1968 Tết Offensive and who had predicted the popular uprising in South Vietnam that never materialized. When Hồ Chí Minh died in 1969 without seeing his dream of a unified Vietnam realized, Lê Duẩn, his chosen successor, became the top decision maker in the Politburo. More offensives were to come.

Chuck was having an early dinner in the dining room of the hotel in Đông Hà that he called home. He had enlisted as an Army intelligence analyst and was posted in Saigon during the Tết Offensive. He had returned to Vietnam to deal with the war's aftermath. He co-founded Project RENEW to clean up American air-dropped munitions, and give assistance to bomb accident survivors and to families disabled by Agent Orange, the toxic herbicide the US military used to clear the jungle.

The hotel in Đông Hà was nondescript. Some might have called it forlorn. Chuck greeted me as an old friend even though we had met only once the previous year at the Fine Arts Museum in Hanoi, where I was organizing an art-in-war exhibition. The presence of a southern gentleman was comforting. Elegant in posture and tone, he reminded me of Jimmy Stewart. A melodious southern twang from his native Georgia camouflaged a razor-sharp wit.

Over dinner, Chuck invited us to join a bomb-disposal team that was going out the following day.

"Unexploded ordnance remains a serious threat to the communities here," he explained. "We get calls on our helpline every day. Of three thousand villages that existed in Quảng Trị Province before the war, only eleven villages had a single building left standing by the end of the war."

"Are you up for that?" I asked Nam.

"And you?" Nam asked back.

"Sure," I answered.

I didn't want to admit to the men that I was scared, and I wanted to see the live ordnance that the women on the Trail detonated.

The blare of a loudspeaker woke me the next morning as dawn broke through the thinly lined curtains of my hotel room. I fumbled around on the bedside table for my cell phone to check the time: 5 a.m. I stumbled out of bed and onto the balcony. The warm air felt tropical. The fog had dissipated. I had arrived in the south of the country. I could see the river and a faint outline of the Trường Sơn Mountains to the west. As I looked down over the streets below, a pickup truck with a megaphone drove slowly through the sleeping city. The bullhorn blasted another announcement. Music followed. Mobile loudspeakers had warned against French military advances in the first war and American bombing raids in the next. But now?

On my way to breakfast, I stopped by the hotel reception to ask.

"Morning propaganda," the man at the front desk replied.

"Morning propaganda?"

"Nobody listens to it anymore. We're so used to it, we don't hear it," he said.

"What are they saying?" I asked.

"Time to wake up. Fathers, get up and get ready to go to work, and provide for your families. Mothers, get up and cook breakfast. Children, get up and get ready for school. Study hard, and make your parents proud of you. Remember mothers and fathers, having two children in your family is enough. You don't need more children than that."

I went to meet the others for breakfast in the hotel dining room. I didn't touch the bland buffet food. Nam, ever positive, piled his plate high with it. Chuck didn't seem bothered either. I ordered a *cà phê đen*.

"We don't have Vietnamese coffee, only American filter coffee," said the waiter.

I skipped breakfast altogether.

Project RENEW was housed in a modest compound on the outskirts of Đông Hà. Bombs of all shapes and sizes decorated the lawn, useless old things that belonged in a César installation of discarded objects. One bomb had been turned into a garden planter.

"Good example of converting military technology to a peaceful use," I remarked.

Chuck showed us around. A floor-to-ceiling map pinpointed the five-million-plus sorties made by American bombers over Vietnamese territory: 956 sorties a day, eighty sorties an hour, one every minute. As I traveled the length of the north of Vietnam, I did wonder what had been left to bomb after the destruction of military installations, factories, fuel depots, bridges, roads, and cities. I was shocked to find out that South Vietnam, the US ally, had been bombed at four times the rate of the North by its own air force and the US Air Force, Navy, and Marines, to rout the Việt Cộng.

Suddenly, somebody from the emergency response team ran into the room.

"We've received a call on our hotline. A farmer has discovered *bombis* in his field. Let's go," she said.

The team jumped into their 4x4s and sped away. We followed. Within a few minutes, we were at the farmer's field close to a new housing development in a suburb of Đông Hà. Chuck introduced me to the man in charge, Lieutenant Colonel Bùi Trọng Hồng. Dressed in military-style khakis, he was a no-nonsense type of guy who instantly gained my trust.

"We're lucky to have him on our team. Bùi Trọng Hồng served with the People's Army for thirty-two years," said the American veteran.

The detonation crew was already in place. A diagram showed the location of the bomb, the detonator, homes nearby, and the ambulance. The team leader in charge of detonation explained:

"A cluster bomblet was found, what we call a *bombi*. *Bombis* are very unstable. They're too dangerous to move. We plan to detonate it in situ. We transport the larger and safe-to-remove bombs to our central demolition site to avoid damaging nearby property. The People's Army was concentrated here during their campaign to liberate Quảng Trị Citadel. Unfortunately, they were detected by the South Vietnamese Army. The US Air Force gave them air support by dropping bombs."

Cluster bombs released a large number of explosive bomblets that were designed to kill people. They dispersed over a wide area for maximum impact and were equipped with time-delay fuses to inflict damage over a long period of time. The insidious weapon was banned by the Convention on Cluster Munitions in 2008, ratified by over one hundred countries. The United States was not one of them.

I was asked to sign a waiver giving my blood type, certifying no allergies to anesthetics and penicillin, and accepting responsibility for any harm that might come to me.

"We have secured the safety cordon. In case of an accident, an ambulance and medic are on standby. The hospital is four minutes away."

I was apprehensive.

"Aren't you afraid?" I asked.

The team leader replied:

"Before, I was afraid. Now, I'm confident. Support from my team is the most important thing. And we have a protocol in place. In eight years, we haven't had a single casualty."

The lieutenant colonel invited me to view the lethal weapon up close. I walked behind him through the field, placing my feet in his exact footsteps. Where there was one, there were others. When we arrived at the site, all that stood between me and the *bombi* was a pink sandbag. Bùi Trọng Hồng bent down, pointing his pen at a small object hidden in the grass. The potentially deadly projectile was the size of a tennis ball. I returned, in his exact footsteps, to the safety of the road.

"Sherry is in charge of detonating the *bombi*," somebody said.

I thought they were kidding. A young woman, a floppy Trail hat on her head with a strap under her chin, led me to a detonator positioned on the road, 300 feet away. The remote-control and long detonator cord reassured me. The wartime bomb-disposal crews in the museum photographs didn't use remote-controls.

"Hold this button down hard," she said, taking my right hand and pushing my finger on it. "When you hear '*ba, hai, một,* fire,' press the button next to it with your left hand."

I pressed so hard that I got a cramp in my finger and struggled to hold the button down while waiting for the "three, two, one," signal to activate the detonator.

"*Ba, hai, một.* Fire!"

A deafening explosion followed. I had kept the button down and pressed the detonator in time. A plume of white smoke billowed up. We were all safe. The lieutenant colonel presented the exploded *bombi* to me wrapped in a pink sack. The shattered pieces of shrapnel lay there, harmless.

"A memento for you," he said.

"The pink matches the color of your running shoes," Chuck remarked.

Within minutes of the explosion, the demolition team was back in their four-wheel drive and on their way to the next job. They headed for an acacia plantation with a high concentration of cluster bombs. We followed.

"How is it possible to clear millions of unexploded cluster bombs?" I asked Chuck, during the drive.

Chuck was surprisingly optimistic:

"Once the Pentagon released their confidential data, we were able to introduce a grid system to detect areas with high concentrations of unexploded ordnance. In the old days, we cleared the land if, say, the city wanted to build a school. But there wasn't a single bomb on the land. We wasted a lot of money. That doesn't happen anymore."

"Is there a government program to de-mine?" I asked.

"The Ministry of Defense in Hanoi could do the de-mining and cover the whole country, but they would have to get out of the mindset that they only do contract jobs for development or infrastructure projects. There, they get paid. But there is nothing in it for them to go find bombs in a farmer's garden," Chuck replied.

"Do they think the United States should pay for it?"

"The ministry doesn't say that, but they would be justified in asking for that," said Chuck.

We crawled along a rough and muddy track. The car kept skidding.

"During the war, we used to sing a song called 'Sloop John B.' by The Beach Boys. Remember the lyrics: 'I feel so broke up, I wanna go home.' What were the other songs, Sherry? The ones you sang stateside?" asked Chuck.

I started humming:

"Where have all the flowers gone? Long time passing ... Girls have picked them every one. When will they ever learn? … Where have all the soldiers gone? Gone to graveyards every one …"

Chuck didn't pick up on it. The song hadn't been popular with GIs.

At the next site, I stood with Chuck in the shade on the edge of the acacia forest. Ngô Thiện Khiết, dressed in a smart khaki uniform, a canvas hat on his head, led the detonating team.

"You can't follow us into the forest. The leeches are out," he said.

I didn't argue. Trail veterans had hinted at blood-sucking leeches crawling into body orifices.

Instead, Bùi Trọng Hồng asked for volunteers to accompany him to the field nearby. He offered to demonstrate how to defuse cluster bombs without a remote detonator, a routine procedure during the war. I volunteered. Nobody else did. I signed another waiver.

"The nearest clinic is six miles away, but we can give first aid here," Ngô Thiện Khiết said gently to reassure me.

I walked even closer to Bùi Trọng Hồng. The survey showed there were bomblets all around us. After a short walk that felt like forever, the colonel bent down, I thought, to show me the *bombi* as he had at the previous site. But he reached for a pair of clippers and cut one of the wires like I had seen it done in the movies. He disabled the weapon so quickly that I had no time to be afraid.

A year later, Chuck emailed to let me know that Ngô Thiện Khiết, who had been in charge of detonation at the second site, had died in an accident. Khiết and his team were conducting a technical survey of a paddy field where rice had just been harvested. They had unearthed five *bombis*. Khiết was recording the GPS coordinates of the fifth *bombi* and marking it with warning tapes so that the demolition team could dispose of it, when there was an explosion. Khiết suffered serious wounds while his team member who was standing thirty feet away was slightly wounded. Both were rushed to hospital. Khiết died shortly after. His team member survived.

## *The Vịnh Mốc Tunnels*

That afternoon, we left to visit the Vịnh Mốc tunnels, where the People's Army had been stationed during the offensives. Ben, an American college kid doing a film on Project RENEW, joined us. We drove through the former Demilitarized Zone. Rice paddies and shrimp-farm lagoons had replaced the moonscape of the war years. On the way, we stopped at the Hiền Lương Bridge, the landmark bridge that spanned the Bến Hải River, the provisional demarcation line in wartime, before continuing north.

The Vịnh Mốc tunnels had become a popular tourist attraction. Brochures advertised the tunnels as bomb shelters built by fishermen to protect their families against the air war. When we arrived at the site, I could smell the sea. The surf was up. We fanned out to visit the tunnels solo. I had discovered the Vịnh Mốc tunnels in *Confidences*, a war drawing depicting the bond between soldiers facing combat stress before the Tết Offensive. They shared coffee, cigarettes, and thoughts in their underground bunker—perhaps even wishes that might be their last.

I walked down a stone pathway bordered by thickets of bamboo. The ocean wind whistled through the razor-sharp leaves. In this landscape of mist and harmony, nothing above ground betrayed the presence of a vast underground network of living quarters, kitchens, and clinics at the shallowest level, coast guard, security police, and people's militias' headquarters at the middle level, and food and ammunition depots buried seventy-five feet underground. I came to the entrance of an A-shaped tunnel, designed to better resist bomb blasts. I ventured inside. Vietnam lived underground in man-made tunnels like these, in the caves of the Trường Sơn Mountains, and in dugouts under village houses. Wartime poems celebrated Mother Earth for protecting civilians and soldiers.

The tunnel was dimly lit by flickering lights nestled in niches in the earthen walls. Within a few yards, I entered a dark, dank world. I felt claustrophobic and short of air. I wished I had brought a guide. I came to a chamber that was little more than a hovel. A sign said it had been a kitchen. The stove, invented during the French War, had air vents to diffuse smoke, so planes could not detect it.

At some point I stumbled upon a panel describing the dingy cavern I was in as a maternity ward. I kept going. In the dark, I lost all sense of direction. A voice in the tunnel ahead cried out:

"Watch out for the steps."

It was Ben, the college kid. I had reached the top of a steep staircase and would have fallen headfirst if it hadn't been for his warning. The steps led to the deepest tunnels, where goods, weapons, and ammunitions had been kept.

I continued my descent. I was sweating and stumbling. Incredibly at this depth, I glimpsed a faint strip of natural light ahead and followed it to an exit. The tunnels were built on a slope and I had reached the bottom of the hill. I walked out into a winter light to a fortified seawall overlooking a stupendous bay. The rough surf of the East Sea rolled in on white sand. I hadn't expected the fishermen's tunnels to be a military fortress by the sea, part of an extensive complex for the North Vietnamese artillery and naval regiments defending the coastline and sea lanes. The garrison, a joint effort by citizens and soldiers, women and men, illustrated the traditional art of war that Vietnam practiced to gain victory against a superior foe: "All people are soldiers," went hand in hand with, "When the enemy comes to the house, even the women must fight."

The rough waters before me were a strategic passage between the coast and Cồn Cỏ island in the Demilitarized Zone, occupied and defended by the People's Army. From the Arcadian beach, boats had supplied the force with weapons, ammunition, and rice.

I walked back up the hill to avoid going through the tunnels, but I was blocked by high and impenetrable fortifications. I reluctantly entered the tunnel system again, somehow retraced my steps in the dark, and ran out of there as fast as I could.

That evening, Nam and I strolled through downtown Đông Hà while Hân took the opportunity to visit family who lived nearby. We were running low on essentials and found a supermarket to stock up on toiletries. It was a happening place. Families were gathered to enjoy ice cream and sweets, and grandparents sat to chat and watch the world go by. I walked down the well-stocked aisles looking for face cream, but I didn't trust the whitening agents contained in every brand. I came away empty-handed.

On our way back to the hotel, we passed by a hairdresser. The open-air shop had room for one client. The stylist gave me the perfect one-dollar haircut in five minutes. I asked her about highlights.

"I don't have any bleach here, but I can get it tomorrow," she said.

"What kind is it?" I asked.

"Pretty strong stuff," she answered.

I couldn't fault her honesty. I decided not to chance it.

Nam took the rest of the night off while I went out for dinner with Chuck to find out why he had come back to Vietnam. So many veterans never wanted to visit. Yet Chuck had returned to a place where he had lost friends for a cause he no longer believed in.

We walked over to the Saigon Đông Hà Hotel, the city's finest, overlooking the river past the statue of Lê Duẩn.

"He was the real hard-liner in the Politburo pushing for the offensives," said Chuck.

The receptionist at the hotel greeted Chuck like a film star and ushered us into a brightly lit dining room that held out some hope of wine. The bottle of Californian white that was presented to us cost a hundred dollars. How about another wine? There was only that one bottle. I settled for sparkling water.

"So, how is the Trail going?" Chuck asked.

"Surprising in so many ways," I replied.

"I went down the Trail by motorbike in 1992. This was before the new road in 2003. I had come back to Vietnam with an old Army buddy. We traveled for thirty days from Hanoi to Saigon and back. There were these deep mountain valleys and creeks. I didn't think we would make it through the creeks. On some sections, we kept going at night because there were no towns to stop in."

"Sounds familiar, even on the new paved road," I said.

I wondered where he was going with this.

"When we did stop, people were wonderful. They let us into their homes and fed us. In one place we stopped, I asked where there was a hotel. Big laugh. So we stayed with the family. We were served this wild animal stuff. I couldn't face it, so told them I didn't eat meat. They called out to a young boy to go down to the river. He caught a fish just for me. We made it all the way to Kon Tum, skirting Laos, when one of my tires got a puncture. We got to an outpost that was a police station. There were a couple of young guys there. All of a sudden, there we were, total strangers, asking them to blow up a tire. It took them a while to remember what their job was. 'Please come in. We need to check your papers,' they finally said. On the wall were all these calendars with buxom beauties. What an isolated existence. They were sad when we left.

"It was during the Trail trip that I started to want to do something. I was astonished by the absence of anger and bitterness. Vietnam was in bad shape. The embargo was on. The economy was in trouble. I had a profound sadness that bordered on anger and bitterness at my own government and at myself for not doing anything courageous about our involvement."

The Trail through the Trường Sơn Mountains had cast its spell on travelers before me, just like Chuck.

"When I flew out of Biên Hòa, at the end of my term," he continued, "I thought, I hope I come back to this country when it's at peace and enjoy these decent people when circumstances are not so threatening. I left Vietnam with one year to go. I wanted to leave the Army, but I was sent to Germany. I calmed down, got my anger and the bitterness out of the way. I was lucky I went to Germany or I might have done something stupid had I gone straight back to the United States."

"When did you start questioning the war?"

"After three months I knew something was badly wrong. After six months, I was convinced. It was a terrible realization. I believed in our government and our country. When I realized it was all lies, it was a big shock. I was in Saigon at the Combined Intelligence Center, near the Interrogation Center. It was a sophisticated operation."

GI protest against the war remained little known during and even after the war. An exception was the "Winter Soldier Investigation" in 1971, a media event sponsored by Vietnam Veterans Against the War (VVAW). Veterans testified that atrocities and massacres were the consequence of the US military rules of engagement, not isolated incidents by rogue soldiers.

"What triggered your opposition to the war?"

"I was in Saigon during the Tết Offensive when the Việt Cộng attacked. The rockets came flying over. It made me realize the magnitude of what we were doing. There was a rain of fire from the sky, night after night. By June 1968, there was almost nothing left of my neighborhood, just blackened rubble and streams of refugees. The Việt Cộng attacked not only our air base, but the Independence Palace and the National Radio Station, even the US Embassy in the center of Saigon."

"Were you the only one to feel this way?"

"No, many of us did. Not all. We used to discuss the events that led to war. We weren't fighting at the front, so we had time to read. We read the Geneva Accords, the promises that had been made by the signatories to hold national elections by 1956 and not kept, and Hồ Chí Minh's speeches, and we would talk about it. I talked to many in the infantry. They didn't have time. They had two concerns: to survive and to make sure their buddy survived."

When he returned home from his trip down the Trail, Chuck kept the promise he had made to himself.

He continued:

"When I got back to the United States, I was offered a well-paid job at the Department of Veterans Affairs in Washington, DC. I had to think seriously before turning it down. I was in my fifties, between jobs and divorced. The main thing was I had no debt. I was able to do it. It was a lucky set of circumstances. Veterans Affairs wanted me to start the following Monday. I went in to see the Secretary of Veterans Affairs. He was a Vet.

—I'm going to do something different. I'm going to Vietnam, I told him.

I thought he would be furious.

—Well, I'll be goddamned. I have another proposition for you. I'll go to Vietnam and take that job and we'll swap! he said in jest, and added:

—Congratulations. That's a great thing to do."

Chuck boarded a plane for Hanoi and opened an office for the Vietnam Veterans America Foundation—an organization he described as "being mildly critical of our policy," with a grant for a rehabilitation project for civilians disabled by unexploded ordnance.

"You actually went through with it?" I asked.

"Yes, I did. It was something my mother and father taught me: 'Listen to people and show some respect.' I attribute what I do today to that simple phrase. Growing up in a racist South, my parents were not racist. They followed social rules, but we were never allowed to use the word 'nigger' in our home. I was a Presbyterian until the day my church asked a black parishioner not to come back. Racist parishioners from the community had threatened the church. Well, that was it for me. I took civic lessons seriously and I believed in these American ideals of basic fairness and justice. I still believe in them. Our government has not reflected those standards. I may be disappointed. I wish it were otherwise, but it's not."

Chuck was confident about the future:

"I have the hope and determination that we can bring closure to this war legacy, at least as far as America is concerned. And that could mean America truly stepping up and accepting our responsibility, and bringing to every province the model for de-mining we have developed, with the ultimate goal that it can be achieved not only in my lifetime but in the next few years."

"War reparations?" I asked.

"We owe a tremendous debt to Vietnam. But the word 'reparations' is too loaded. That term is too sensitive. I try to avoid words like reparations and guilt. Responsibility: that's a positive term. It means you accept what you did and try to compensate those you harmed. I see most Americans of goodwill are ready to do that and deal with the terrible tragic problem of Agent Orange, and the millions who were exposed to dioxin. We should at least give the Vietnamese the same status we give Americans. Vietnam is such a huge scar on America's psyche.

"I realized a long time ago there are so many things wrong and unjust in the world. We have to pick out a small corner of the world and do the best we can in a small way. We should take more small steps that make a difference.

"I have a lot of admiration and respect for the Vietnamese. Particularly their ability to forgive. To have them welcome and embrace us ... It's incredible that the Vietnamese welcome us back here. They have an underlying Buddhist belief in harmony. Pragmatic, too: once it's over, it's over. Look to the future. And I don't know if they believe it, but they all say that Hồ Chí Minh told them:

'Don't ever forget that the American people are our friends.'

"I think the Vietnamese respect our ideals. We don't follow those ideals. I wish we did. The Vietnamese are too eager to welcome us back. They put too much trust in us as a counterbalance to China. We are using them as pawns. They should know that the Americans don't keep their promises. We make problems worse. In some cases, we destroy countries. Look at Iraq, the cradle of civilization. We don't have a record that's at all encouraging."

We walked back to the hotel through the empty streets of Đông Hà. The night air was sweet. On the Trail I had met an American veteran who offered redemption for a war that had none.

Artist unknown, *Sniper*, ink on paper, 1968.

At Project RENEW, Đông Hà, Quảng Trị Province.
Heroine Hoàng Thị Mai who served with the Youth Volunteer Corps.

It was perhaps no coincidence that it was in Quảng Trị Province, which had seen the greatest destruction and loss of life, that I came face-to-face with an emotion that foreign visitors to Vietnam rarely hear expressed: "hatred" (*căm thù*) for the foreign enemy.

The following morning, I went back to Project RENEW to meet women veterans from South Vietnam who had served on the mountainous Trail. I discovered that US bombings of Allied territory had delivered fear and loathing, not freedom and democracy.

The women arrived smartly dressed in tailored dark-green military uniforms decorated with rows of medals, their long dark hair elegantly tied back in buns. I congratulated myself for having worn that morning the one smart linen blazer in my limited Trail wardrobe.

Ngô Xuân Hiền, Project RENEW's director of communications and a former People's Army officer, introduced the veterans as friends of his late mother who had served with her during the war. Good-looking, wearing combat boots, and with a commanding yet easy manner, he chaired the meeting and served as the interpreter. We took our seats at a round table. Nam and Hân were there and Chuck joined us later. The tea on the table was served. I raised my cup, pretending to drink.

Colonel Lê Kim Thơ, who had accompanied the women veterans, opened the discussion. The senior officer had served with the Trail Command and had been in charge of coordinating logistical and fighting units. He spoke with authority, crediting the Trail and the women who had defended it with North Vietnam's victory.

"Our biggest obstacle was the US Air Force. We had to fight to overcome that. We built the roads through the mountains. When one road was discovered, we built another. The Trường Sơn Mountains have been the backbone of our country for many generations. The United States had to deploy all the modern weapons of warfare to try to destroy the Trail. Over four million tons of bombs were dropped over the Trail in Vietnam, during sixteen years. But they couldn't cut the Trail. It was especially hard for the women who defended the Trail. They were responsible for carrying rice and ammunition between stations, opening the road when it was blocked, and caring for the wounded. They didn't have enough clothes—two women shared one pair of trousers. They used parachutes from US flares to make clothes. And they didn't have enough rice, a day's ration was only fifteen grams [half an ounce]."

Fifteen grams of rice fits in a nail-polish jar.

The women shared their memories, taking it in turns. Nguyễn Thị Nguyệt, softly spoken and poised, described her hard labor on the Trail with a transportation team. She talked of heavy loads, illness, and hunger, but also of friendship and camaraderie:

"I was assigned to the first station on the Trail. In the evening, we prepared guns and ammunition for transportation the next day. The nearest station was two days away on foot, the farthest station was ten days away. On short trips, we women carried sixty-pound loads; the men, ninety pounds. On longer trips, we carried fifty-five pounds; the men, seventy. A team of three hauled the two-hundred-pound guns. We climbed high mountain peaks. We crossed rivers and went through valleys. We cooked rice in the morning. Because of US planes, we had to be careful not to be detected. Sometimes the whole company got malaria and nobody could cook. That's a painful memory. We couldn't stop to help the sick. The fighting was too fierce. We had to keep moving. I saw people dying on the road. Despite the hardship, nobody deserted. There was a feeling of solidarity in the team. Without that care for each other, we wouldn't have survived. But people still died because they lacked food."

Phạm Thị Kim Oanh, dignified and reserved, who had served with a bomb-disposal team, added her harrowing recollections:

"My first most painful memory was when I was filling in a bomb crater. A blast [from an unexploded bomb] blew me away. I woke up in the clinic. I was only slightly injured. But there I was told that some of my team workers had been killed.

"My second was a B-52 strike during a musical performance. They bombed right over our headquarters. Twenty-six in my team were killed. I collected up all the pieces of my friends."

She fought back tears as she relived the unspeakable trauma. Then, wistfully, she added:

"And this happened at the place where we had been enjoying music a few minutes before."

Her words were sparse, but I felt implicated in her pain.

Tragedy had shattered the young life of Hoàng Thị Mai, the third veteran of the group and the last to speak. She was fifteen when the Americans bombed her village in Allied South Vietnam. The village, like many in the South, was suspected of being sympathetic to the Việt Cộng. Hoàng Thị Mai remembered the fateful day when the planes attacked Ái Tử, midway between Đông Hà and Quảng Trị City:

"My dad was killed. My older brother was killed. My brother-in-law, too, was sacrificed. After the attack, I wanted to follow my younger brother into the jungle. He convinced my mother to let me go, even though I was so young. He told her I would be safer if I joined the forces fighting against the Americans than if I stayed with her. So, I enlisted with the militia in 1965. I had developed hate. That's why I left home, to fight against all the US attacks. I was so furious and angry. Because I had a strong hatred, I was given an AK-47 and I was trained to become a sniper. The Americans then took the land they had bombed where my village was and built an airfield there.

"In 1967, I went back for more training and became a nurse. I was at the Battle of Quảng Trị in 1972 during eighty-one days of fighting. There was so much killing and suffering."

Her voice hardened as she remembered. I felt her anger was directed at me. The polite mask offered to foreign visitors had slipped.

She added:

"I was in the war for ten years. If you didn't shoot the enemy, the enemy would shoot you."

"Do you feel hatred now?" I asked.

She said she didn't, but she had struggled to forgive.

"The war is over. The two governments have normalized relations. I know the Americans feel sorry for what they did. American veterans say they were told they were bringing civilization to Vietnam. Veterans I have met say they are sorry. We now meet as friends. We should forgive," she said.

I could only guess that her ability to forgive came from an inner strength, a Buddhist belief that anger "harms me not them," a desire to move forward, or simply because they had won the war.

We could have gone on talking, but we hoped to cross the border into Laos later that day before closing time. I thanked the veterans for sharing their stories. As we stood up to leave, something powerful happened. Nguyễn Thị Nguyệt, the first veteran to speak, came toward me to embrace her former enemy. We held each other for a long time. Phạm Thị Kim Oanh joined us. Hoàng Thị Mai, the sniper who at the age of fifteen had lost loved ones in a US air strike, initially kept her distance, then she too joined our communal embrace. The veterans from both sides smiled for my camera, and we said our farewells until we meet again.

Chuck drove with us for the few miles to Quảng Trị City, east of Đông Hà. After the sparsely populated Trường Sơn Mountains, the busy South Vietnamese towns of Khe Sanh, Đông Hà, and Quảng Trị City along the provisional demarcation line told of civilian suffering and loss. The towns home to Allied headquarters and close to combat bases were shelled by North Vietnamese artillery and bombed by American planes supporting the ground troops.

We drove through the narrow streets of Quảng Trị City to a junction packed with people, bicycles, mopeds, and cars. Chuck pointed to the ruin of a red brick wall. I didn't know what I was supposed to be looking at.

"It's the only original part of the nineteenth-century city wall that survived," said Chuck.

During the 1972 Spring Offensive, Quảng Trị City, a town of some 30,000 people, had been reduced to rubble by North Vietnamese shelling and American bombing, its nineteenth-century citadel flattened. Hoàng Thị Mai, the sniper-turned-nurse, had cared for the wounded here. The *People's Army Newspaper* compared the "three-hundred-and-twenty-eight thousand tons of lethal weapons dropped [in and around Quảng Trị City] to the equivalent of seven nuclear bombs dropped on Hiroshima and Nagasaki in 1945."[49]

The journalist Craig R. Whitney described in the *New York Times* what was left of the town when he went there after the battle:

"The Citadel, only six months ago a splendid if crumbling nineteenth-century fortress with thick, red brick walls surrounded by a moat, is no more. It is possible to see where the walls stood, but they are chewed up and broken by the force of countless seven-hundred-and-fifty and two-thousand-pound bombs that American planes dropped ... to enable South Vietnamese troops to fight their way back in. Inside the walls nothing—not one tree, no building, not even a bunker—is left standing. Outside, stretching east, west, and south as far as the town once did, there is nothing but rubble, bomb craters, and shredded trees."[50]

We continued on to what had once been a church, on Route 1A at a Trail junction baptized "T-junction of fire." The pitiable ruin of Long Hưng Church reflected an orgy of violence. The steeple had been obliterated. The wreckage was scarred with bullet holes. A wretched Star of Bethlehem clung to the portico. We stood inside its remains in silence.

"They kept the church as a remembrance," said Chuck.

"Hoàng Thị Mai mentioned this morning that her village was bombed and civilians killed to clear the land for a US military airstrip," I said.

"We did that all the time. Only once civilians were dead, the US military identified them as Việt Cộng. If they didn't die, they became Việt Cộng anyway," Chuck replied.

US rules of engagement gave the right to bomb South Vietnamese towns and villages if they gave any material support to the Việt Cộng, conditional on prior approval from the South Vietnamese official in charge and a warning to the villages, usually with air-dropped leaflets. One leaflet read: "If the Việt Cộng in this area use you or your village for this purpose [to hide], you can expect death from the sky. Do not let the Việt Cộng be the reason for the death of your loved ones." Another warned: "The US Marines will not hesitate to destroy immediately any village or hamlet harboring the Việt Cộng."[51] But the warnings, when they were given, gave no clue as to when the bombings might come.[52]

The Vietnamese government estimates two million civilians lost their lives across both sides between 1954 and 1975.[53] In contrast, the US government asserts that its bombings of North Vietnam killed 30,000 civilians in collateral damage, with no responsibility or liability for the perpetrators.[54] There are no statistics of how many civilians in South Vietnam were killed by disproportionate US fire-power, rules of engagement, or massacres.

Fifty years on, American television documentaries, publications, and popular historical websites have begun to accept the Vietnamese government's estimate of civilian war dead published in 1995, dismissed as propaganda for decades. There is growing recognition, too, of US responsibility for its part in the tragedy and for the need to pay compensation for past wrongs.

Ken Burns' and Lynn Novick's ten-part television series *Vietnam War*, which first aired in 2017, brought a balanced perspective. Nick Turse, in his book *Kill Anything That Moves: The Real American War in Vietnam,* published in 2013, concluded from his research into previously unused US military archives "that the intentional killing of civilians was quite common in a war that claimed two million civilian lives, with over five million civilians wounded and eleven million refugees ... It was generally due to heavy firepower not microlevel atrocities ... The US rules of engagement and massive disregard for civilian life led to a huge number of civilian casualties."[55]

Benjamin A. Valentino, in his book *Final Solutions: Mass Killing and Genocide in the 20th Century*, concluded that US and South Vietnamese military actions in South Vietnam caused more—or as many—civilian deaths as Việt Cộng terrorism. He estimated that "Allied suppression of the National Liberation Front (NLF) caused between one-hundred-and-ten thousand and three-hundred-and-ten thousand civilian war dead; NLF terrorism led to between forty-five thousand and one-hundred-and-eighty thousand civilian dead."[56]

It was quiet in the car as we drove west on Route 9 toward the Laotian border. Even Hân wasn't cracking jokes. We stopped at a military cemetery on Route 9, one of seventy-two in Quảng Trị Province. Some graves had a name, military rank, photograph, date of birth, and death; many were marked "name unknown." Chuck paid his respects to former enemies, young men and women like him who had fought for their country.

He struck the temple bell. "Show some respect," learned from his parents, had brought him back to Vietnam.

After we said our goodbyes to Chuck, we continued along Route 9 to Lao Bảo, the sleepy town on the border with Laos. We were all excited to be going to Laos. Nam and Hân had never been. I had visited Luang Prabang and Vientiane in the north, but I hadn't explored southeastern Laos which was off the beaten track. When we arrived in the town, Hân, the master chef with a nose for good food, chose a busy open-air restaurant for our late lunch. A delicious chicken in a spicy soup was brought to the table. As coffee was served, I consulted my trusty map. I hadn't planned our next stop. I had been too exhausted by the savagery of the past.

"Where should we stay the night?" asked Nam.

"I vote for Xepon. It's just down the road," said Hân.

The town had been at the center of the Laotian Trail. In the wake of the Tết Offensive, Allied forces launched an attack against it to disable the road network through southern Laos.

"My uncle fought there with the South Vietnamese Army. But he never talked about it. Too painful. They had to retreat," said Nam.

"We can stop at the Ban Dong War Museum. No doubt it celebrates the communist victory," I said.

"I'm ready. It's important to get the other side," said Nam.

Hân was on the winning side but, as far as he was concerned, it was a long time ago.

At the next table, border guards toasted to a happy event.

"*Một, hai, ba: Yo!*" they cheered, raising their beer mugs and downing the golden brew in one go.

More beer cans were stacked up on the table, at least four or five for each of them.

"I bet nobody will be at the border station this afternoon!" said Hân.

We all laughed and hoped for an easy crossing into Laos.

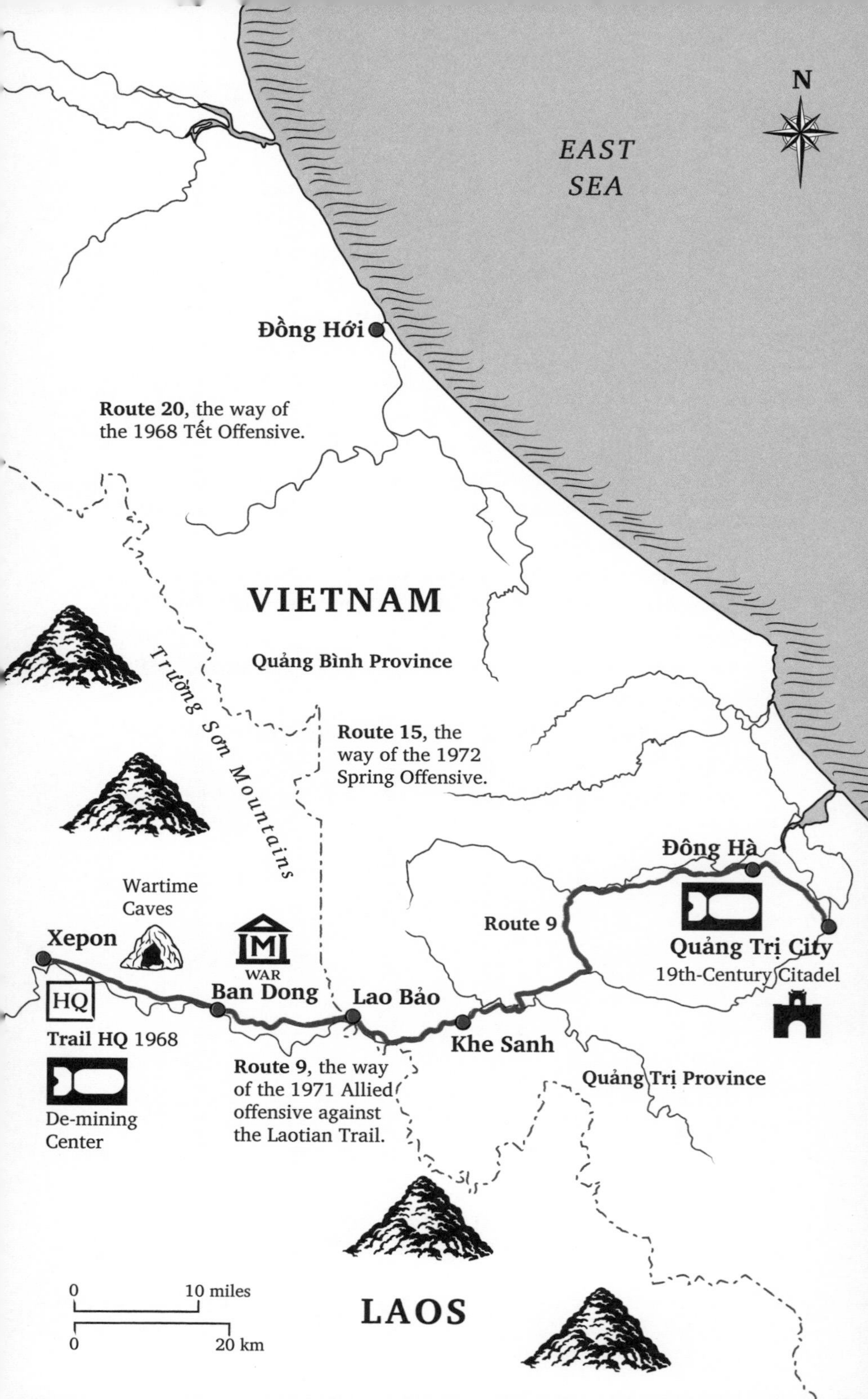
N
EAST
SEA
Đồng Hới
Route 20, the way of
the 1968 Tết Offensive.
VIETNAM
Quảng Bình Province
Trường Sơn Mountains
Route 15, the
way of the 1972
Spring Offensive.
Đông Hà
Route 9
Quảng Trị City
19th-Century Citadel
Wartime
Caves
Xepon
WAR
HQ
Ban Dong
Lao Bảo
Khe Sanh
Trail HQ 1968
Route 9, the way
of the 1971 Allied
offensive against
the Laotian Trail.
Quảng Trị Province
De-mining
Center
0
10 miles
0
20 km
LAOS

Chapter 7

# *ĐÔNG HÀ, VIETNAM TO XEPON, LAOS*

*The way of the 1971 Allied offensive, floral wallpaper, and golden Buddhas.*

*Xepon, the hub of the Laotian Trail, had been the Trail Command headquarters during the 1968 Tết Offensive.*

*Between 1969 and 1971, with Vietnamization in place, South Vietnamese ground forces supported by US air power were sent in to attack the Trail bases in Laos and Cambodia, to stop possible future North Vietnamese offensives. Congress had banned US troops from entering the neutral countries, but not South Vietnamese troops.*

*In February 1971, the South Vietnamese Army was airlifted into Laos to launch Operation Lam Son 719 against Xepon. The attack failed and the South Vietnamese Army was forced to retreat.*

*The Trail Commander ended the Laotian campaign on a high:*

*"Not only did the Trail network not get clogged up, we doubled the delivery of goods to the battlefields and the time to the destination was faster, cut by half."*[57]

*After the victory at Xepon, the Politburo began planning for the 1972 Spring Offensive.*

All Trail roads led to Xepon, Laos.

"Vietnam was so intense," said Nam.

"Exhausting," I agreed.

"I feel relaxed here," Nam added.

"I was laughing so much crossing the Lao border, wondering how I was going to talk to people," remarked Hân.

"I should have brought my uncle's wartime dictionary," said Nam. "It was army-issue and pocket-sized with phrases like: 'Where is the enemy?' 'Don't shoot!' 'Can you teach me to dance?'"

The border crossing had gone smoothly. Hân drove and we walked across alongside women in colorful silk sarongs and fitted blouses with narrow shawls draped across the bodice.

We continued west on Route 9 toward the town of Xepon, our destination for the night. On the western flank of the Trường Sơn Mountains, the horizon was open, the rivers were wide, and the air was crisp and dry. The weight of the past lifted with the fog. But the war caught up with us soon enough when we reached Old Xepon. The Allied assault began on February 8, 1971. South Vietnamese ground forces were flown in by US helicopters and dropped along Route 9 between Ban Dong and Old Xepon. Old Xepon was obliterated. The US Air Force dropped 52,000 tons of bombs and napalm on the area. Between 1,000 and 12,000 South Vietnamese, between 2,000 and 13,000 North Vietnamese, and 253 American soldiers were killed. Thirty Americans were reported missing in action. The number of civilians who lost their lives was not recorded.

After the war, what was left of Old Xepon was abandoned. A sign half-hidden from the road pointed to the forgotten town. Away from the trucks thundering down Route 9, a peaceful hamlet lay on the banks of the Xepon River, close to the confluence with the Banghiang River. A few wooden houses had been rebuilt on the riverbank. It was difficult to imagine there had ever been a town here.

Goats grazed by the edge of the blue river, the Trường Sơn Mountains rose in the east. I had left the reflective dark wood and black-and-red lacquers of Vietnamese temples. A small pagoda bathed in the saffron and iridescent gold, white, and silver of Laotian Buddhism. Metallic paper cutouts in the shape of leaves and hearts in gold, silver, bright pink, and green shimmered in the light.

We sat on the pink tiled floor of the holy place. A monk entered the pagoda followed by a rush of children coming to pray after school.

There were no memorials to the fallen. A golden Buddha draped in a saffron robe protected the place. The Buddha's right hand rested on his knees, pointing toward the Earth. His left hand lay on his lap with the palm facing upward. I didn't know one *mudra* from another.

"Buddha is defying the temptations of the demon Mara. It is the moment when enlightenment triumphs over darkness," Nam whispered in explanation.

We left the pagoda as the monk began chanting, and stepped out into the sunlight. A lone war relic stood on a grassy knoll, close to a Bodhi tree. The walk-in vault of reinforced concrete and bricks had withstood artillery shelling and aerial bombings. What had it contained? Who had built it and when? The French? The vault seemed too grand and well-fortified for a small colonial outpost. A French company prospected for gold here in 1929, but there were no reports of a hoard. The Việt Minh? At the end of the French War, Xepon was a hiding place for "Việt Minh caches of arms, some buried, some hidden in caves," as their forces withdrew from the south of Vietnam, Laos, and Cambodia and moved north to Hanoi. The People's Army? North Vietnam had reportedly printed wads of new banknotes before the 1968 Tết Offensive in the event of victory, but the cash was delivered to the secret Trail Command headquarters built 650 feet into a mountainside near Xepon, not to a bank safe in Old Xepon.[58]

At 4 p.m. we arrived at the Ban Dong War Museum to find it was open. The museum commemorated the 1971 Route 9–Southern Laos victory. A monument celebrated the "friendship" between the Vietnamese and Laotian communist forces who had pushed the South Vietnamese troops back over the border.

Tanks, cannons, and bombs were displayed in the museum grounds. Lao folk music played at top volume on an old-fashioned ghetto blaster. Women in sarongs danced around a campfire. The rhythmic beat, repetitive dance steps, circular hand rotations, and graceful hip movements were hypnotic. Laos, with its most gentle soft music and dance inherited from the Khmer, was the last place on Earth that a benevolent god would allow a war.

A black chauffeur-driven car with dark windows pulled up in front of the museum. A high-ranking Vietnamese military official stepped out of the front passenger seat. He held the back door open for an elderly gentleman. The two men had traveled twelve hours to get here. The older gentleman was a veteran. Nam asked the military official if we could talk to him about his time in the war.

"Please go ahead. He's my father," said the military official, smoothing his father's hair with his hand. It was tousled after the long car journey. They hadn't expected to meet anyone here.

I reached for a comb in my pocket and handed it to him. The son thanked me and gently tidied his father's hair.

"I was on the Trường Sơn Road that went through Laos," said the older gentleman.

"Is this your first time back to Laos?"

"Yes, it's my first time, and also my last because of my age. I am seventy-six years old. My purpose in coming is to find my brother. He died here in 1967. But I can't recognize anything. Everything has changed."

"Is your brother buried here?"

"No, he's not buried. We're looking for him. We're asking people who may know where his regiment fought and where they died."

"Have you had any leads?"

"Not yet."

The wandering souls inhabited Laos. Veterans and relatives from the north and the south of Vietnam and from the United States came to Xepon looking for lost loved ones. An estimated 300,000 North Vietnamese, an unknown number of South Vietnamese, and 1,587 American military (and civilians), according to the POW/MIA Accounting Agency of the US Department of Defense, are missing in action in Vietnam, Laos, and Cambodia.

I wanted to spend more time with the elderly gentleman, but his son indicated our short meeting was over. Perhaps he didn't want to cause further distress to his father, perhaps he was weary of foreigners. We took a couple of pictures together to remember our brief encounter, but his son declined the opportunity.

"He might run into trouble if he is photographed with foreigners," said Nam.

Shades of the past.

We continued on Route 9 to meet a Laotian veteran who had fought on the North Vietnamese side. The track to the village was dry. We arrived in time for the evening shower. A cold wind was blowing but village life carried on outside. The place had electricity but no running water or indoor cooking facilities. Women in sarongs washed at the communal water pumps. Satellite dishes graced the rooftops. Hard rock blasted from a newly built opulent house. Girls and boys carried firewood piled high over their heads. Grandmothers squatted, lighting fires to cook the evening meal. Chickens, pot-bellied black pigs, and well-fed, tan, husky-like dogs roamed around freely.

Mr. Vannaseng was a cheerful sixty-six-year-old, recently retired from the civil service. He was born in the village and had lived here during the war. When he turned eighteen in 1965, he enlisted with the People's Army out of self-preservation, not obligation or ideology, or that's how he remembered it.

"I joined the People's Army so I could carry a gun to protect myself and my family. I wanted to sign up, for protection. I served in an intelligence unit. They bombed every day, everywhere," he said, holding out his arm in a sweeping gesture all around him.

"Who?"

"The Americans. The North Vietnamese didn't have any MiGs [Soviet jet fighters] down here," Mr. Vannaseng replied.

"Where did the women and children live?"

"We all lived together with the People's Army soldiers, Lao fighters, and women and children in the rock caves and tunnels."

On the Laotian Trail, at a river near Xepon.

Aerial bombardments then and now did not distinguish between civilians and fighters.

"Were you wounded?"

"No. But three times I was trapped under the ground. I nearly suffocated. My friends pulled me out," he said.

"How did you feel in the war?"

"Scared."

People had different ways of expressing past traumas. Most Vietnamese veterans said they weren't afraid.

"Can we visit the caves?"

"You have to walk about three miles into the mountain."

"Will you take us there?"

"You have to get permission from the Vietnamese police."

"In Laos?"

We gave the cave visit a miss.

Mr. Vannaseng was happy with how his life had turned out after the war. He had a large family and lived comfortably on his pension.

"I have eight children. Four sons and four daughters. And this is my wife," he said.

He pointed to an attractive woman of a certain age. A tartan turban covered her hair. She stoked the flames of the campfire in preparation for the evening meal.

"Your wife is good-looking," I remarked.

"Old," he replied, laughing.

Mr. Vannaseng asked to have our picture taken together. He stood to attention. He wrote down his address in Laotian script on my notebook. Hân presented Mr. Vannaseng with a case of Lao beer, having guessed that he would prefer beer to sweets. The village campfires flickered in the waning light.

We drove back to Route 9 and on to New Xepon, the new town built a few miles away, to spend the night there. When we arrived at the Vieng Xay Hotel, a welcoming pink guesthouse, there was nobody behind the desk to greet us.

"Are you coming here for tourism?" a man in the reception area asked. Kelvin was a computer salesman from Guangzhou, on business from the southern Chinese city.

"A road trip," I replied.

"Good way to get away," he said.

"That's one way of looking at it," I remarked.

I settled into an armchair to wait for the hotel receptionist. We had time. Eventually, the receptionist showed up to take us to spacious rooms. After the rat and used condom in Khe Sanh, the flowered wallpaper lifted my mood. Later, we went to investigate the night market along Route 9. We chose an assortment of dishes from stalls that offered freshly cooked vegetables, grilled chicken, and pork. We skipped the rat livers that were stewing in a large pot over an open fire. Nam bought some sticky rice and a coconut sweet with banana and tapioca for dessert.

We brought our delicacies back to the hotel restaurant but Hân declined to join us.

"I'm sorry. I don't think it's right. You shouldn't bring a takeout to a restaurant," said Hân.

"I know it's rude. But I don't think they'll mind," Nam replied.

Nothing was coming between Nam and his coconut sweet. We missed Hân that evening, but the hotel's amiable cook wasn't offended. He brought cutlery and plates for our picnic from the night market. He even served us *laap* from the kitchen. The Laotian national dish was a tasty blend of minced chicken, chili peppers, fresh mint, lime juice, and ground toasted rice.

As Nam tucked into his coconut dessert, I took out the map to indulge my evening ritual.

"What's the plan for tomorrow?" he asked.

"What about experiencing a Trail gravel road, the real thing?"

"Any nice hotels on the way?"

"No. But I hear the Laotians are hospitable. There are homestays if we get stuck," I answered.

Nam didn't sound as excited about the idea as I was.

"Sounds rough. I've just come back from a month at the ashram in northern India where there was no hot water and no creature comforts," he said, laughing. "But I'm game. I know you want to immerse yourself in the Trail experience."

Back in my room, I studied the People's Army map I had photographed at the Ban Dong War Museum. At the end of 1971, the People's Army left Xepon to advance south to the Trail station near Salavan, in preparation for the 1972 Spring Offensive against Kon Tum and the Central Highlands in South Vietnam.

According to the military map, several tracks and gravel roads were built to connect Xepon to Salavan. I settled on Route 23 that traveled across the high Laotian plateaus on the western flank of the Trường Sơn Mountains. Marked in red, it appeared as the main artery for the infantry, artillery, and tank units on their way to Salavan. The region was a basin of endless rivers, flowing west to the Mekong River. I had been warned there were few bridges. I was counting on the winter season when the water was low to be able to ford the rivers. The Banghiang River was the widest river on my route and was difficult to cross even in the dry season. I checked my paper map. It showed no sign of a bridge over the Banghiang. Google Earth revealed the bombed remains of the old iron bridge lying on the riverbed. And Google Maps issued the warning:

"Sorry, your search appears to be outside our current coverage area for driving."

Read: no bridge.

I prayed to the sun gods that the levee would be dry.

I sent a short email to my husband:

"Much more peaceful in Laos and we have seen our first sunset after ten days of solid gray skies in Vietnam. All good, but feeling less operational until tomorrow when I can get a local SIM card as we're heading out on a rough road! Signing off for now and not sure when we will be able to talk next. Missing you."

I woke up at 2 a.m. and couldn't get back to sleep. Would we be able to cross the Banghiang? How about the other rivers? Was I being careless? Should we have hired a special vehicle? What if we got stuck? Who would rescue us? Would there be a phone signal?

Roosters crowed through the night. As I drifted into a shallow sleep, I dreamed of Hồ Chí Minh. The only detail I remembered in the morning was that he had blue eyes. Over breakfast, Hân said he hadn't slept well either. He had dreamed that he had added opium to his vodka.

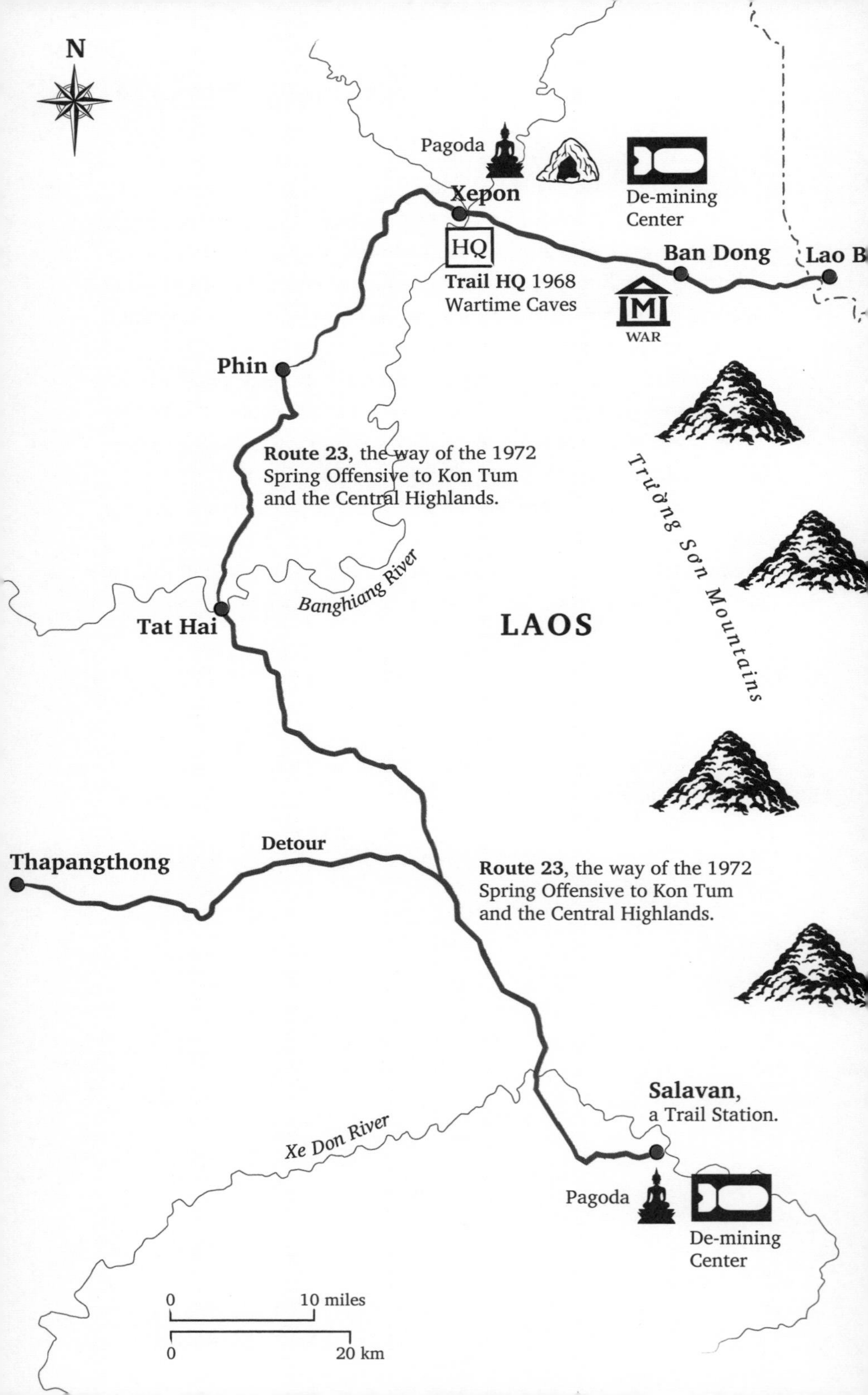

N
Pagoda
Xepon
De-mining
Center
HQ
Trail HQ 1968
Wartime Caves
Ban Dong
Lao B
M
WAR
Phin
Route 23, the way of the 1972
Spring Offensive to Kon Tum
and the Central Highlands.
Trường Sơn Mountains
Banghiang River
Tat Hai
LAOS
Detour
Thapangthong
Route 23, the way of the 1972
Spring Offensive to Kon Tum
and the Central Highlands.
Salavan,
a Trail Station.
Xe Don River
Pagoda
De-mining
Center
0
10 miles
0
20 km

Chapter 8

# *XEPON TO SALAVAN, LAOS*

*The way of the 1972 Offensive, a gravel road, and fording rivers.*

*The Trail Command began planning the 1972 Spring Offensive in May 1971. In the run-up, Group 559 had been promoted to Trail High Command in 1970, adding infantry and artillery units to its command. The Trail network expanded after the 1968 Tết Offensive: the Laotian Trail stretched south of Xepon to Salavan, Attapeu, and across the Trường Sơn Mountains to Kon Tum in South Vietnam.*

*The Trail Commander wrote in his memoir:*

*"[Our victory in Khe Sanh] was of great significance. We extracted the 'anchor' of the enemy's strategic position on the Trail that locked the whole network. By opening that lock, we were able to expand the eastern Trail network in North Vietnam [east of the Trường Sơn Mountains] and connect it to the western Trail network in Laos [west of the Trường Sơn Mountains]. By December 1969, a gasoline pipeline from the Mụ Giạ Pass to Xepon was completed. To see gasoline flowing through the pipeline to Xepon directly was a great event, a great joy … I had witnessed the bitter hard days, when delivering a drop of gasoline to the battlefield cost bowls of sweat, even blood. Our soldiers in the early years had to carry gasoline in backpacks liable to catch fire."*[59]

*The scrubby brushes and stunted trees of the dry plateaus between Xepon and Salavan presented the Trail Commander with a new challenge:*

*"We started building new 'covered roads' through Laos in 1971. By January 30, 1972, they stretched along the entire route."*[60]

*Soldiers 40,000 strong, hundreds of tanks, and thousands of trucks carrying heavy anti-aircraft artillery, and surface-to-air missiles left Xepon on Route 23, and parallel tracks, for the Trail station near Salavan.*

We headed west on Route 9 to the junction with Route 23. The infantryman Mạnh Minh was advancing on that same road in the months before the 1972 Spring Offensive. He was about to start college to study engineering when he was drafted into a Trail infantry division.

In a letter to his father, he wrote:

"Route 9 was the most dangerous crossing. It was like an empty beach, trees were low, and there was a lot of dust. Yesterday, at about 9 a.m., observation planes spotted our unit. Fifteen minutes later, fighter jets arrived and bombed us for thirty minutes. A bomb exploded close to my truck. I jumped out before it burst into flames. Luckily, no one was injured. We waited until 5 p.m. that afternoon before crossing the road."

Earlier that morning, when I could not get back to sleep, I had found Mạnh Minh's letters to his father online on a blog with thousands of messages looking for lost relatives and friends. A schoolfriend had posted the letters in Mạnh Minh's memory.

Youth Volunteers, women and men, left Vietnam with the regular troops for Laos. They joined transport, sapper, artillery, and infantry battalions, medics, nurses, and cultural troops heading on Route 23 for Trail station number 39, close to the town of Salavan.[61]

As we turned off Route 9 onto Route 23, a grader was flattening the red earth. Was I too late for the gravel road? Giant trees lay felled and forlorn by the roadside, their leaves shriveled and covered in red dust. A strip wide enough for a two-way highway had been cut through the jungle.

We drove on the new road to Tat Hai on the Banghiang River. Suddenly, the river appeared before us. It was very wide and very deep. My prayers to the sun gods had gone unanswered. The new bridge that was being built was still under construction.

"Oh, ferry!" Hân shouted.

A motorized platform was heading our way after dropping off a truck on the opposite bank. Hân drove the car onto it to cross the fast-flowing river. On the far side of the river, the car hurled itself up the steep bank onto a sandy white track, the "beach" that Mạnh Minh had described in his letter home. The wide road had vanished. We crawled through a maze of dry grassland and desiccated trees. Deep grooves, gullies, ditches, potholes, and protruding tree roots slowed our advance until we arrived at a track wide enough to be Route 23.

"Gravel," said a confident Hân, who had been looking out for the Trail roads' trademark.

The sparsely forested high plateau was as dry as bone under the midday sun. We crossed a dusty, shrubby, flat terrain without any tree cover. The "trees were low and there was a lot of dust," Mạnh Minh wrote.

The Trail Command had built giant trellises to cover hundreds of miles of roads. Tanks were hidden under individual contraptions made of bamboo and foliage. Vehicles dragging branches swept away their tracks. Even so, I wondered how thousands of fighters, and hundreds of trucks and tanks, could have advanced through the semi-desert undetected from the air.

Wooden houses on stilts lined the road. A pickup truck was parked in the shade under each house. Cows grazed alongside satellite dishes. Only the tumbleweed was missing to evoke the desolate setting of Wim Wenders' *Paris, Texas*. A kid sold watermelons at a junction. Snack, I thought. Hân said no, the watermelons had been sitting in the sun and would make us sick. We reached a larger village. Palm-thatched houses with bamboo screens stood next to brightly painted cement houses in fluorescent greens, pinks, purples, reds, and oranges. Here, too, there were pickup trucks and television satellite dishes on every home. Apart from a few cows, there was no sign of farming.

"They don't even have a vegetable garden. What do the villagers live on?" Hân wondered.

We veered out of the village onto a track. The GPS showed it as Route 23. As we entered a thick wooded area, the track narrowed down to a path.

"There's gravel. This is a Trail route," said Hân.

It may have been a Trail way, but we were lost. The thicket was dense. Branches crowded in on the car, scratching and scraping the windows, until we were forced to stop: we were on the edge of a cliff. We made a U-turn.

On our way back, we crossed a lone motorcyclist, a People's Army helmet on his head and a fetching pink scarf around his neck, embroidered with purple, yellow, and red flowers. I coveted his scarf. Minh was a Vietnamese traveling salesman with a developed sense of fashion. He crisscrossed the high plateaus on a dusty Mad Max-style vintage motorbike, stripped down to its steel frame. The bike, usually piled high with duvets, blankets, pots, and pans, was empty. Minh was on his monthly trip to collect cash from customers who bought on credit. Amiable and helpful, he greeted Hân as a fellow countryman.

"You're on the Trail network, but this is a footpath. Here's a Trail road you can drive on," he said, and showed Hân on the map.

Minh followed us to make sure we were headed the right way. A short way along, Hân stopped at a fork in the road. The GPS was confused. Minh suggested he ride with us in the 4x4 to the town where he lived, a couple of hours from Salavan. He dropped his motorbike off at a friend's house in the next village. I paid the guy sixty dollars to take Minh's bike to Thapangthong the following day. A bargain if it got us back on a Trail road that led to Salavan.

Minh sat in the back seat next to Nam and directed us to the road to Thapangthong. The sandy track gave way to layers of dried lava rock as we approached a river. On the bank, a young water buffalo stood forlorn in the dry landscape. There was no sign of its mother. The water was low. Hân steered the vehicle successfully between submerged boulders and crags to reach the other side.

Minh was enjoying the air-conditioning in the car. He talked nonstop. He came from Nghệ An Province where he had worked as a policeman. He had come to Laos to earn enough cash to send his son to police academy. He lived in Thapangthong in a rented house that he shared with his brother. They divided the territory between them. Minh covered the villages, and his brother, the Salavan area.

I asked him how people in the villages could afford pickup trucks and satellite televisions when there was little farming and logging.

"They send the girls to work in factories in Thailand," Minh replied. "But there is a big problem with the sex trade. A Vietnamese guy from Kon Tum was arrested recently. He was picking up girls in the villages here, promising them regular jobs, and sending them for sex to Thailand. There's also a lot of drug trading."

"Opium, heroin, cocaine?"

"No, pills."

He asked why we were driving to Salavan on Route 23 when we could have taken the highway. I told him about the Trail and the war.

"You're in the right place. Vietnamese television was here shooting a documentary about the Trail a few weeks ago. The crew found the hooks for the soldiers' hammocks in tree trunks," Minh explained.

"Do you want to stop to look for the hooks, Sherry?" Nam asked.

"I'll survive without them, thanks," I replied.

Minh continued:

"We Vietnamese, we fight. The Lao are peace-loving people. For example, the other day, I was playing cards. My opponent lost and accused me of cheating. I was so offended that I started a fight.

In Vietnam, I would have ended up in jail. Here, I was fined. I bought a pig for the town chief for four hundred and fifty thousand *kip* (fifty-five dollars), and a cow for the community. My neighbors each got a share of the cow. Everybody was happy."

The main street into Thapangthong was lined with open-air shops selling Chinese Lunar New Year lanterns. Minh suggested lunch at his regular Vietnamese restaurant on the edge of the small town. We shared spicy chicken, clear soup, and vegetables.

"Are you and Nam married?" Minh asked.

"No," Nam and I replied in unison.

"You're younger than him?"

I smiled. Minh had earned brownie points. Nam frowned.

"What's life like in Thapangthong?" I asked.

"Business is good but there are a lot of Chinese. They bring their entire families to stay. The problem for me is that the Chinese sell their goods much cheaper. We're about two hundred Vietnamese in town. Most are hairdressers and traders."

"What else happens here?" Nam asked.

"The town has ten brothels," he revealed, smiling.

"Good for you," joked Hân.

"I go to Vietnam once a month to see my wife and renew my visa," said Minh.

It was time to get directions to Salavan. We had a choice, Minh explained: a partly paved road to Salavan or a shortcut on a dirt track. I opted for the shortcut. Minh estimated that we would be in Salavan in two hours.

We exchanged greetings before parting.

"Meet again soon. *Hẹn gặp lại.*"

The track was deceptively smooth until we came to a narrow bridge made of wooden planks that stretched over a dry creek. The track got rougher after that and we were soon back to potholes, ruts, and bumps. At the next creek, there was no bridge. It had been washed away. Hân crested down the gorge and struggled to get the car back up the other side. At our third bridge, a watchman dressed in military fatigues signaled for us to stop.

"I'm checking vehicles," the guard explained.

"What are you looking for?" I asked.

"Trucks carrying heavy loads. They're not allowed to cross. The bridge is too weak," he answered.

The single-lane track we had been traveling on was a main thoroughfare for goods being transported south, just as it had been during the war.

"You can go. The bridge will hold," he said to reassure us, as he moved out of the way to let us through.

We moved cautiously onto the pontoon and continued our advance. On the outskirts of a town, we stopped for a short break and watched kids playing volleyball. The scene depicted in a war drawing had seemed so incongruous I wondered whether the artist had imagined it, until I chanced upon it in this remote place on the Laotian Trail.

We drove on for another hour. Suddenly, we arrived at a paved highway.

"Eureka!" I cheered.

"Looks promising!" said Nam.

The vanishing sun painted pink and orange stripes on the blue wash of nature's canvas. A tabletop mountain rose in the west, its hard edges delineated against the luminescent sky. The soft limestone shapes of the Trường Sơn Mountains were a distant memory.

But our moment of euphoria was short-lived. The good stretch of road ended abruptly. More bone-shaking potholes. More ravines. More wobbly bridges. And we had run out of light. We advanced blindly through the darkness. I checked the GPS but there was no signal. We arrived at bridge number ten. But instead of crossing it, Hân drove down a steep ravine into the creek.

"Why didn't you cross the bridge?" I asked. "We're never going to make it to Salavan tonight."

"Too dangerous. Last week, a Vietnamese bus crashed near here.

On Route 23, between Xepon and Salavan, Laos.

On Route 23, a watchman oversees the crossing of a bridge.

The bus fell into the riverbed. In the dark, the driver didn't see that the bridge didn't go all the way across. The passengers and driver were all killed," Hân answered.

I looked back at the bridge that Hân had avoided. It hung in midair, halfway across the creek.

I wondered why Minh had suggested this way. Suddenly, the GPS came back to life. It showed we were nearing Salavan. Our headlights shined on the deep waters of the Xe Don River. The river was as wide and as high as the Banghiang River that we had crossed that morning by ferry. The Xe Don was a tributary of the Mekong that joined the mother river at Pakse. It flowed during the dry season and had been used as a Trail waterway. But there was no ferry. I now understood why friends had mentioned their regiments crossed rivers in the nude. Soldiers took off their clothes, wrapped them in plastic, and floated them across to keep them dry for the onward journey.

"Let me find a stick and check how deep the water is," I suggested.

I didn't have time to open the car door. Hân drove the 4x4 into the flowing river and hit a rock hidden underwater. The car stalled. Hân floored the accelerator. The car hurled itself over the ledge and landed on sand. It stalled again. We were in the middle of the river. And then, it happened. We began sinking in what felt like quicksand. We were stuck. And we kept sinking. The water level started rising until it reached the height of my side window. The current that had appeared gentle in the headlights from the riverbank felt swift, rocking the car. I imagined I heard rapids ahead. Hân let out a high-pitched war cry. He shifted into first gear, floored the accelerator, and freed the wheels from the sucking sand. The 4x4 advanced forward. I relaxed. Too soon. We crashed into another boulder hidden beneath the surface. There was a loud bang. We stalled again. Karen Carpenter was singing on the CD player: "We've only just begun to live ... A kiss for luck and we're on our way ... " Hân floored the accelerator again. The 4x4 heaved itself up, lurched across the water, and onto the bank to safety.

I looked behind me. Nam was meditating.

After our ten-hour odyssey, Salavan appeared as a dreamy safe haven on the banks of a tranquil Xe Don River. A Vietnamese café served cold Lao beer and fresh river shrimps. We had crossed the Xe Don River near "a large People's Army ammunition dump," targeted by B-52 strikes.[62] The area was full of unexploded ordnance.

Over dinner, we talked about dogs. It started with Minh's story about the Lao being a peaceful people, the Vietnamese fighting among themselves, and him having to buy a pig for the village chief that was more expensive than dog. Dog meat, not dog as in pet.

"There's a big dog trade from Laos for dog meat," said Nam, who was upset about it.

I hadn't given it much thought. But now that Nam mentioned it, I had noticed well-fed dogs all along Route 23. They were friendly and greeted their owners, wagging their tails.

"How can people kill their own pets?" Nam asked.

"Dog owners don't kill the parent-dogs who are their pets. They sell the puppies for dog meat," Hân replied.

Dogs fetched 150,000 *kip* or roughly seventeen US dollars each.

"Even worse," I said.

"The Vietnamese were forced to eat dogs during the famine of 1945–1946 that killed two million people. People were desperate, they ate insects, rats, dogs, anything," Hân explained.

"The famine was fabricated by Hồ Chí Minh," Nam remarked.

"No, by the Japanese and the French. The Japanese forced the farmers to hand over their rice to feed their troops, and the French carried out the orders," said Hân.

"You're right. I was thinking of the Land Reform of the fifties," acknowledged Nam.

Hồ Chí Minh's Land Reform policy of 1955 had led to the execution and imprisonment of thousands classified as landlords or enemies of the state. Denounced in the Rectification of Errors campaign, the policy was ended in 1957.

"What do you think about Minh's view of the Vietnamese?" I asked.

"He's right. Vietnamese are always fighting. They have too much pride. You can't joke about certain things or people fight. If you hurt their pride, they fight," replied Hân.

"That's why Uncle Hồ was determined to fight. The Americans and the Europeans put him down. Woodrow Wilson didn't even answer his letter," said Nam.

In 1919, at the end of World War I, Hồ Chí Minh wrote to the US delegation to the Paris Peace Conference to ask the president to pressure the French to relinquish their colonial hold on Vietnam. His letter was left unanswered, as were his letters twenty-seven years later, asking President Truman for his support in Vietnam's war of independence against the French. The United States instead supported the French colonial power in their war against him.[63]

"We're all beat. I vote to stay here for a couple of nights," one of us said.

"Seconded."

"Me too."

We found a hotel in the center of town. It looked nothing like its description in the guidebook because it was an entirely different hotel, even though the owner insisted it was the same one. None of us could read Laotian script. We capitulated and adopted the purpose-built cement block as our home for the night.

A giant pike swam alone in the fish tank in the lobby. The sealed windows of the rooms in the upper floors gave me claustrophobia, so I opted for one on the ground floor. I opened up my laptop to finish reading the letters of infantryman Mạnh Minh that had been posted online. Mạnh Minh wrote to his father that he had been "badly wounded" during a battle and moved to a military clinic. Both his legs were amputated.

The letter read:

"I! Child away from the family.

Thank you to all the women doctors and comrades who brought my letters to the Socialist North and to my family.

THANK YOU & THANK YOU SO MUCH! The one who has gone away. Mạnh Minh."

It was his last letter. Mạnh Minh's family received it after the war. The hospital where Mạnh Minh was recovering had been bombed. Mạnh Minh did not survive.

Before turning off my laptop, I checked Thapangthong on Google Maps. The thirty-mile detour to drop off Minh had added several hours to our trip. But without Minh we probably wouldn't have made it to Salavan at all that night.

I put the light out and got some sleep.

The following morning, we went in search of the office of the Norwegian People's Aid (NPA), in charge of de-mining unexploded ordnance in the area. The secret air war over Laos, on steroids for the entire war, had turned Laos into the most heavily bombed country per capita in the world. In the lead-up to the 1972 Spring Offensive, the Trail station near Salavan had been a prime target.

Phongsavai—Bob to foreigners—directed the NPA's office in Salavan. He greeted us with a relaxed smile and easy manner.

"There are eighty million live bombs out there. Most of them are *bombis*. Two hundred and seventy million bombs were dropped, or over three million bombs per square kilometer. Thirty percent didn't detonate," Bob said.

"Did you say eighty million live *bombis*?" I asked.

I couldn't get my head around the six-, seven-, and eight-figure numbers in this war.

"Yes. The People's Army couldn't go directly south through the former South Vietnam, so they negotiated with Laos to open the border and went via Route 9 and the Trail in southern Laos.

The American bombs followed," is how Bob put it.

I asked Bob how he got the job.

"I come from a family of farmers in northern Laos. When I was young, we used to play *pétanque* with the *bombis*. I was a naughty boy. I was injured many times. You see, my finger was almost cut off," he said, holding up his pinkie to show me the scar. "That day, I was carried to the hospital. When I woke up, I was happy. I was alive! My granny was afraid I was going to die. So she sent me to be a monk for a few years. The temple paid for my education. I didn't want to be a farmer, like my father and granny. After graduation, I got a job with a mine-clearing company."

Bob invited us to join a team clearing a forest on the Xe Don River, a few miles downriver from our crossing the previous night. He took one look at our 4x4 and offered us a ride in his high-powered amphibious vehicle.

"So yesterday you came down the Ho Chi Minh Trail?"

I didn't mention our detour and dangerous river experience from the night before.

"Yes, sort of."

"The rocky road," said Bob, referring to the gravel.

We sped across the Xe Don River and continued on a rough track at high speed. A woman sitting on her porch waved as we drove by. The villagers chopped wood for house repairs and firewood in the forest where the cluster bombs had been detected.

The team leader gave us the drill:

"If you see an item, please don't pick it up. If you want to take a photograph, please ask. You're not allowed to smoke. If there's an explosion or accident, please stay calm. We will take you to the medic and to a safe place. An ambulance is parked in the forest."

We signed the waivers.

"Any leeches?" I asked, knowingly.

"No, it's the dry season," the team leader replied.

It was midday. Giant dry leaves crunched underfoot. We walked in silence. I kept close to Bob when suddenly we came to an ominous hole in the ground where a large snake could have easily been hiding.

"That's where the rat lives," said Bob.

"The bamboo rat, the one people eat?" I asked, reassured.

"Yes."

Earlier, when Nam had seen a cuddly bamboo rat for sale at a roadside market, we made a U-turn to rescue the animal but we were too late to save it. It had been sold.

The bomb technician ahead of Bob was swinging a metal detector. I was not with a bomb-disposal team. I was following a survey team in charge of detecting cluster bomblets, on a virgin path that hadn't been cleared for our visit. The metal detector came to a halt. I stopped inches away. The detector beeped continuously. I was standing on a patch of newly discovered *bombis*. The technician remained calm and recorded the site in his GPS.

We came to a sandpit piled high with bomblets.

"Isn't it dangerous to move the *bombis*?" I asked.

*Bombis*, I had learned, were usually detonated in situ because they were too unstable.

"We carry them in a bucket filled with sand," Bob answered.

"Why don't you detonate each one where you find it?"

"It takes too long, there are so many. We dig a pit like this, collect all the explosives, and detonate them all together. Some organizations don't allow this because it's too dangerous. We need a remote. Now we have to use cables, and it takes time," he explained.

I made a note to ask about the cost of a remote-control detonator with an asterisk: "Buy remote detonator, top priority." It was delivered to the NPA a few months later.

We left the forest and the unexploded ordnance in the sandpit. It was scheduled for demolition the following day.

On the drive back to Salavan, Bob dropped us off to visit a farmer who had been injured by a bomblet. Mr. Keun was at home when we called. The young father was sitting on a rope bed in the shade of the house. Soft-spoken and visibly unwell, he no longer farmed since his injury. His three-year-old daughter clung to him, happy to have her father at home.

"*Sawadee*," he said, greeting me.

I asked about the accident. He smiled a gentle smile and explained how it happened:

"I was collecting food in the forest when I saw the *bombi*. I used *bombis* to catch fish for the family. I had caught fish many times. It worked well! But this time I was unlucky. When I picked up the small bomb it exploded in my hand. A friend took me to hospital on his motorcycle. But I lost my right hand. That whole side of my body hurts, I can't hear in that ear, and my eyes burn. Before the accident, I was strong. I worked in the field growing rice and I was building a new house. Now I can't work. My wife grows the rice and I look after my daughter and the house. I'm learning English so I can find another kind of job."

He handed me an English-language comic book.

"You can get a job as a security guard with an NGO. That's how I started my career," said Noukone, the NPA interpreter who had accompanied us.

We left Mr. Keun on that hopeful note. His young daughter peeked out from behind her father and hazarded a smile and a wave.

That evening over *laap*, we talked about mortality and doing what we needed to do now. We had checked out of the hotel with the lonely pike in the fish tank and moved into an enchanting B&B built in pagoda-style at the foot of the Bolaven Plateau. After dinner, we held a late-night war council on the terrace of my bungalow.

"Where did the People's Army go from here?" asked Nam.

"They went west, all the way to the Mekong River," I said.

During the war, Laos was a divided country. Eastern Laos was controlled by communist Pathet Lao forces allied with Hanoi; western Laos was held by anti-communist Royal Lao and American forces. The Royal Lao Army airborne and ground forces, and CIA-led forces had been stationed in Pakse, a city eighty miles away on the Mekong River where we planned to spend the following night.

I wanted to explore the westernmost reach of the Trail, the Bolaven Plateau, and the mighty Mekong. The communities who farmed the fertile highlands had come under fire from US bombing and North Vietnamese artillery fire.

I had another reason to want to reach the Mekong River. The night before my departure for the Trail, a most erudite and charming friend who had grown up in Laos had urged me to visit the magical temple of Wat Phu on the banks of the Mekong. His father had been a nationalist who supported Hồ Chí Minh and the Việt Minh's fight for independence from French rule. But when Maoist hard-liners gained power within the Vietnamese Communist Party, the family left Vietnam and settled in Laos. Later, he studied at the École des Beaux-Arts in Paris and made the French capital his home. I had long been an admirer of his artworks, imaginary maps of the soul which traced abstract paths from suffering to redemption.

We were walking along Hoàn Kiếm Lake in Hanoi on our way back from a *đàn nhị* concert at the Hanoi Opera House. I was enraptured by the concerto for the ancient bowed string instrument, an epic orchestral work by a contemporary Chinese composer. But my artist friend lamented the Chinese influence on Vietnamese culture. He preferred the soulful and intimate classical Vietnamese compositions for the *đàn nhị*, accompanied by flute and drums, to the grandiose sound we had just heard.

"I cry when I listen to *chèo* music," he said, referring to the Vietnamese musical tragicomedies that dated to the eleventh century.

We stopped at the romantic Temple of the Jade Mountain on a small island in the lake. The temple was dedicated to the warrior who repelled invasions by the Mongols and the Yuan dynasty that ruled over much of China in the thirteenth century.

"If the Russian faction of the Vietnamese Communist Party had won over the Chinese faction, Vietnam wouldn't be communist today," he reflected. "And if the Vietnamese communists had been influenced by the Soviets instead of the Maoists, they would have culture now."

He paused and continued:

"When you're doing the Trail, will you be going to the temple of Wat Phu on the Khmer imperial road? If it isn't on your route, it should be."

The temple overlooking the Mekong was the northernmost temple of the Khmer Empire and had been built at about the same time as Angkor Wat.

I trusted his aesthetics completely and added the temple of Wat Phu to my itinerary.

It was a prescient move.

On Route 23, tabletop mountain at sunset between Xepon and Salavan.

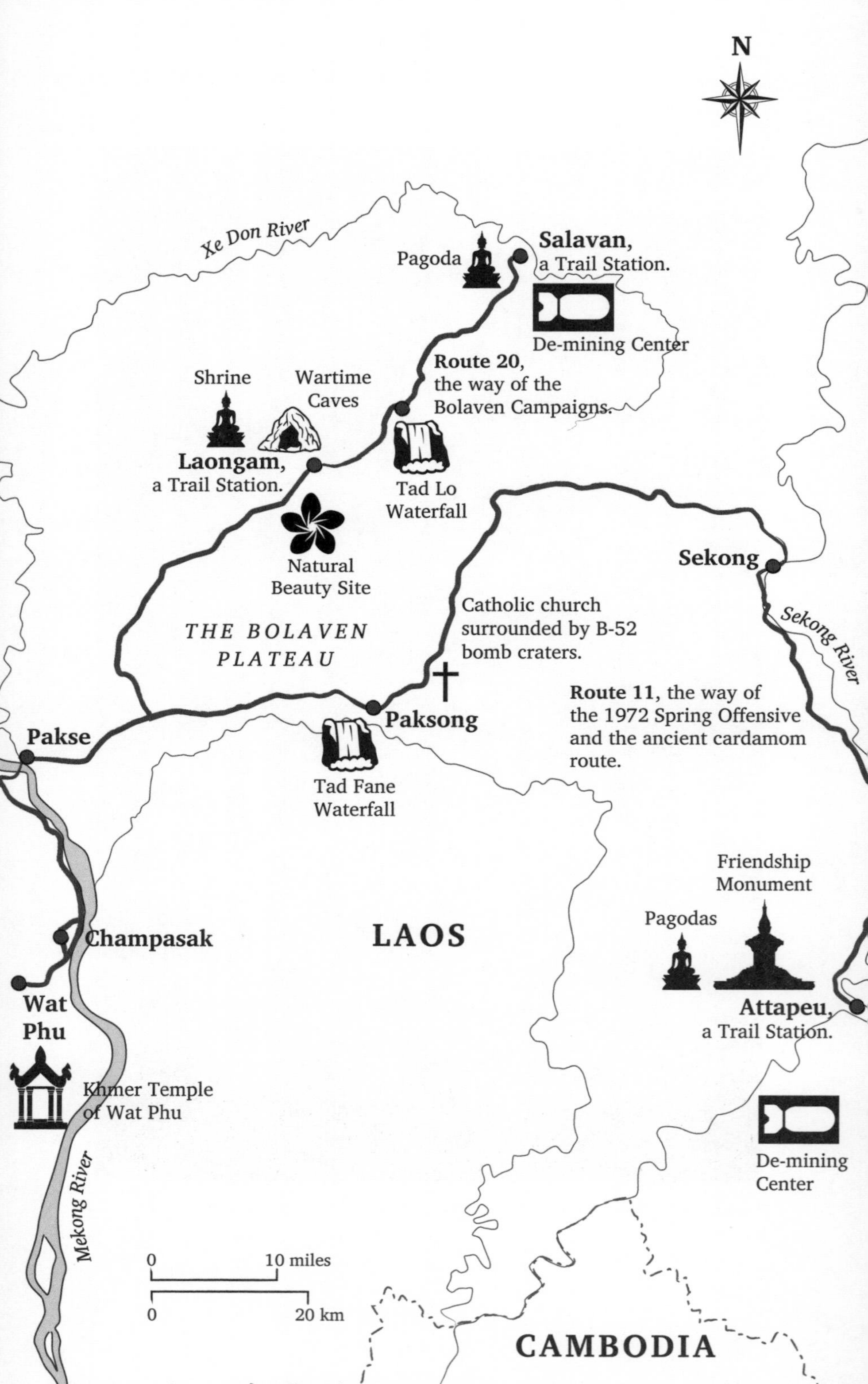

N
Xe Don River
Pagoda
Salavan,
a Trail Station.
De-mining Center
Route 20,
the way of the
Bolaven Campaigns.
Shrine
Wartime
Caves
Laongam,
a Trail Station.
Tad Lo
Waterfall
Natural
Beauty Site
Sekong
Sekong River
Catholic church
surrounded by B-52
bomb craters.
THE BOLAVEN
PLATEAU
Route 11, the way of
the 1972 Spring Offensive
and the ancient cardamom
route.
Pakse
Paksong
Tad Fane
Waterfall
Friendship
Monument
Pagodas
Champasak
LAOS
Wat
Phu
Attapeu,
a Trail Station.
Khmer Temple
of Wat Phu
De-mining
Center
Mekong River
0
10 miles
0
20 km
CAMBODIA

Chapter 9

# *SALAVAN TO ATTAPEU, LAOS*

*The way of the Bolaven Campaigns, the Mekong River, and the magical Khmer Temple of Wat Phu.*

*The Trail Command extended its logistical network westward, across the Bolaven Plateau to the banks of the Mekong River, to contain the Royal Lao Army and CIA-led forces who threatened the Laotian Trail.*

*Brigadier General Soutchay Vongsavanh, who was in charge of the Royal Lao Army during the Bolaven Campaigns in Champasak Province, wrote in his memoir:*

*"The US Air Force conducted a massive interdiction campaign," as the People's Army "shifted its logistics system westward into the Mekong and Bolaven regions, tucked up against and inside this relatively dense population area … The Bolaven became a bloody battleground for the remainder of the war … Many Lao and North Vietnamese were killed … It became a haunted place to the Lao."*[64]

"Bad things go out, good things go in," said the young woman wrapped in a bright sarong, with fragrant frangipani flowers in her hair.

She knotted a cotton bracelet around my wrist as she delivered the Buddhist blessing. The knot tied body and soul together.

It was early morning outside the hotel. Women distributed bracelets and flowers to the joyous sounds of Lao pop music. The tabletop mountains of the Bolaven Plateau rose on the horizon.

The sheer cliffs and flat tops had the angular shapes of the Grand Canyon.

We had breakfast in the shade of a gazebo set in the hotel's lush tropical gardens. Hân prepared a *cà phê đen* with freshly ground Vietnamese coffee he had bought in Khe Sanh.

"Delicious. Tastes like vanilla," I said.

"The coffee beans are roasted in chicken fat to give them extra zest," Hân explained.

"No comment," I replied.

Undeterred, I drank my morning coffee.

We left for Pakse after breakfast on Route 20, following the way of the People's Army's first Bolaven Campaign. We planned to stop in Laongam, invited by Noukone, the NPA's effusive translator. We drove up the ridge of the Bolaven Plateau. Crops and flora grew abundant in the volcanic soil. In the thin air of the high plateau, the hyper-realistic reds of poinsettias, yellows of giant daisies, and magentas of bougainvillea were sharply delineated against a cerulean sky. Deep crags and crevasses were covered in luxuriant vegetation. Towering waterfalls crashed into gaping sinkholes.

At the Tad Lo Falls, I stood in the refreshing spray on monumental chunks of molten lava sculpted into tactile rocky shapes, immersed in color and beauty. Trail soldiers, depicted in blue-wash ink drawings, crossed the river on black lava boulders, as white water thundered beneath their feet.

When we arrived in Laongam, Noukone's wife offered us sun-filled papayas from this land of plenty. Crates packed with the delicious fruits were being loaded onto a truck that would take them to market in Pakse.

Noukone had grown up here during the war:

"There was a lot of fighting in the Bolaven Plateau, especially here in Laongam. The Soviets supported the Pathet Lao and the People's Army. Saigon's troops joined the Royal Lao and Thai, supported by the United States."

He couldn't forget the menacing sounds of his childhood.

"All night, trrrrrrrrrr, trrrrrrrrr, and sometimes during the day. They bombed all the time, trrrrrrrrrr, trrrrrrrrr. People hid in caves. Would you like to visit the caves?" he asked.

"Yes," we said in unison.

In this land of simple abundance, the people who farmed the rich volcanic soil of the high Bolaven Plateau had paid the price of the superpowers' proxy war.

The Laotian writer Theap Vongpakay, in his novel *The Storm of Life*, wrote of the colonial oppression that led the Pathet Lao to Marxism, to the alliance with Hanoi, and to war:

"I was living in the place where mud smelled bad and under oppression. There was no other better way than fighting."[65]

Riding through lush banana plantations and peanut fields, we parked in a forest and set out on foot for the caves. Up an arduous path—I put the *bombis* out of my mind—we reached a highland of black lava rock that looked down onto a vast caldera below. Sandstone deities draped in yellow silk stood watch, immersed in glittering gold and silver paper offerings. The violent explosion of a massive volcano millions of years ago had created the primeval Bolaven ridges and mesa.

We continued on the path under high-canopy trees, crisscrossed with giant tree roots, until we reached an overhanging rock. High up in the rock face, slits like the stone windows of medieval castles overlooked the road from Salavan. A ladder led to the narrow cave entrance. The space inside was confining, the rock too low for even a child to stand in. Incense sticks burned in stone niches, flickering lights in the dark space.

"Young people now come here for love," said Noukone, breaking the silence.

"Feels safe," I said.

"It wasn't. If one bomb had hit, the whole thing would have collapsed or blown up. Either the B-52s didn't discover it or the hill never took a direct hit. People from the villages hid in these caves, if they could make it in time."

Over 350 villagers hiding in a cave had been killed in Tham Piu in the north of the country, near the Plain of Jars, a site covered in mysterious stone jars from the Iron Age.

"Did you hide here?"

"No, my village was too far away. We didn't have time. We hid under our house."

On the way back to Laongam, fishermen offered us barbecued fish caught that morning in the scintillating emerald-turquoise lake. Tempting as it was, Noukone suggested we taste some culinary delights in town.

"I don't eat the blood dishes, but if you want to try them we have two restaurants in the village. After the goat and duck are cooked, the blood is poured over the warm dish," said Noukone.

Nobody wanted to taste blood. We ended up at the local grocery store. On her stove behind the counter, the owner cooked a mean *laap* of minced chicken, chili, lime juice, *padaek* or Lao fish sauce, mint, and a mix of fragrant fresh herbs with mysterious flavors.

I made a note:

"Go back to Laongam for the best *laap*, in the shop before the big yellow house that belongs to the Prime Minister's nephew."

"In Vietnam, we also have goat and duck blood dishes. Another delicacy is bull testicles. They make your 'gun' stronger," said Hân.

"Is 'gun' a Vietnamese slang word?" Nam asked.

"Yes. You mash the testicles into the vodka and add Chinese medicine herbs," Hân replied.

"A Bullshot!" I said, delighted with my discovery of the origins of the drink. But the vodka and beef consommé cocktail was so late-fifties Manhattan Upper East Side that nobody around the table had heard of it.

The food brought back wartime memories for Noukone:

"We couldn't cook during the war. The conditions were hard.

We never had *laap*, never. We wrapped chili inside a rice ball. That made us less hungry. We also smoked a long pipe that made you less hungry. The Vietnamese soldiers gave us a special food, sticky rice with meat wrapped in banana leaf. Around New Year, we received two rolls and cut them into pieces to share with the whole family."

"*Bánh chưng*!" Hân and Nam said in unison, with delight. The sticky rice cakes made of glutinous rice, bean paste, and pork belly are a Vietnamese New Year delicacy.

We said our goodbyes to Noukone and continued westward on the Bolaven Trail, for the short drive to Pakse. Past delicately carved spirit houses and gleaming gold pagodas, a church appeared after a bend in the road. There was an air of celebration. A Vietnamese deacon enveloped in black robes, a white clerical collar around his neck, came out to greet us. Personable and outgoing, he was proud of the new church that was being consecrated that evening.

"We built a new church because the foundations of the old church were damaged," he said.

"How?" I asked.

"By bombs during the war. Come, have a look," he said.

There was no escape from the war.

The old church, on the edge of a coffee plantation, was made of wood. All around it were bomb craters, deep and wide, as though the Earth had been hit by a cataclysmic shower of meteors. The small church had been spared.

"B-52s," said the deacon. "I'm keeping the old church as a war relic."

As if on cue, crepuscular rays lit the holy place. We followed the deacon to a grotto dedicated to the Virgin Mary. Water flowed down the rock face into a pool, dark and deep.

"Many people died here," he said.

"Who were they?" I asked.

"Vietnamese soldiers."

"Where?"

Nguyễn Văn Hoàng, *Early Morning River Crossing*, watercolor, February 28, 1972.

*Above*: Nguyễn Văn Hoàng, *Crossing the River,* watercolor, December 2, 1971.
*Opposite*: On the Laotian Trail, at the Tad Lo Falls, Bolaven Plateau.

"There's a cave deep underground. It took a direct hit. After the war, the communists sent the priests to jail. Our church land was confiscated and stolen by the locals," explained the deacon.

The deacon stood by the water's edge and sang a hymn from the Catholic liturgy of my youth. Children who had followed us joined in. He prayed for the souls of the Vietnamese soldiers who had fought and died here for a belief that had persecuted his religion.

"I have a friend who was here during the war. He would be happy to share his stories," the deacon said as we walked back to the church.

Nguyễn Văn Hồ owned the coffee plantation next door. He had the energetic demeanor and wiry build of a man who managed and worked the land. He'd been caught here during the war, between 1965 and 1971, unable to leave. Like Noukone, what he remembered most was the roar of the B-52s:

"We lived underground. Four years, underground. We dug a shelter underneath our house. We had little food. The bombings were intense. I never saw fighting. I hid in the shelter. I did see B-52s flying above. And I heard the explosions. We wanted to leave but the path through the forest was too difficult for my mother. It was dangerous, too. My aunt left through the forest. She was injured when she stepped on a *bombi* that blew up. Finally, there was a break in the fighting in 1971 and we made it to Savannakhet. When we came back after the war, everything was destroyed. There was nothing. We had to clear our land. That was the most dangerous. There were big bombs that hadn't exploded and *bombis*. The *bombis* were vicious. Many in my family were injured by shrapnel. For the first ten years, we had to cope on our own. After that, the government gave us some help to clear the land."

"Didn't the People's Army force you to join them?" asked the deacon.

"They encouraged me to join the Youth Volunteers, but I wasn't interested. I didn't want to go into the military. My uncle had been a soldier with the Việt Minh and fought against the French. They didn't force me. They encouraged me. When they had extra food, they gave it to me. That's what I mean by encouragement. I told them I had to take care of my mother. My father died when I was young and my mother wasn't in good health."

"They forced the Lao, though. I have friends in the ethnic groups. They had no choice. They had to join the People's Army as laborers," said the deacon.

The deacon invited us to attend evening Mass. But I faced a mutiny, so we said our goodbyes and headed for Pakse.

Pakse was a surprisingly popular place, and the hotels were either full, too shabby, or too glitzy. We drove around the city in circles for so long that we missed the sunset over the Mekong. We ended up at the Mekong Paradise Resort where we made up for the sunset with a convivial dinner over a few bottles of Lao beer, sweet and mellow. Flowers decorated the table.

"They're plastic!" Hân said.

"They're from Vietnam," the Laotian waiter fired back in Vietnamese, as he filled Hân's glass.

Back in my room, I stretched out the full length of the map on the terrace that overlooked the mighty river. I had reached the westernmost point of the Trail network. I was tempted by the blue night and hypnotic river to sleep in the hammock on the terrace. But gigantic voracious mosquitoes buzzed round me. When a fuzzy flying beast caressed my cheek, I retreated inside.

The mysterious temple of Wat Phu that had escaped the war beckoned.

Nam and I took a boat downriver to Champasak and Wat Phu the following morning, while Hân drove. The boatman handed me the helm. I glided down the sacred river. The calm surface masked treacherous undercurrents. The scarred earth of Quảng Trị and

Savannakhet Provinces receded. The cicadas were singing, the Mekong was flowing, and Lao music was playing.

At the River Lodge Hotel, eco-pavilions set in landscaped rice paddies stood on the river's edge. A few tourists milled around, enjoying a winter vacation. We had agreed to spend a slow day, the first in our relentless pace down the Trail. That evening, I watched the languid Mekong, unconcerned by human folly. I transcribed my notes from my conversations with the Trail veterans in Quảng Trị Province. In the enchanted night, the words of suffering and hatred liquefied, losing their hard edge, to communicate the common bonds of light we sought to forge out of the darkness of human history.

I woke before dawn the following morning. A molten sun rose over a quiet Mekong, a fisherman, and his boat. Hân was at the ready to drive to Champasak to catch the monks' morning procession. Champasak's resplendent pagoda was gold, white, and red in the distilled morning blue. The Morning Alms was humbling. Empty bowls in hand, saffron-clad monks moved from house to house asking the devoted for rice, their sustenance for the day. A woman knelt on the road and spooned rice into a monk's bowl. The monk gave her a blessing in return. The rituals offered her reassurance. The saffron robes had lost some of their harmonious luster after a Laotian monk had informed me that women had to be reborn as men before they could aspire to become Buddha. Since he was only a novice, perhaps he was mistaken?

The magical temples of Wat Phu lay seductively on the slopes of Phou Kao mountain, high above the Mekong. After days on the pitiless Trail, Wat Phu offered a respite from the turbulent memories of war. The temples had escaped the war, either by design of the warring sides, or by chance. I approached the sacred complex by the grand imperial road that connected the mother temple in Angkor Wat to the holy site at the confines of the Khmer Empire. The cruelty of ancient wars had evaporated with time. All that was left was the beauty of old stones. Had the Khmer come as liberators or as conquerors? The stories of Khmer engineers and slaves building the road; of archers and soldiers far away from home, advancing astride elephants; of Brahmin priests carrying their gods; of Apsara dancers and Khmer cultural troops and of Laotian civilians, happy or fearful to see the new arrivals, were lost in time.

I walked solo in a trance of the senses on sun-bleached stone blocks from the Mekong River to the beguiling ruined temple. Bordered by imposing sandstone columns with lotus-shaped finials, the causeway was constructed in the straight line of imperial Roman roads, connecting the vast reservoirs of the lost city that had once stood here.

Collective memories were etched on the many ways that criss-crossed the Earth: military roads, pilgrims' ways, and trade routes, traced for war, beliefs, or money. The Trail was distinctive for having been built mostly or partly during war. Few logistical systems had been constructed with such determination during a conflict. Even Roman military roads that corresponded to military advances were formalized and consolidated at the end of wars, during periods of stability.

I arrived, hot and parched, at the tumbledown grand temple dedicated to the Hindu god Shiva, destroyer of all evil, decorated with the sensual corbeled arches, the heavy stone portals, the carved bas-reliefs of deities, and the blind windows with colonnettes of Khmer architecture. Nam, who had driven here with Hân, was waiting for me, sitting on an ancient stone. Refreshed, he was ready to climb the steep stepped walkway to the sanctuaries built high above the plain overlooking the Mekong, bordered by scented frangipani about to bloom, offering the promise of spring. The upper sanctuaries were richly decorated. A Dvarapala, a Hindu temple guardian with the characteristic top-knot hair, fleshy lips, and smile of the Khmer, stood guard, clasping a menacing mace with both hands, combining charm and cruelty.

Buddhas were draped in silky yellow and gold capes. The Hindu temple had become a Buddhist monastery in the thirteenth century. Exquisite offerings were delicately fashioned into conical shapes made from banana leaves and decorated with frangipani. A stone carved into the shape of a crocodile was thought to have been the site of human sacrifices.

I sprinkled some holy water on my forehead from a sacred spring. The water flowed along a stone aqueduct and bathed the *lingam* in the sanctuary below.

I stayed for a while, under the spell of the enchanted place.

That evening, back at the River Lodge, I lit a Chinese paper lantern and watched it float up into the mystery of a universe without borders.

*In the winter of 1972, the People's Army left Salavan and the Bolaven Plateau to launch the 1972 Spring Offensive against Kon Tum.*

*The military convoys advanced on Route 16, along the Sekong River, immersed in the stunning scenery the artists remembered. They stopped at the Trail station near the Laotian southern town of Attapeu. The People's Army had seized control of the town in 1970, giving the Trail access to the Central Highlands in South Vietnam, and to neighboring Cambodia.*

The following morning, we left the languid Mekong for the drive to Attapeu, where we planned to stay the night before crossing the border the next day for Kon Tum.

I was reminded that Trail routes used ancient trade ways and

French colonial roads. Route 16 had been the "cardamom route" in the seventh century. The fragrant spice used in traditional medicine and cuisines was grown on the Bolaven Plateau. Traders from the Champa kingdom, present-day central and southern Vietnam, carried the spice to Vijaya, the Champa capital on today's Vietnamese coast, from where it was shipped to India and the Middle East. The Champa controlled the trade in spices and silk in the East Sea until the tenth century, when they were conquered by the Đại Việt Empire to the north. The track became a paved way under French colonial rule and was part of the road network built at the beginning of the twentieth century to connect French territories in Indochina.

Under a cerulean sky, the Trường Sơn Mountains, marking the border with Vietnam, appeared on the eastern horizon like old friends. To the west, the cliffs of the eastern ridge of the Bolaven Plateau towered high above the plain.

We stopped on the banks of the Sekong River to look for Siamese crocodiles, but there were none lazing in the sun. Crocodile meat had been a rare delicacy for artist Trần Huy Oánh and his unit when they had reached the river.

We continued on to Attapeu. At the entrance to the town, we were greeted by a golden victory monument celebrating the wartime alliance between Vietnamese and Laotian communists. Brothers stood arm-in-arm, the People's Army soldier wore a helmet on his head, the Pathet Lao had a Maoist soft cap on his, raising their AK-47s in triumph. The war memorial was next to a stupa, a Buddhist place of meditation that contained sacred relics. The socialist realist style of the old Soviet Empire looked improbable in this golden Buddhist land far from the frozen banks of the Moskva. Leaders fighting against a colonialism that enslaved them had been enticed by communism which promised them social justice and freedom from oppression.

The conflicting ideologies of capitalism and communism that had originated in the industrial towns of Europe—the *isms* of the twentieth century—had swept across the Eurasian continent to clash and erupt into a murderous conflict.

The fading sun poured liquid gold over the sparkling white and gold stupa. Women in sumptuous white, coral, and pale blue silks lay evening flower offerings at the holy shrine.

In preparation for the 1972 offensive, the road builders had constructed an all-weather road from Attapeu through the high passes of the Trường Sơn Mountains to the border with Vietnam and Cambodia. This was the road we followed the next morning.

As we left the Laotian Trail for the drive back to Vietnam, we headed for Kon Tum and the Central Highlands, a region situated on the direct path of tropical depressions and cyclones. The Trail Commander wrote in his memoir how the monsoon rains, flooding, and landslides had been as challenging and devastating for those traveling on Trail tracks and roads as American bombs.[66]

Sunrise on the Mekong River near Champasak, the westernmost point of the Trail.

LAOS
VIETNAM
N
Friendship Monument
Nongphatom Lake
Natural Beauty Site
Attapeu,
a Trail Station and departure of the Sihanouk Trail through Cambodia.
Kon Tum Cathedral
Kon Tum
De-mining Center
Pleiku
Mekong River
Route 14,
the way of the 1975 Spring Offensive.
Kraceh,
last Station on the Sihanouk Trail.
CAMBODIA
Buôn Ma Thuột
Victory Monument
Lắk Lake
Hunting lodge of Emperor Bảo Dại
Trail Command Headquarters 1975
HQ
Nha Trang
Saigon River
National Liberation Front Headquarters
HQ
Route 14
Dalat
Natural Beauty Site
Tây Ninh
Route 13
Route 1A, the way of the 1975 Spring Offensive.
Củ Chi Tunnels
Phan Thiết
Natural Beauty Site
HO CHI MINH CITY
FINE ARTS
EAST SEA
Mekong Delta
0
50 miles
0
100 km

Chapter 10

# *ATTAPEU, LAOS TO KON TUM AND PHAN THIẾT*

*The ways of the 1972 and 1975 Spring Offensives, tasting blood dishes, and the last Emperor's hunting lodge.*

*The People's Army launched its offensive on March 30, 1972. In response, the United States resumed its bombing of North Vietnam.*

*The offensive was the largest logistical operation of the war. The deployment was estimated at three times that of the Tết Offensive. Between 200,000 to 300,000 troops, supported by tank units, advanced on three fronts: from North Vietnam, on Quảng Trị Province, again; from Cambodia, on An Lộc, fifty miles north of Saigon; and from Xepon and Salavan in Laos, on Kon Tum and the Central Highlands.*

*Could the Trail supply that many troops? Could the Trail withstand the onslaught of the renewed US bombings of North Vietnam? The Trail Commander reported shortages of food, ammunition, and of men and women. Under attack from B-52s, and lacking reinforcements and ammunition, the People's Army was forced to retreat from Kon Tum.*

*The Trail Commander wrote in his memoir:*

*"The lack of food on the battlefield was very dangerous [particularly on the Quảng Trị Front]."*[67]

*North Vietnamese military deaths during the offensive were estimated at between 40,000 and 100,000, South Vietnamese casualties at 39,587 killed and wounded, and US military deaths at 759. The number of civilians who lost their lives on both sides is unknown.*[68]

*Four years after peace negotiations began in October 1968, and millions of war dead, wounded, and refugees later, both sides were ready for compromise.*

⛩

We arrived in Kon Tum in the early evening to discover a town with a nostalgic French air. A neo-Gothic church steeple graced the skies; trees that lined the boulevards were pruned French-style; women in conical hats sold baguettes in the market; and open-air eateries along the quay were decorated with the green, blue, and white fairy lights of *guinguettes* along the Seine.

The pleasant town in the former South Vietnam had seen plenty of fighting. During the 1972 Spring Offensive, the Allied military headquarters in the town was attacked by North Vietnamese artillery and tanks, and defended by American B-52 bombing.

Thomas McKenna, an advisor to the South Vietnamese infantry division who was in the city during the battle, described the bombing of the town center:

"During just twenty-five days, B-52s alone dropped sixty million tons of bombs around Kon Tum. Tactical air fighters dropped additional millions of pounds of bombs both inside and outside the city … the air was filled with the smell of cordite, smoke, and rotting bodies."[69]

Kon Tum held thanks to US air support. The People's Army retreated. The Trail had been overwhelmed.

We strolled along the quay and settled on a fish restaurant. A few tables away, an older gentleman was having a beer with two friends. In the dark, and from a distance, I thought he could be a former American soldier.

Nam and I went over to talk to the trio. Don Stille introduced himself as an American veteran. He was visiting Vietnam with his son and grandson.

"It's my third time back to Vietnam," said Don.

Tall and softly spoken, with white hair and a mustache, Don was open and friendly. He was a retired engineer who lived in Grand Rapids, Michigan with his family and wife of fifty-one years, his "high-school sweetheart." He had enlisted to support his country, and served one tour of duty as a ground radio operator in 1967–1968. He was stationed with the Military Assistance Command, Vietnam in the town of Bến Tre in the Mekong Delta, and at the airfield in Cheo Reo not far from Kon Tum, from where Forward Air Controllers flew out. The controllers provided guidance so that air strikes hit the intended target and did not injure friendly troops.

"Why did you come back?" I asked.

Don replied:

"Because I love the people. I felt that we let them down when we left. We let down the South Vietnamese and the Montagnards [the hill tribes] who helped us. While I was stationed in Bến Tre, I befriended a family and coached basketball at the local school. In 2007, I returned to look for my friends. I wanted to see how they were doing and if the town had been rebuilt. My search was in vain, but I made new friends, had a pleasant visit with a combatant from the other side, helped the local orphanage. When I go back to visit, people come over and embrace me in the street. But I have a friend who was in the infantry. He never wants to come back here."

Don had served in this foreign place, halfway across the world, out of patriotism, duty, and a sense of adventure to help the South Vietnamese defend their country against communism. He felt responsible for their betrayal when US forces pulled out.

Don was based in Bến Tre during the 1968 Tết Offensive. When the Việt Cộng attacked the South Vietnamese forces and the US military headquarters in the town, the US Army, Air Force, and Navy were called in to defend them. Don believed the US media had misrepresented the events:

"As for our bombing of Bến Tre, I never want to hear that saying again: 'It became necessary to destroy the town in order to save it.' I was there and we didn't target civilians in the town. I was talking to those pilots. They targeted the jungle across the river. It wasn't the town."

The quote was attributed to an unidentified US major in an Associated Press dispatch reprinted in *The New York Times,* and became a rallying cry for the anti-war movement. The news item went on to comment that "[the major] was talking about the decision by Allied commanders to shell the town regardless of civilian casualties, to rout the Việt Cộng."[70]

The author of the dispatch was war correspondent Peter Arnett. The major has never been identified.

"Did you feel bad about the bombings?" I asked.

"Not at the time. It was war," he replied.

Don explained the challenges he and his pilots faced:

"We bombed troops in enemy areas and what appeared to be enemy encampments in the jungle. Towns and villages were never targets while I was there in the provinces in which I served. Avoiding harming civilians was difficult of course. The Việt Cộng hid with the villagers and were in the towns. Outside Bến Tre, the Việt Cộng were using a church to store ammo and as a place in which mortars were launched at our airfield, planes, and crew members. The church was not part of a town or village. My pilots kept asking me: 'Can't you find a way to bomb that church? Mortar fire is coming at us from there. We're tired of it.' But we had difficulty bombing the church. I talked to the province chief—he was of that religious denomination—and he said 'no way' are we going to bomb that church. So I chose a set of coordinates about a thousand meters from the church and asked for a thousand-meter radius—normally we asked for one hundred, two hundred and fifty, or five hundred meters around a target center. The pilots bombed the target and, sure enough, there were massive secondary explosions!

"I worked with the fighter pilots to help them do what they could not to injure civilians. Pilots came in at least twice to tell me they didn't follow orders because they saw children in the target area. I put down on the log that they didn't bomb because of the weather or some other reason."

But, Don agreed that people were caught in the firepower targeting the Việt Cộng:

"When the B-52s came in and bombed, I could feel the ground shaking from fifty miles away. The helicopters then came in. The people who were still alive were so deafened by the explosions that they didn't hear them and they were all killed by helicopter fire."

Don continued:

"On this trip, I have been visiting Montagnards here and in Buôn Ma Thuột. I was very concerned about their plight after reading several stories about their difficulties after the war. One reported that the government treated them terribly, cutting off women's breasts and men's Achilles tendons."

"The atrocities may have been misreported," I suggested.

"I don't think so. When I got to Vietnam during the war, I was told that the Việt Cộng came into the villages and routinely killed a baby or a child to terrorize the people. I never saw that myself. But I did see a South Vietnamese strung up. He wasn't mutilated, but we heard stories that the Việt Cộng were killing people and mutilating them. You should hear what the Việt Cộng were saying about us, that we were cannibals and raped women."

For Don, it came down to intentions:

"If I was on my farm and the Chinese invaded the United States, I would have a hard time believing they were coming to help. We certainly had trouble with rural areas; they were not on our side. But I think we had honorable intentions. I don't think we went in to colonize. The protesters could be against the war, but it didn't mean they had to call us 'baby killers.' If you want to change the course of a war, you should target the politicians, not the young soldiers who are doing their duty. There is no such thing as a humane war. If you are going to do it, you have to just go in. Protest and concern for human rights in war prolongs the war and makes it worse."

"Have you been to the north of Vietnam?" I asked.

"I don't feel like visiting the North," Don replied.

We toasted to the end of wars. Don was taking the bus the next morning to visit his Vietnamese friends, a veteran who had come back to make amends for the betrayal of an ally.

I woke up the following morning with a sore throat, my body's warning sign of physical and mental exhaustion. Nam bought some antibiotics at the pharmacy and brought them back to the hotel. Don had recommended a visit to the splendid French colonial church in town. Rows of coffee beans outside the church roasted in the white hot sun. Built in 1913, the church's aesthetic reflected consonance in a land marked by conflict. The facade's dark wood with gold trim and triangle motifs was the color of Confucian temples, a wraparound French colonial porch was shaded by the sloping roof of hill-tribe dwellings, and a grand nave was illuminated by graceful arched windows. Parishioners dusted church benches in preparation for the evening service.

We held our final council in the coolness of a church pew. I pulled out my map. We were approaching the end of the Trail. We were headed for Buôn Ma Thuột in the Central Highlands, the way of the 1975 Spring Offensive, the final offensive of the war.

*After the Paris Peace Accords were signed on January 27, 1973, US troops left South Vietnam in March, and US planes stopped bombing North Vietnam, South Vietnam, Laos, and Cambodia. The Trail's "greatest obstacle," the US air war against North Vietnam, and against the Việt Cộng in South Vietnam, had come to an end.*

*But the fighting between North and South Vietnam continued. The Politburo began planning the final offensive. Their first target was Buôn Ma Thuột in the Central Highlands.*

On Route 14, the 1975 victory monument in Buôn Ma Thuột, Đắk Lắk Province.

*The Trail Commander wrote:*

*"At the end of November, I was informed that the Politburo had officially decided to build the East Trường Sơn Trail [through South Vietnam, east of the Trường Sơn Mountains] ... My main concern was how to speed up the building work ... The East Trường Sơn Trail was a huge construction site employing four divisions, five engineering regiments, and many Youth Volunteer units ... The main difficulty at this time was a shortage of cement, steel, and asphalt ..."*[71]

*The Trail Command headquarters moved south of the Bến Hải River to oversee construction—close to where the first mission in 1959 had crossed the provisional demarcation line to deliver fifty guns. The Trường Sơn forces, 500-strong in 1959, numbered 120,000 combatants and Youth Volunteers by 1974. Anti-aircraft defense weapons, mobile armored tanks, and Soviet surface-to-air missiles had replaced hand-me-down AK-47s. Within nine months of beginning work on the East Trường Sơn Trail, the Trail Commander was ready. All-weather roads and parallel pipelines had been built through South Vietnam. The pipeline network stretched over a thousand miles from the Chinese border to within seventy-five miles of Saigon, with over a hundred refueling stations, and large oil-storage facilities at key stations.*

*The Trail Commander met with General Giáp in Hanoi in early February 1975. He wrote in his memoir:*

*"Giáp gave me a warm and friendly greeting ... and said: 'The Politburo is ready to start the transport to ensure the liberation of the South.'"*[72]

I had developed a strong connection to the Trường Sơn Mountains and wanted to follow the range all the way to the south.

"Let's take Route 14C along the mountains," I suggested.

"Not enough time. But Route 14 to Buôn Ma Thuột is fast. It's a main highway," said Hân.

Hân had to get home for New Year's Eve and so did Nam.

"OK, guys, Route 14 it is," I conceded.

Route 14 had been the main way of the 1975 Spring Offensive. Between 270,000 (the North Vietnamese estimate) and one million North Vietnamese soldiers, over 1,000 artillery pieces and 320 tanks advanced south on Routes 14 and 14C to Saigon, the capital of South Vietnam.

I was intrigued to follow the road that the Trail Command had built right in the enemy territory of South Vietnam. How did they do it? After the United States left Vietnam, the South Vietnamese Army still numbered over one million soldiers, equipped with 1,500 artillery pieces, 2,000 tanks, 1,500 aircraft, and over 570 warships.[73]

"Where should we spend the night?" Nam asked.

"I have a special place. It's a little out of town. A surprise," said Hân.

I was sorry my traveling companions were leaving. The challenge that lay ahead had nothing to do with topography. The South Vietnamese diaspora in the United States, Canada, and Australia talked openly about the war years, and had published numerous accounts, novels, and memoirs. But those who stayed in Saigon after 1975 did not share their "shaded memories" easily.

We left the désuet charm of Kon Tum by Route 14 for Buôn Ma Thuột. The People's Army aimed to capture the city in preparation for their final advance on Saigon. Heavy artillery, 65,000 troops, and close to sixty tanks advanced on Buôn Ma Thuột, coming from Laos, Kon Tum, and Pleiku.

Route 14 was a mess of roadworks. There were no traffic lights and no road markings. Hân practiced the avoidance dance he had perfected on Route 1A earlier in the trip. We drove through Pleiku. There was nothing to entice us to stop there. The US and South

Vietnamese Air Force base nearby had been hammered by Việt Cộng artillery at night. During the day, South Vietnamese military aircraft flew missions against the North Vietnamese positions on the Trail in Cambodia.

We drove by fields of pepper trees and coffee plantations, and stopped for lunch at a roadside restaurant recommended by Hân who had once worked on a coffee plantation nearby. The restaurant specialized in the goat-blood dishes that we hadn't tasted in Laos. The congealed goat blood came served in a bowl decorated with freshly chopped peanuts and herbs, and looked like an appetizing raspberry mousse. I dipped in the tip of my chopstick to find to my surprise that it tasted like an exquisite consommé.

We drove through the center of Buôn Ma Thuột on our way to our mystery destination for the night. Contemporary office buildings and hotels lined wide boulevards. In the center of town, tall conifers were bright with Christmas lights. Worshipers at an evening Mass filled the church and spilled onto the parkland around it, their voices united in songs of praise. Across from the church, the victory monument commemorated the "liberation" of Buôn Ma Thuột after a short battle. A People's Army tank made of cement stood in place of the original tank that was housed in the town's museum. Annual victory celebrations were held at the monument.

Don Stille's words resonated:

"We let them down."

The fall of Buôn Ma Thuột in March 1975 opened the Trail's way to Saigon. The Battle of Buôn Ma Thuột had been bloody, bitter, and decisive. The chaotic withdrawal of the South Vietnamese Army, followed by a long line of refugees crammed into buses and vans, was remembered as "the convoy of tears." Tens of thousands perished when they were hit by People's Army artillery and South Vietnamese aerial strikes.

The mystery destination was shrouded in darkness when we pulled up at the front gate. I sensed a lake nearby. We had arrived at the former hunting lodge of Emperor Bảo Đại, Vietnam's last emperor. The lodge overlooked Lắk Lake. After Bảo Đại abdicated in 1945, he served as chief of state of the State of Vietnam (South Vietnam) from 1949 until 1955 when he left Vietnam. He lived in exile in Paris until his death in 1997.

After the lodge was destroyed in a fire, it was rebuilt in 2001 in an architectural style that defied definition. Hân and Nam insisted I take the emperor's bedroom. Maybe they knew something I didn't. That evening, I sat down at the emperor's desk. The pace of the Trail had been intense. Beauty created in war had led me to the Trail, to the devotional shrines of the mountain Trail, the mystical caves of Phong Nha, and the gritty gravel roads of Laos. Remembrance and storytelling had brought a measure of redemption. Each encounter had given meaning to my journey: forgiveness, an embrace, a prayer and a song, and a desire to repair the legacies of war.

Excited tourists peered through the glass doors of the imperial bedroom as I woke up the next morning. Nobody had warned me that the imperial lodge was a favorite tourist attraction open to visitors. I jumped out of the imperial bed and ran to the imperial bathroom to get dressed.

Whether I had slept in the actual bed of Bảo Đại, Vietnam's thirteenth and final emperor, was far from certain. But the visitors didn't share my skepticism and were impatient to view the imperial suite, bed, and bathroom.

I had just finished putting on my war paint when the museum guard unlocked the door to let the tourists in.

After 1,500 miles on the road, I planned to stop for a few days' rest in the beach town of Phan Thiết. Phan Thiết had been "liberated" on April 19, 1975, a month after Buôn Ma Thuột.

I had discovered the town in a war drawing that recorded the liberation of POWs by the People's Army. Scribbled on the back of a red cigarette pack, the artist's exuberant black magic-marker strokes had expressed his feverish anticipation of the end of a long war.

On the way, we broke the journey in the delightful hill station of Dalat, known as a honeymoon destination, where we spent the night. On the outskirts of the town, we stopped on the banks of Tuyền Lâm Lake where the image of a lone fisherman, enveloped in the fog of war, became the emblem of my Trail journey—misty and mysterious.

During the war, the former French hill station had been home to senior government officials, and escaped destruction. The South Vietnamese Army had already left the town when the People's Army entered the city a few days later on April 3, 1975.

We visited Crazy House, a trippy hotel where the Flintstones would have felt at home. The architect was the daughter of Trường Chinh (1907–1988), an influential Politburo member during the French and American Wars, who became Secretary General of the Communist Party in 1986. The cultural czar was remembered for promoting art for the people in his 1948 manifesto: *Marxism and Vietnamese Culture*. His daughter, Đặng Việt Nga, had followed in his footsteps. Her eclectic building had popular appeal and had become a major tourist attraction.

The following morning, we traveled along another beautiful and dangerous mountain road to reach Phan Thiết. We held our farewell lunch at the beach hotel where I planned to spend a few days.

"Nam, I'm taking up yoga. I was impressed by how calm you were during the trip, when I was hanging on for dear life!" I said.

"I don't want to disappoint you, but I was praying like mad, and my wrist mala was going really fast! In yoga philosophy, if you die with the lord's name on your lips, you'll be liberated. I was scared to death to even look at the road! Luckily, our Rambo got us through!" Nam replied.

"Thank you for trusting me with your life!" said Hân.

We said emotional goodbyes. Nam was flying back to New York from Ho Chi Minh City the next day, and Hân was setting off for the long drive back to Tĩnh Gia. I waved as they drove off in opposite directions: one to the north, the other to the south.

I collapsed on a deck chair on the windswept beach. I approached the Trail's denouement with foreboding as I prepared for the final leg to Ho Chi Minh City to travel with my friend Nga to the once elusive Việt Cộng headquarters at the end of the Trail.

Would I only find bitter memories in the southern city?

At the end of the war, those who stayed in Saigon experienced the full weight of retribution. The economy collapsed. Shops and businesses were nationalized or shut down. Fuel was rationed. Families were torn apart when loved ones were sent to reeducation camps. South Vietnamese military, police, and intelligence officers, civil servants, and others connected to "reactionary parties" were interned.

After the economic reforms of 1986 introduced a socialist market-orientated economy, the city began to recover and became the thriving commercial and financial center that it is today.

I fell into a long afternoon sleep.

I woke up at dusk in time for dinner. The only guests at the beach hotel that evening were three cheerful ladies from Siberia, who were spending their winter holiday in the warm land of the old socialist ally. A live band was playing retro music. I drank wine, the women drank vodka. So much of it, in fact, that we ended up on the dance floor doing the Twist together to tunes from the sixties.

TIMES SQUARE

Chapter 11

# *HO CHI MINH CITY AND THE VIỆT CỘNG HEADQUARTERS*

*The end of the Trail and the road to reconciliation.*

*The People's Army, the Trường Sơn forces, and the National Liberation Front advanced on Saigon from the northwest, east, and southeast.*

*A lasting image of the fall of Saigon for Americans is of men, women, and children desperately clambering over the wall of the US Embassy to be evacuated to ships waiting offshore. President Gerald R. Ford later called the evacuation "a sad and tragic period in America's history."*[74]

*A lasting image for the South Vietnamese is of their soldiers discarding their boots and uniforms when enemy troops entered Saigon.*

*A lasting image for the victors is of a North Vietnamese tank, flying the reunification flag, smashing through the gates of the Independence Palace, the seat of the government of the Republic of Vietnam.*

*The Trail Commander wrote in his memoir:*

*"At 5 p.m. on April 26, 1975, the General Offensive against Saigon, the capital of South Vietnam, began … At 11:30 a.m. on April 30, the 66th Infantry Regiment and the 203rd Tank Regiment proceeded to the Independence Palace. President Dương Văn Minh and key figures of the Saigon government surrendered unconditionally … In that extremely sacred moment, the Trường Sơn soldiers … their uniforms red from the dust of the roads … occupied the Independence Palace, the last enemy holdout. The Ho Chi Minh Road Campaign was victorious. The South was completely liberated. The forces of the Trường Sơn–Ho Chi Minh*

The twenty-first-century skyline of Ho Chi Minh City at night.

*Road Campaign had successfully completed their extremely important mission. [The main reason for our victory was] the speed of the roads over thousands of miles to carry out the largest military operation in the history of the liberation wars of our nation."*[75]

Trần Thị Huỳnh Nga was at home in Saigon on the morning of April 30, 1975, when the communist tanks rolled in:

"On April 30, the Việt Cộng are happy. But that day was a day of great suffering for the Saigonese. I saw many things that day. I could see over Saigon from the terrace of my third-floor apartment. I lived in the center of town opposite the main hospital. I saw the defeated South Vietnamese soldiers; they took off their clothes and their shoes and they were running. Their faces were pitiful. They died on the sidewalks of Saigon. Many, many, many."

We were sitting in the sunlit living room of Nga's townhouse in Ho Chi Minh City (HCMC), where I was spending the last few nights of the trip.

During the war, Nga lived in Saigon, "the pearl of the East," as she called it. She had a good job with Air Vietnam and had married for love into a prominent southern family. Her husband was a fighter pilot with the South Vietnamese Air Force. They had been married for only nine months when, in December 1971, he was shot down in the border area with Cambodia and reported "missing in action."

Nga explained why she chose to stay in Saigon with her young son when the war ended in 1975 and so many left South Vietnam:

"My husband's family left. But I stayed to wait for my husband. I was convinced he was being held as a prisoner of war by the North and that he would return to us. I was twenty-four years old. I had faith in happy endings. I couldn't imagine what was going to happen. They closed down businesses and shops. People were expropriated. There was no work. I looked after thirteen members of my family."

The following morning, I took a taxi with Nga and her son to visit the war cemeteries. The place I had known in the early nineties had been dark and silent, full of whispers and secrets. We drove through a gleaming city, self-confident and prosperous, with luxury shopping malls, high-rises for young professionals, and restaurants where lunch cost 200 dollars a head. Glass and steel towers were profiled against a futuristic skyline. Wealth had papered over wartime divisions or so it seemed.

The memorials to the combatants who had fought against each other were less than a mile apart. The cemetery for South Vietnamese soldiers had been closed for thirty years at the end of the war; relatives and friends banned from visiting the graves of loved ones. The place remained difficult to access. I had volunteered to go alone, but Nga insisted they accompany me, even though they risked harassment by the authorities after the visit.

We first stopped at the HCMC Martyrs' Cemetery. The Việt Cộng cemetery was on Route 1A, the main highway to Hanoi. Monkey trees and flowers in bloom lined stone paths and perfectly manicured green lawns. Water sprinklers refreshed sculpted hedges. Women wearing conical straw hats for protection against the sun swept the leaves off the grass. Immaculate white tombstones were arranged around box-tree hedges. Worshipers brought yellow chrysanthemums, red candles, and baguettes.

We got back in the cab to look for the military cemetery of the South Vietnamese soldiers, about a mile away. There was no road sign. We drove along the highway, turned left past an industrial park, continued down an unmarked road, and stopped to ask for directions at a roadside stall.

"Look for a blue door," said the owner.

We reached a high wall topped with barbed wire. The blue gate was padlocked. A policeman opened the gate. The taxi drove in and stopped in front of the security post. Nga went into the police station while we waited in the taxi. She signed our names in a register and wrote down the purpose of our visit: "Looking for my husband's tomb 'missing in action' in 1971."

"The police keep track of people who visit the cemetery," she explained, when she came back out of the station to join us. "But they've granted us permission. We're in."

I was grateful for their company. The cab parked at the entrance. We set out on foot. A security guard came with us to look for the grave. The sight that unfolded before me was one of desolation. The place bore the full weight of revenge. About 18,000 soldiers who had fought on the South Vietnamese side were buried here.

"They destroyed other military cemeteries," said Nga.

The land was forested with straggly trees, thin and sad. There were no immaculate lawns, no clipped box trees, and no paths between the graves. We walked through rubble and earth, shuffling through layers of dead leaves. Unmarked headstones lay derelict face down. Mounds of earth lay uncovered. Tombstones had been removed and recycled to build homes.

Occasionally, there was a new gravestone with a photograph, name, date of birth, and military rank.

"The Việt Kiều have rebuilt their relatives' tombs," said Nga.

We were the only ones there. The guard motioned that he might have found Nga's husband's grave. We knew it was unlikely, but we followed him to the 1971 section.

A vast crumbling monument stood at the center of the cemetery. An obelisk rising to the merciless heavens, a memorial to the fallen soldiers of the South. The statue of the South Vietnamese general that had once towered over the cemetery had been torn down. We walked up stairs to the main altar. Our minders camped themselves at the bottom of the stairs to keep watch.

"This is history. You must record this," said Nga.

Photographs were strictly forbidden. Another guard on a motorbike kept circling around us to make his presence known. As he disappeared from view for a few seconds, I timidly hazarded a few photographs. Nga told her son to film the desolate scene with his video camera. Fearful, he refused. We looked at each other.

"I'm ready to leave," I said.

"Me too," said Nga's son. "This isn't right. They shouldn't leave the cemetery like this."

But Nga took out the offerings she had brought: mandarin oranges, yellow chrysanthemums, and incense. She stepped up to the altar and carried out the rituals commemorating the fallen. Unafraid to disobey police rules, she filmed her son as he paid his respects to the fallen and to the father he never knew, who had died in a bombing mission against the Trail.

Our minder on the motorbike had disappeared. The other two sat quietly at the foot of the stairs, content with the tip that Nga had given them for showing us around.

As we sat on the wall that surrounded the monument, Nga talked about her husband's disappearance:

"I was in the hospital. I had given birth to our son. A cousin came to tell me my husband was 'missing in action.' He wanted to give me hope. He probably knew the truth. In 1972, I went to Da Nang to look for my husband during a POW exchange. Many pilots came back, but I didn't find him. I know that eighty percent of POWs during the war were South Vietnamese and twenty percent were American. The northerners don't accept that this was a civil war. The Việt Cộng always talk about the war against the Americans. I know that was not the case. My husband served with the South Vietnamese Air Force in Pleiku for six months in 1971. Every week, he told me how many missions his squadron flew to bomb Việt Cộng positions in the Central Highlands."

After her husband was reported "missing in action," Nga and her young son moved in with her parents. The apartment overlooked the Saigon General Hospital.

Nga, overwhelmed by her visual memories, continued:

"Every day, many South Vietnamese soldiers died in battles.

Every day, many were wounded. Every day, many families came to the hospital looking for their dead. And every day, many helicopters brought the wounded to the hospital. The Hanoians always talk about the suffering caused by the American bombings of Hanoi in 1972. How about Saigon? The Việt Cộng attacked the center of Saigon every night with their artillery. 'Boum, boum,' all night long. Who did they want to kill? Americans? We were the ones living there. We filled sacks with sand and put them on top of furniture. The whole family hid under the dining-room table and the couch.

"On April 30, 1975, the day the Việt Cộng entered Saigon, trucks drove around the streets all day long to pick up the bodies of soldiers who had been killed. The Việt Cộng brought all the dead to the mortuary of the Saigon hospital opposite my house. I saw many, many dead. That same night they dragged bodies along the sidewalk, and threw them onto the trucks as if they were rice sacks. The bodies were all twisted. The trucks drove them out of Saigon. They dug a huge common grave and dumped all the dead there. Many families whose sons died don't know where they are. Suffering was not only in Hanoi but also in Saigon. Our economy is stronger than the North's, but our suffering is the same."

Nga mimicked the grotesque positions of the bodies she had seen being brought to the hospital on that fateful day. She began to cry. I had never seen her cry in the twenty years I had known her.

She continued:

"When I lost my husband, I was too young. I know that war brings violence. You want to move on, but you can't forget. It's within you. The new generations don't understand. My generation, we see both sides. Now, when I meet people from the North they are friendly, they look happy. I wonder why they don't think of the people who died by their hands. They only talk about their fight against the Americans. I don't understand why my friends from the North don't see they fought against us, their brothers and sisters from the South. Imagine a soldier from the North and a soldier from the South, in graves side by side. They ask each other: '*Nous sommes morts pour qui? Pour quoi?*' 'We died for who? For what?' They both answer: '*Pour rien.*' 'For nothing.' That's our story."

Nga was upset that her northern friends did not acknowledge that the Vietnam War had been a civil war. She believed that true reconciliation could only come through recognition and acceptance of responsibility, not denial.

"Had you ever visited this cemetery before?" I asked.

"No. I will ask my artists to paint the tombs white," she answered.

A few months after our visit, the local authorities renovated the cemetery in time for the fortieth anniversary of the war. The forest was cleaned up and the gravestones painted white as Nga had imagined.

As we prepared to leave, I heard a car approaching. I started to panic. I thought it was the security police. But Nga had ordered the taxi to follow us inside the cemetery, in case we were detained. As the guard opened the gate, I breathed a sigh of relief. I felt immense fatigue.

"The spirits of the dead are following me," I said.

"You believe that?"

"I don't know if I do, but I feel drained," I replied.

"If they follow you, they are blessing you. They know you are working hard on their behalf."

The following day, Nga and I set off for the drive to the Việt Cộng headquarters at the end of the Trail with her friend, the artist Huỳnh Thị Kim Tiến. Warm and with an easy sense of humor, Huỳnh Thị Kim Tiến had invited us to join her on her first visit back to the military camp that had been her home during the war. She had gone to a school set up for the children of senior Việt Cộng officers. The minibus drove down a dusty track of packed red earth that ran along the Cambodian border through a primeval forest of high-canopy trees. The vast forest, roughly ninety miles from Ho Chi Minh City, had been the domain of the "elusive" Việt Cộng headquarters until 1967.

We entered the forest I had discovered in the drawings. I was overwhelmed by the majesty of the forest. The density of the high trees created a protective umbrella against the planes sent to destroy the camp. I imagined a soldier reading a newspaper in a hammock, a woman sewing a button on a pink shirt, another painting her friend posing with a gun.

The minibus stopped at the site of the reconstructed "Traditional Houses of the Central Office for South Vietnam (COSVN) during the Period against the Americans, 1961–1975." The National Liberation Front of South Vietnam (NLF), or Việt Cộng, was its military arm.

Hồ Chí Minh and the Politburo had launched the Trail in 1959 to support the guerrilla war waged by the women and men who had lived here and who had been their comrades-in-arms during the French War. The mobile "Bamboo Pentagon," targeted by US and South Vietnamese ground and air forces, had moved several times within the forest, and over the border to Trail bases in Cambodia. President Nixon—who ordered the secret 1972 bombing of neutral Cambodia—justified it later to the American people as a necessary military action to destroy the "headquarters of the entire communist military operation in South Vietnam."[76]

We set out on foot with a guide. The forest floor was shaded. There was little undergrowth and it was easy to walk on the path. I gently poked a giant termite mound with a stick, revealing thousands of insects. We reached a jungle lodge. The wood and bamboo structure, the guide explained, was the Việt Cộng equivalent of the Situation Room in the White House, where intelligence meetings were held. The roof was thatched with oblong leaves sewn together and wrapped around the bamboo structure in thick layers, to provide cover against the monsoon rains. Huỳnh Thị Kim Tiến had been silent. The leaves brought back nostalgic memories.

"My job was to collect and dry the leaves for the roofs of the lodges. The selection was important," she said.

She chose a plant from the undergrowth. To the untrained eye, there was nothing that distinguished it from the foliage around it. She picked off a leaf.

"This was the special leaf. Keep it as a memento," she said, handing it to me.

I tucked the precious offering into the pocket of my jacket, to add it to the shrapnel from the *bombi*, the pink sack, cinnamon-scented incense sticks, and other keepsakes I had been offered along the Trail.

She continued:

"I was young when I came here. Thirteen. I missed my grandmother. She looked after me when my mother was sent to jail. My father was killed by the Diệm regime. After, in 1959, my mother was imprisoned [by Diệm] for five years, for political activities. After her release in 1964, she worked for the National Liberation Front in this section of the forest. But I was too young to live with her. The senior officers lived alone without their families. It wasn't suitable for children. I was sent to school in another section of the forest where I studied art. I never saw my mother."

My heart sank for her lost childhood. It must have been hard for mother and daughter to live so close without seeing each other. Outwardly, Huỳnh Thị Kim Tiến bore the wounds of childhood lightly. She expressed her sadness about the past in her art. On a previous visit to her studio, she had shown me her painting of a girl, wounded, forlorn, and alone in a forest of tall trees that sheltered the tombstones of her friends.

We followed the guide to the jungle lodges of the Việt Cộng High Command. The revolutionary women and men had lived in spartan conditions in one-room huts within walking distance of each other. Bound by a common history, they joined Hồ Chí Minh's Indochinese

Huỳnh Thị Kim Tiến, *In the Forest*, oil on canvas, 2000.

Oil lamp at the NLF headquarters.

*"My job was to collect and dry the leaves for the roofs of the lodges."*
Huỳnh Thị Kim Tiến

Reconstructed lodge at the NLF headquarters, Tây Ninh Province.

Communist Party in the thirties, fought the war of independence against the French in the forties and early fifties, and established the NLF in 1961.

We arrived at the bungalow of Võ Văn Kiệt (1922–2008), a senior member of the Central Office for South Vietnam and commander of the forces in Saigon and surrounding areas. The lodge was built from rain-forest materials. The trapezoid roof was made from the dried leaves that Huỳnh Thị Kim Tiến had collected. Inside was a traditional rope bed. A bomb shelter dug under the hut led to escape tunnels. Even crouching, I could barely squeeze into the tunnel that made the Củ Chi tunnels seem spacious. These were the simple fortifications used against the high-tech war waged by the United States and South Vietnamese.

We continued in the silent forest along the path to the jungle lodge of the People's Army officer, sent down the Trail from Hanoi in 1964 to command the NLF. Zigzagging trenches surrounded the dwelling.

"The tunnels and trenches defended us against the Americans. The open escape trenches were built in a zigzag, never in a straight line. Better protection from the planes," said Huỳnh Thị Kim Tiến.

"Did you do the digging yourself?"

I could not imagine the petite artist excavating bagfuls of soil. I was wrong. She was a prizewinning digger and proud of it.

"I dug a trench a day, twenty-foot-long and four-foot-deep. I was small, but strong," she said, laughing.

I strayed off the path to check out the depth of the trench.

"Be careful of snakes. Don't walk in the leaves," said the guide.

I jumped back on the path. The forest was home to a venomous snake that the GIs had nicknamed "two-step" for the distance you could walk after being bitten before you collapsed.

At the next jungle lodge, Nga pointed to a pond filled with stagnant rainwater. A sign next to it read "B-52 bomb crater."

The guide explained:

"It was unlikely the Americans would choose to attack the same place. So they built their houses next to old bomb holes. When the basins filled with rainwater, they were used as fishponds."

We reached the last lodge. It was simply furnished with a bamboo-slatted bed, a desk, and a chair. On the desk were a green Army satchel, a pair of glasses, a watch, a pack of cigarettes, a Toshiba radio-cassette player, and an oil lamp.

We sat at the desk of the senior Việt Cộng officer to cool down. In the early years before the Americans discovered the base, Huỳnh Thị Kim Tiến remembered her life as a teenager in the Việt Cộng camp as pretty "boring:"

"Life in the forest was the same every day. The days were long. We got bored. We never went into town, we stayed in the forest. Our huts were the same as this one. But we lived in dormitories in a communal house. So did the soldiers. The sexes were segregated. Then the American soldiers raided the base in 1967. (The attack, code-named Operation Junction City, was the largest airborne operation since World War II, supported by tank and infantry divisions.) We were temporarily evacuated to Cambodia. That was my scariest time. I had gone to a waterfall to bathe. I took the bus back to base camp. I was walking from the bus stop when I was spotted by a helicopter. As soon as I heard it, I hid under a tree. The helicopter hovered above me for a long time. I was terrified. Luckily, the helicopter didn't spot me and left. During the Tết Offensive, we were ordered to stay at the base and fight. Most of us were trained to use a weapon to protect ourselves. I was bombed. Many of my friends died. But I was too young to understand anything. What I remember most was how much I missed my grandparents and my family."

A few years later, Huỳnh Thị Kim Tiến left the Việt Cộng base on the Trail for Hanoi.

"Why?" I asked.

"I was selected to go to art school in Hanoi in 1971," she answered. "I walked from the South to the North to study at the Hanoi College of Fine Arts. I was sad to leave my friends behind. But my team leader, a musician and songwriter, reassured me that I would see them again. He told me my duty was to study in the North and to return to the South after graduation to liberate the people."

Huỳnh Thị Kim Tiến traveled 900 miles (a twenty-five-hour drive today), on foot and in trucks, through Cambodia and southern Laos, crossing into North Vietnam north of Route 9 and the provisional demarcation line, and on to Hanoi.

"Did you know how tough it was going to be?"

"Older soldiers had told me life was hard during the journey. They were undernourished and sick."

"Were you afraid to go?"

"No, I was in a group. We were in it together. It took us three months to get to Hanoi. I walked through Quảng Bình Province, and up the Trail to the Phong Nha Caves where you were. We walked thirty miles a day. I was lucky. I wasn't bombed. So we could travel during daylight. We woke up at 5 a.m., bathed, had breakfast, cooked rice for lunch, and walked until 1 p.m. After our lunch break, we walked until 4 or 5 p.m. to reach the next station. I did go through forests burned by napalm.

"I didn't draw at all during the journey. I was too tired and I was sick most of the time. My worst memory was when I woke up with malaria. That day, I felt very weak but I kept on walking until I made it to a Trail station. We stayed overnight. When I woke up the next morning, I still felt very ill, but I left with my team. I didn't want to stay at the Trail station on my own. A wounded soldier in my group who was going north helped me and carried my backpack part of the way."

"You should have rested at the clinic," said Nga.

"If I didn't go with my group, I would have had to stay behind, and there were only men there."

I wasn't getting it.

Huỳnh Thị Kim Tiến elaborated:

"I was afraid because I was intact [a virgin]."

At the end of the war, Huỳnh Thị Kim Tiến returned to Saigon, renamed Ho Chi Minh City. She married Quách Phong, another war artist, had children, and worked for the HCMC Fine Arts Association. Part of her family live in the United States.

"My American grandson who lives in Boston asks me: 'Granny, why did you fight against the Americans?'" she said, smiling at the irony of history.

Nga had listened to her friend tell her story. While Huỳnh Thị Kim Tiến studied in the Việt Cộng camp under attack from the US and South Vietnamese Air Forces, Nga was studying in Saigon under attack from Việt Cộng mortar fire. The year Huỳnh Thị Kim Tiến left on the Trail for the Hanoi College of Fine Arts, Nga's husband was shot down over Cambodia near Memot, fifteen miles from where we were. After the war, the women worked together at the Fine Arts Association in HCMC where they became friends and collaborated on art exhibitions.

We walked back through the forest. Our driver was waiting by the minibus. Huỳnh Thị Kim Tiến directed us to a shrine built in memory of her childhood friends. She and her husband, along with other veterans, had funded the memorial. We left the Việt Cộng headquarters, drove past the Cambodian border gate, and continued along a dirt track. The shrine, built in pagoda-style, amidst rice fields, was newly painted in brilliant red, yellow, and gold, and sparkled in the flat, dry plain. Golden Buddha statues stood in the sanctuary filled with light.

The names of her schoolfriends were inscribed on a bronze plaque. Huỳnh Thị Kim Tiến approached the altar with offerings of incense and gifts. Nga followed. I watched with admiration and respect the widow of a South Vietnamese fighter pilot shot down by Việt Cộng artillery presenting oranges, apples, and flowers to those who had fought against her.

When we got back to HCMC that evening, Nga explained:

"When I followed Mrs. Kim Tiến to the altar, I read the names of those who died in the forest and the places where they were born. I was surprised that most of them were born in the South, and that they had sacrificed their lives to liberate the people of the South from what they were told was a life of pain and persecution.

"But after listening to Mrs. Kim Tiến talk about her childhood earlier today, I realized why the young Việt Cộng believed the communist propaganda. They lived in the forest, in the revolutionary zone, and never ventured outside that forest, and every day they were told to hate the American imperialists who had invaded Vietnam, and to free the South Vietnamese from an oppressed and miserable life. They didn't know what was going on in the outside world. When I stood in that place of worship built in commemoration of Mrs. Kim Tiến's school friends, in my heart there was no hatred toward them. I understood they were indoctrinated and died believing in their cause."

The Trail, the military road that had become a pilgrim's way, did not disappoint.

The next day, I made my way back to the HCMC Fine Arts Museum where I had discovered the war drawings that had led me to the Trail. Nguyễn Toàn Thi, the director of the museum at the time who had been a Việt Cộng artist, had assembled the collection.

I walked by Louis Vuitton and Prada stores, along Lê Lợi street, and past the Bến Thành market. I negotiated mopeds and cars swirling around the centerpoint and reached the Blue Space Contemporary Art Center in Lê Thị Hồng Gấm Street. I had spent many hours in Nga's gallery while I was archiving and photographing the museum's collection of war drawings. How quickly the once-present becomes the past.

The grand villa next door that housed the HCMC Fine Arts Museum had been restored to its former glory. As I walked through the majestic entrance, the place was unrecognizable. I almost missed the naked light bulbs and peeling paint that had accompanied the thrill of my discoveries. The dragon-lion that guarded the Trail's mountain shrines was the theme of a temporary exhibition complete with state-of-the art lighting, wall text, and captions, the hallmarks of the packaged culture that graced museums around the world.

I wandered through the galleries but there was no sign of the collection of war drawings. The fragile paper records of the conflict had been stored away. I felt the tiny scar on my elbow.

On a trip to Vietnam a year earlier, I had been riding in heavy midday traffic on the back of Nguyễn Toàn Thi's moped. We were on our way to visit a war artist. His moped skidded and crashed. I fell off the bike onto the road beneath a whirl of mopeds. Nguyễn Toàn Thi cradled my head, keeping it off the tarmac, to protect me. A man, barefoot on the burning tarmac, pulling a wooden cart heavy even for oxen, came over to say he was sorry, that his load had caught the moped by accident, the poverty of a life so hard marked on his face. He was terrified we would report him to the police. Nguyễn Toàn Thi told the man not to worry, that he would do no such thing, and gave him a few *đồng* to comfort him.

"Are you all right?" he asked me.

"Yes," I replied, dazed.

I managed to get up. My head was spinning. But I was unhurt except for a gash on my elbow that would leave a small mark.

"A memento," he said.

Land of mementoes and wandering ghosts, of tragedy and optimism, of despair and resilience.

The following day, as I boarded the plane for my flight back to New York, I felt I was leaving, not going home.

On the Ho Chi Minh Trail, nature had restored what we had destroyed. I held onto the beauty of the white sandy bays, of the swells of the strong sea, and of the misty peaks of the mystical Trường Sơn Mountains.

Trần Trung Tín, *She Couldn't Study*, oil on photographic paper, Saigon 1981.

# *EPILOGUE*

"You must have had to work out some bad karma, to go on that crazy trip we did on the Ho Chi Minh Trail," said Nam, when we met up a few years later.

"I've moved on from war art to peaceful landscapes, if that's what you mean. Something good must have happened," I replied.

While accounts of the Vietnam War have focused on the divisiveness for Americans, I came back from the Trail with a new understanding of the differing perspectives of the opposing sides: through the stories of the women from the North and from the South, their bravery, pragmatism, and ability to forgive after traumatic events that we who live in peaceful times cannot imagine; the memories of the artists who drew them under fire; the tales of those in Laos who lived under the bombs; and the accounts of the American veterans who had the courage to return to Vietnam to "do something," when their own government has done little to redress past wrongs.

I learned that the women in the war drawings played a dominant role in defending their homes and communities against American bombings. The Long-Haired Army in the South, and the Youth Volunteers and women in the Three Responsibilities Campaign in the North were not a historical footnote: they were central to North Vietnam's victory. In protecting the Trail, they were safeguarding their children, their neighborhoods, and their places of work. Their collective war record is testimony to their bravery. The mother too traumatized to breastfeed after picking up body parts following a bombing raid represented for me the woman in North Vietnam who protected home and country, not the vicious communist sniper of US war propaganda.

After the war, these same women encouraged a culture of forgiveness for the foreign enemy that contributed to their resilience and ability to rebuild, move forward, and make Vietnam the success that it is today. Some, like the veteran and film actress Kim Chi, continue the fight for social justice they went to war for with the same courage and fearlessness they showed in their youth.

Their forgiveness is not an absolution, but seeks recognition and a measure of responsibility from the US government who bombed them. I wanted to share the powerful stories of the American veterans who took responsibility where their government didn't—for the harm done through our bombings, for our betrayal of an ally, or for their friends who died in Vietnam. One veteran assisted Vietnamese victims of unexploded ordnance and Agent Orange; another built kindergartens; another brought friendship, and many more have made positive contributions.

I went on the Trail journey because I cared that a government that claims to bring democracy and human rights to the world—and preaches it to others—was partly responsible for two million civilian war dead in Vietnam and hundreds of thousands more in Laos and Cambodia. Fifty years on, the United States hasn't done enough—although the government is cleaning up dioxin hot spots and assisting in clearing live bombs. US denial of responsibility in Vietnam led to similar deceptions in Iraq, Afghanistan, and in today's drone wars.

As we reexamine the dark legacies of colonialism and racism, I would like to see in the United States a museum where children can learn the failings of past American military interventions and explore radical new ways to encourage democracy and human rights; a national memorial to our fallen allies; and a visual commemoration of, if not an investigation into, the number of Vietnamese civilians whose deaths we are responsible for.

I gained an understanding of the bravery of the women in the former South Vietnam in the face of retributions after the war. They provided for their extended families when their husbands, brothers, and sons were killed or missing in action, and when those who returned lost their jobs or were sent to reeducation camps. The war widow who stepped up to the altar of former enemies without hatred came to symbolize for me the women in the South, not the Miss Saigon of popular culture abandoned by her American lover.

It was the art collector Doris Lockhart Saatchi who said that "the kind of art you end up liking is entirely an autobiographical thing ... you go for works that have some kind of personal resonance, some kind of association with your own life."[77]

During the war, there were fighters on both sides who carried out atrocities and massacres. I was drawn to the art created in war for its depiction of the humanity of the majority of young soldiers, both women and men, who faced a reality that civilians cannot understand, in the words of the defender of the Dragon's Jaw Bridge:

"If you don't kill them, they kill you."

This destruction of young people's humanity leads to the post-traumatic stress suffered by my father and so many combatants on so many battlefields. I began to accept and forgive the divisiveness that broke my family, I stopped wanting to change the past—an irrational but obsessive desire—and I started down my own path to compassion and reconciliation.

The stories collected along the Trail, reflecting the many truths, memories, and legacies of the Vietnam War, will I hope bring us a step closer to the realization—in the words of the novelist Herman Wouk (1915–2019) in *War and Remembrance*—that "war is an old habit of thought, an old frame of mind, an old political technique, that must now pass as human sacrifice and human slavery have passed."[78]

The author with General Võ Nguyên Giáp (1911–2013), at his residence in Hanoi, March 31, 2006. General Giáp was the architect of the Indochina and Ho Chi Minh Trails, and of Vietnam's victories against the French and the Americans.

## DOING THE TRAIL

We covered close to 2,000 miles out of the 10,000 miles of Trail roads. We traveled on paved highways, double- and single-lane roads, original Trail gravel tracks, and forded rivers.

Our itinerary followed the way of the North Vietnamese People's Army offensives and the Trail's expansion south from Hanoi to Ho Chi Minh City (HCMC), the former Saigon.

We traveled south from Hanoi to the Phong Nha Caves, and on to Khe Sanh, where we crossed the border into Laos to Xepon. We continued through southeast Laos to Salavan. Going west, we drove across the Bolaven Plateau to the Mekong River, and on to Attapeu. From Attapeu, we traveled to the Vietnamese border and continued on to Kon Tum. From Kon Tum, we journeyed to HCMC and to the mobile headquarters of the Việt Cộng in Tây Ninh Province, on the Cambodian border.

### *PLACE NAMES, SITES, AND ROADS ON GOOGLE MAPS*

While Google Maps recognize most place names without diacritics, including the commune, city, district, and province names will improve your search accuracy.

*Xã* commune
*Thành phố* [*tp*] city
*Huyện* district
*Tỉnh* [*tt*] province

### *SITES*

*Bảo tàng* museum
*Nghĩa trang Liệt sĩ* military cemetery
*Chùa* pagoda (usually Buddhist)
*Đền* shrine, temple
*Nhà Thờ* church
*Khu di tích lịch sử* historic relic

### *ROAD DESIGNATIONS*

AH Asian Highway, road designation added in 2003
*Quốc lộ* [*QL*] route
*Đường tỉnh* [ĐT] provincial road
*Ngã ba* junction
*Đèo* pass
*Cầu* bridge
*Sông* river
*Núi* mountain

## ITINERARY

### CHAPTER 1

I spent a few days in Hanoi getting over jet lag, visiting the Vietnam National Fine Arts Museum, meeting Trail veterans, and welcoming my traveling companions.

Day 4, we left Hanoi for Hòa Bình Province where Trail recruits did their military training before the trek south. We stopped for the night at the Mai Châu Lodge in the scenic Van Village (Tòng Đậu, Mai Châu, Hòa Bình), a three-hour drive (86 miles) from Hanoi.

### *SITES*

The Vietnam National Fine Arts Museum in Hanoi (66 Nguyễn Thái Học, Ba Đình, Hanoi) has a wonderful collection of drawings and paintings that include depictions of the Trail.

The Ho Chi Minh Trail Museum or *Bảo tàng Đường Hồ Chí Minh* (QL6,

Yên Nghĩa, Hà Đông, Hanoi) illustrates the story of the Trail with military maps, war photographs, artifacts, memorabilia, weapons, and an assortment of US bombs.

Mường Studio or *Bảo Tàng Không gian Văn hóa Mường* (Tây Tiến, Hòa Bình) is a heritage and contemporary art site. The complex includes reconstructed royal Mường stilt houses, a museum of Mường artifacts, and installations by contemporary artists.

The Mai Châu Viewpoint or *Chiềng Châu, Mai Châu, Hòa Bình*, an hour and a half (38 miles) from Mường Studio, overlooks a spectacular valley, and marks the beginning of QL15, the mountainous Trail road where the road to war began. There are traditional villages and organized tourist activities in the area.

**CHAPTER 2**

Day 5, we left the Mai Châu Lodge for the coastal city of Thanh Hóa and the Dragon's Jaw Bridge. We traveled on QL15C through the foothills of the Trường Sơn Mountains to the coastal Trail Route QL1A. It's a poetic four-hour drive (102 miles) through bamboo forest, lush jungle, and villages of stilt houses. We stopped in Thanh Hóa to visit the Dragon's Jaw Bridge and a Trail veteran. From there, it's a one-hour drive to Tĩnh Gia (27.5 miles), where we had dinner with Hân's family and spent the night at the Ngọc Linh Villas on the beach.

*SITES*

The Hồ Citadel (Tây Giai, Vĩnh Lộc, Thanh Hóa) is a three-and-a-half-hour drive from the Mai Châu Lodge. The fourteenth-century fortress built of limestone blocks is a UNESCO World Heritage Site.

The Temple of Lady Triệu or *Đền Bà Triệu*, located on QL1A (Triệu Lộc, Hậu Lộc, Thanh Hóa), is dedicated to the woman warrior who led a popular rebellion against the Chinese in the third century AD.

The city of Thanh Hóa is a pleasant coastal town with a notable statue of Lê Lợi, the emperor from Thanh Hóa Province who ended Chinese rule in the fifteenth century. Vietnam War memorials include a Soviet-style victory monument and a Buddhist pagoda dedicated to the mothers of the fallen.

The Dragon's Jaw Bridge or *Cầu Hàm Rồng* over the River Mã was a strategic crossing point. Targeted by US fighter jets in over 800 sorties, it was destroyed in 1972. The bridge was restored in 1973 after the Paris Peace Accords. It was constructed by the French in 1904 following blueprints by Gustave Eiffel, who built the Eiffel Tower in Paris.

The Thanh Hóa Museum in the city has a collection of Đông Sơn bronze drums and other artifacts from the Bronze Age. Đông Sơn Village, close to the Dragon's Jaw Bridge, gave its name to the Bronze Age civilization that stretched across Southeast Asia and southern China.

The coastal town of Tĩnh Gia (Tĩnh Gia District, Thanh Hóa Province), off QL1A, has a pleasant beachfront.

## CHAPTER 3

Day 6, we left Tĩnh Gia at 7:30 a.m. for the 225-mile drive to the Phong Nha Caves (Sơn Trạch, Bố Trạch, Quảng Bình) where we spent two nights at the Saigon Phong Nha Hotel in Sơn Trạch. Trail Route QL15 was built in 1965 to speed up supplies to the South, and to avoid US bombings of the coastal Trail Route QL1A. The drive to the Phong Nha-Kẻ Bàng National Park is meant to be spectacular. Clearly, I am the wrong person to give you advice for this segment of the trip, since we drove the last couple of hours of the route in the dark.

Day 7, we visited the Phong Nha Caves and a Trail veteran who served on the Mụ Giạ Pass.

### *SITES*

In the coastal city of Vinh, we stopped at the Xô Viết Nghệ Tĩnh Museum or *Bảo tàng Xô Viết Nghệ Tĩnh* (Đào Tấn, Cửa Nam, Vinh). The history museum chronicles the communist-led rebellions against French colonial rule that took place in the thirties, and were a forerunner to the French or First Indochina War (1946–1954), Vietnam's war of independence.

A short drive (10 miles) from Vinh is the childhood home of Hồ Chí Minh, Vietnam's independence hero and first president. The Historic Relic and Museum of Kim Liên or *Khu di tích lịch sử Kim Liên* (Kim Liên, Nam Đàn, Nghệ An) includes a Confucian temple dedicated to Hồ Chí Minh, the house where Hồ Chí Minh spent his formative years, and the house of his grandparents.

The Đồng Lộc T-Junction or *Ngã ba Đồng Lộc* (Quốc lộ 15, Đồng Lộc, Can Lộc, Hà Tĩnh) was a Trail station and choke point for the military truck convoys heading for the mountain passes to Laos. The site includes the Tombs of Ten Youth Volunteer Heroines Martyred at the Đồng Lộc T-Junction or *Khu mộ 10 nanh hùng liệt sĩ TNXP hy sinh tại Ngã Ba Đồng Lộc*, a Soviet-style victory monument, and a Buddhist tower pagoda. The Historic Relic and Museum of Đồng Lộc or *Khu di tích lịch sử Ngã ba Đồng Lộc* illustrates the history of the women who served on the Trail.

The Khe Ve Junction or *Ngã ba Khe Ve* (Hóa Thanh, Minh Hóa, Quảng Bình) is at the heart of the Trường Sơn Mountains, 52 miles from the Đồng Lộc T-Junction. The Trail Command moved its Hanoi headquarters here in 1965 to oversee construction of the Mụ Giạ Pass and the expansion of the Trail network into Laos.

From the junction, drive up the Mụ Giạ Pass or *Đèo Mụ Giạ*, the first motorized mountain pass built into Laos that was considered invincible by the US Air Force.

In Sơn Trạch, we took a boat to the entrance of the Phong Nha Caves in the Phong Nha-Kẻ Bàng National Park or *Khu du lịch sinh thái Phong Nha-Kẻ Bàng*, a mile up the Son River. The headquarters of the Trail High Command during the 1972 Spring Offensive were located in this area. The network of over 300 caves and grottoes hid a floating pontoon, and served as an ammunition depot and hospital. Today, the national park is a UNESCO World Heritage Site. The mountains and caves date to the Paleozoic Era, some 400 million years ago. The Sơn Đoòng Cave, discovered in 2009 by British and Vietnamese explorers, is considered the largest cave in the world.

Inscriptions, *lingams*, and altars from the Champa Kingdom have been found in the caves. The ancient Indochinese kingdom lasted from the second to the seventeenth centuries AD and extended over the central and southern regions of Vietnam.

There are many outdoor activities in the area, including hiking, kayaking, canoeing, and ziplines.

**CHAPTERS 4 and 5**

Day 8, we left the Saigon Phong Nha Hotel and drove up Route ĐT20, the way of the 1968 Tết Offensive, to visit a mountain shrine. We traveled on Route QL15 to Khe Sanh, the site of the US Marine Combat Base built to stop infiltration from the Trail. This section of the road was the way of the 1972 Spring Offensive. We arrived at Khe Sanh Village after dark. The journey from the Phong Nha Caves to Khe Sanh (140 miles) took us nine hours, including stopovers. There were no hotels, roadside stands, or food shops.

*SITES*

The Cave of the Eight Youth Volunteers or *Di tích lịch sư Hang 8 Cô TNXP* (ĐT20, Tân Trạch, Bố Trạch, Quảng Bình) is six miles from the Saigon Phong Nha Hotel. Route ĐT20 to the Laotian border was built by Youth Volunteers in 1966 to ease heavy traffic on the Mụ Giạ Pass. It's a two-hour drive to the Laotian border (70 miles). The mountain pass was the main track used by the infantry, artillery, and tank units of the People's Army during the 1968 Tết Offensive.

QL15 leaving the Phong Nha Caves going south to Khe Sanh is a dramatic mountainous Trail road. Stops included a viewpoint overlooking Làng Mô Village (Trường Sơn, Quảng Bình); the Khu Đăng Pass or *Đèo Khu Đăng*, where a sign commemorates the Fortieth Anniversary of Group 559, the engineering corps tasked with building and defending the military supply network; the B-52 bomb site we never found, twelve miles from the pass; and the Sa Mù Pass or *Đèo Sa Mù*, the highest pass on this section of the Trail.

**CHAPTER 6**

Day 9, we drove to Đông Hà in the afternoon to visit Project RENEW, the de-mining center in Quảng Trị Province, and to meet with veterans from the opposing sides. From Khe Sanh, it was a short drive on Route QL9 to Đông Hà and Quảng Trị City, the former sites of US and South Vietnamese combat bases where major battles took place in 1968, 1972, and 1975. We arrived in Đông Hà in the early evening and spent two nights there.

Day 10, we went out with Project RENEW's bomb-disposal teams. In the afternoon, we visited the former DMZ and the Vịnh Mốc Tunnels.

Day 11 in the morning, we met with Trail veterans, saw more military sites, and headed west along Route QL9 to Lao Bảo on the Laotian border. Check the border closing times.

*SITES*

In Khe Sanh, we visited the museum that commemorates the seventy-seven-day siege by the People's Army of the US Marine Combat Base during the 1968 Tết Offensive or *Di tích lịch sử Sân bay Tà Cơn* (Tân Hợp, Hương Hóa, Quảng Trị).

The city of Đông Hà is a good base to see military sites in the former DMZ. In Đông Hà, we visited the Project RENEW Visitor Center that tells the story of UXOs in Quảng Trị Province. Heading north, stop at the Trường Sơn National Martyrs' Cemetery or *Nghĩa trang liệt sĩ Trường Sơn* on QL15 East. Crossing over to QL1A, the Hiền Lương Bridge spans the Bến Hải River that marked the provisional demarcation line between North and South Vietnam after the 1954 Geneva Accords. The History Museum of the Hiền Lương Bridge or *Bảo tàng lịch sử Cầu Hiền Lương* contains war artifacts and photographs.

The Vịnh Mốc Tunnels (Vĩnh Thạch, Vĩnh Linh, Quảng Trị) are a half-hour drive northeast of Đông Hà on QL1A. The underground North Vietnamese military fortress is vast and overlooks the East Sea.

Follow the beautiful coastline back south to the Long Hưng Church or *Nhà thờ Long Hưng* in Quảng Trị City on QL1A that was kept as a war relic.

Visit the Quảng Trị Citadel, the site of the bloodiest battle of the Vietnam War during the 1972 Spring Offensive. The citadel was started during the reign of Emperor Gia Long (1762–1820), the first emperor of the Nguyễn dynasty, and completed in 1837 by his son Emperor Minh Mạng (1792–1841). Gia Long unified what is now modern Vietnam in 1802 and founded the Nguyễn dynasty, the last of the Vietnamese dynasties. The citadel is one of several European-style military fortresses in Vietnam. Almost entirely destroyed during the Vietnam War, it has been recently restored.

Heading west on Route QL9, visit the Martyrs' Cemetery or *Nghĩa trang liệt sỹ đường 9* (Quốc lộ 9, phường 4, Đông Hà, Quảng Trị). From there it's an hour-and-a-half drive to Lao Bảo (Hướng Hóa, Quảng Trị) on the Laotian border. As you enter the town, turn left on Lê Thế Tiết Street to the ruins of the Lao Bảo Prison or *Khu di tích Nhà tù Lao Bảo*, an infamous French colonial jail for political prisoners. QL9 leads straight to the border gates.

**CHAPTER 7**

Day 11 in the afternoon, we crossed the Vietnamese–Laotian border. Formalities took an hour. We drove (78.5 miles) to Xepon, where we spent the night at the Vieng Xai Hotel. Xepon was the Trail Command headquarters during the 1968 Tết Offensive.

*SITES*

The Ban Dong War Museum is situated on 9E in the town of Ban Dong, ten miles from the border. The museum commemorates the joint victory by the People's Army and the communist Laotian forces against the 1971 offensive by South Vietnamese ground forces backed by US air support.

Old Xepon is a hamlet on the banks of the Xepon River, a tributary of the Banghiang River. The town was obliterated during the 1971 Allied offensive against the Laotian Trail. There is a small Buddhist pagoda, a banyan tree, and the ruins of a mysterious bank safe.

Look for the secret headquarters of the Trail Command during the 1968 Tết Offensive dug into a mountainside near Xepon.

**CHAPTER 8**

Day 12, we left Xepon for Salavan on Route 23. The original Trail gravel road was the way of the 1972 Spring Offensive. On the way, we got lost and ended up in Thapangthong. The tracks, bridges, and river crossings were hazardous. We arrived in Salavan twelve hours after leaving Xepon (132 miles) and stopped there for two nights. Estimated driving time has been cut to five hours since the opening of the new bridge over the Banghiang River at Tat Hai in 2018.

Day 13 in Salavan, we went out with the Norwegian People's Aid bomb-disposal team.

**CHAPTER 9**

Day 14, we left Salavan along the northern ridge of the Bolaven Plateau for the city of Pakse on the Mekong River, the westernmost point of the Trail. The People's Army followed this route during the Bolaven Campaigns against the Royal Lao Armed Forces and CIA-led forces headquartered in Pakse. We spent the night at the Mekong Paradise Resort.

Day 15, we took a boat down the Mekong to the River Lodge Hotel near Champasak where we spent two nights.

Day 17, we drove from Champasak to Attapeu (84 miles). We followed Trail Route 16 along the southern ridge of the Bolaven Plateau. We stopped at the Tad Fane and Tad Yuang Falls and stayed the night in the charming town of Attapeu.

*SITES*

The Bolaven Plateau is a spectacular volcanic highland of crags, sinkholes, and waterfalls. We visited the Tad Lo Falls, 20 miles from Salavan. In Laongam, take a local guide to hike to the mountain caves where villagers took refuge from the bombings. Drive to Pakse in time to catch the sunset over the Mekong River.

In Champasak, we caught the monks' early morning Alms Procession. South of the town, we visited the Khmer Temple of Wat Phu. The temple complex over the Mekong was built between the eleventh and thirteenth centuries and is a UNESCO World Heritage Site. It is the northernmost temple of the Khmer Empire that built Angkor Wat in Siem Reap, Cambodia.

Visit Attapeu, a town of golden pagodas, stupas, and war memorials situated between the high ridges of the Bolaven Plateau and the Trường Sơn Mountains.

**CHAPTER 10**

Day 18, we traveled from Attapeu to Kon Tum on a beautiful four-hour drive over the Trường Sơn Mountains to the border with Vietnam, and on to Kon Tum (122 miles). This was the way of the 1972 Offensive against Kon Tum and the Central Highlands. The border crossing at Bờ Y was quick and easy. From the border, it's an hour and forty-five minutes (50 miles) to Kon Tum where we stopped for the night.

Day 19, we set off for Buôn Ma Thuột on QL14, the way of the final 1975 Spring Offensive. After the 1973 Paris Peace Accords, the Trail High Command constructed highways and pipelines right through the Central Highlands of South Vietnam. The five-hour drive (142 miles) was uninspiring after the spectacular landscapes of the Trường Sơn Mountains and Laotian plateaus. There were roadworks and heavy traffic. We spent the night at Emperor Bảo Đại's former hunting lodge overlooking Lắk Lake (Liên Sơn, Lắk, Đắk Lắk).

Day 20, we made our way from Lắk Lake to the scenic town of Dalat, once a French hill station.

Day 21, we took a spectacular but treacherous mountainous road (100 miles) from Dalat to the beautiful beaches of Phan Thiết. The People's Army and National Liberation Front (NLF) forces "liberated" the coastal town shortly after Buôn Ma Thuột. They advanced on Saigon from Buôn Ma Thuột in the north on QL14 (200 miles) and from Phan Thiết in the northeast on QL1A.

Day 24, I left Phan Thiết on QL1A, the way of the 1975 Spring Offensive, and arrived in HCMC in the evening, where I met Nga, my new traveling companion.

*SITES*

Between Attapeu and the border, we took a side trip to Nongphatom Lake, a volcanic lake in the Trường Sơn Mountains. The track off Route 11 was hazardous and the round trip took three hours. The lake was an R&R destination for North Vietnamese soldiers. But Laotians believe the lake is inhabited by a monster and never bathe in it.

In Kon Tum, we visited the Kon Tum Cathedral or *Nhà thờ chính tòa Kon Tum* (Nguyễn Huệ Street, Kon Tum). There is a museum and orphanage attached to the church. From the church, walk to the equally notable Kon Tum Seminary.

In Buôn Ma Thuột, we stopped at the 1975 Victory Monument.

The last emperor's hunting lodge on Lắk Lake is worth a visit. The area is scenic and there are elephant rides across the shallow lake. Elephants were used on the Trail to transport military supplies to the Việt Cộng before the tracks were motorized.

In Dalat, visit the colonial architecture of the town, the landscaped golf course and lake, and the eccentric Crazy House Hotel.

On the peninsula of Phan Thiết, enjoy white sandy beaches and the multicolored sand dunes of Mũi Né.

**CHAPTER 11**

Day 25 in HCMC, we went to the military cemeteries of the opposing sides. The HCMC Martyrs' Cemetery or *Nghĩa trang Liệt sĩ Thành Phố Hồ Chí Minh* and the Bình An People's Cemetery of the South Vietnamese Army or *Nghĩa trang Nhân dân Bình An* are ten miles out of the city center on either side of QL1A. The latter cemetery has been recently renovated.

Day 26, we traveled to the mobile Việt Cộng headquarters on the Cambodian border, three-and-a-half hours (86 miles) from HCMC.

Day 27, I visited the HCMC Fine Arts Museum, whose collection of war drawings had inspired my Trail adventure.

*SITES*

The Central Office for South Vietnam (COSVN) or *Trung ương Cục miền Nam* (Tân Lập, Tân Biên, Tây Ninh) is located in a primeval forest on the Cambodian border. The COSVN directed the NLF in South Vietnam. We visited the reconstructed jungle lodges of NLF senior officers and the network of tunnels. Created in 1961, the southern commanding agency reported to the Politburo in Hanoi. The COSVN moved several times during the war, including over the border to Cambodia.

The HCMC Fine Arts Museum (97A Phó Đức Chính, Phường Nguyễn Thái Bình, Quận 1) is housed in adjacent handsome mansions once owned by a wealthy Vietnamese–Chinese family. The museum has permanent collections of war drawings, paintings, sculptures, and ceramics.

**WHAT YOU WILL NEED**

*BUY A LOCAL SIM CARD FOR YOUR CELL PHONE*

Do not use data roaming unless you want to remortgage your house.

*TRANSPORTATION: BY CAR*

Rent a four-wheel drive with an experienced driver and a reliable GPS. Alternatively, join an organized tour operator specializing in road trips on the Ho Chi Minh Trail.

Expect heavy traffic on Vietnam's highways, challenging conditions on paved mountain roads, and difficult-to-hazardous conditions on unpaved tracks. In Laos, the highways are well maintained and have little traffic. But original Trail tracks, bridges, and river crossings require a qualified off-road driver and a four-wheel vehicle equipped for rough terrains.

*BY MOTORCYCLE*

Travel agents, including Explore Indochina in Hanoi, organize motorcycle tours on the Trail's rough roads.

*ON FOOT*

Read the story of Virginia Morris's incredible voyage on foot before you think about doing the same: *A History of the Ho Chi Minh Trail: The Road to Freedom.*

### *WHEN TO GO*

The dry season between November and March is the best time to go, but it can be cold and foggy in the mountains in the north in December and January. The timing of your trip will depend on your interests, whether they be outdoor activities, museums, and heritage sites, religious and cultural festivals, commemorative war anniversaries, or photography. December and January, for instance, are not optimal for photography in the north of Vietnam.

### *UNEXPLODED BOMBS*

Do not explore anywhere on foot without a local guide.

### *VISAS*

Check visa requirements for both air and overland travel at your local Vietnamese, Laotian, and Cambodian consulates.

### *CURRENCY*

US dollars can be easily exchanged into *đồng*, the Vietnamese currency in Vietnam's major cities, and into *kip*, the Laotian currency, at the Lao Bảo border.

### *LANGUAGE*

Few people speak English once you leave Hanoi. Make sure your driver has good English-language skills. In Laos, hire guides on site who speak the local dialects.

### *ACCOMMODATION*

Hotels were reasonable and plentiful except on the mountain sections of Route QL15 in the north of Vietnam and on Route 23 in Laos. Homestays, by all accounts, are hospitable to travelers. Camping on the Trail's mountainous roads is not organized, but some tour companies include it. Camping solo is not advised due to unexploded ordnance and other hazards common in mountainous tropical terrain around the world.

### *FOOD*

There are many restaurants offering culinary delights. Beer is available. If you want wine, bring your own.

### *EQUIPMENT*

Temperatures between north and south vary sharply in the winter months. Pack warm clothes for the north and tropical-weather clothes for the south. Bring hiking boots to trek the walking trails in the Phong Nha-Kẻ Bàng National Park.

### *HEALTH*

As of November 1, 2020, there were strict travel restrictions due to COVID-19. Vietnam was not allowing entry or issuing visas to foreign nationals, except for those traveling for official or diplomatic purposes. The country reported one of the world's lowest COVID-19 infection rates and only 35 deaths due to the virus.

When travel resumes, check your insurance for medical coverage—including for COVID-19 and possible emergency medical evacuations—in Vietnam and Laos.

## INTERVIEWS AND NOTES

### *INTERVIEWS*

The author conducted interviews between November 2014 and January 2015 during her journey down the Trail, and updated them in 2020. Interviews from visits to Vietnam before 2014 have also been included. Alphabetical listings are accompanied by a short biography, followed by the place and date of the interview.

Lieutenant Colonel Bùi Trọng Hồng. National Technical Officer, UXO Survey and Clearance Program, Project RENEW. Đông Hà, December 16, 2014.

Đặng Xuân Khu. Veteran who served with the People's Army. Ban Dong, December 18, 2014.

Deacon of the Catholic church near Paksong, Laos. Paksong, December 21, 2014.

Hân Mai's parents-in-law. Veterans who served with the Youth Volunteer Corps (TNXP) and the People's Army. Tĩnh Gia, December 10, 2014.

Hoàng Thị Mai. Veteran who served with the Youth Volunteer Corps. Đông Hà, December 17, 2014.

Huỳnh Phương Đông (1925–2015). Artist, Deputy Director of the Fine Arts Department of the Ministry of Culture and Information (1977–1988), and veteran of the National Liberation Front (NLF). Ho Chi Minh City (HCMC), January 3, 2015.

Huỳnh Thị Kim Tiến. Artist and graduate of the Hanoi College of Fine Arts who attended high school at NLF headquarters (1964–1971) in Tây Ninh Province in the former South Vietnam. HCMC, January 9, 2015.

Mr. Keun. Rice farmer wounded by a *bombi*. Salavan, December 21, 2014.

Kim Chi. Film actress and veteran who served with the NLF in the former South Vietnam. Hanoi, December 6, 2014.

Judd Kinne. Veteran who served as 1st Platoon Commander, Kilo Company, 3rd Battalion 1st Marines (1967–1969), investment banker, and former Executive Vice President of KimEng Holdings. Singapore, November 30, 2014.

Colonel Lê Kim Thơ. Veteran who served with the People's Army. Đông Hà, December 16, 2014.

Lê Lam. Artist and veteran who served with the NLF in the former South Vietnam. HCMC, January 17, 2002.

Lê Quang Luân. Artist and veteran who served with the People's Army in an anti-air defense unit. HCMC, January 6, 2015.

Lương Xuân Đoàn. Artist, President of the Vietnam Fine Arts Association, and veteran who served with the People's Army. Hanoi, December 7, 2014.

Lieutenant Colonel Ngô Thị Tuyển. Veteran who served with the Youth Volunteer Corps, and Heroine of the People's Armed Forces. Thanh Hóa, December 10, 2014.

Ngô Thiện Khiết (1971–2016). Team Leader, UXO Survey and Clearance Program, Project RENEW. Đông Hà, December 17, 2014.

Ngô Xuân Hiền. Communications and Development Manager, Project RENEW. Đông Hà, December 17, 2014.

Nguyễn Thanh Bình. Artist and veteran who served with the 304th Division (Đoàn 304), Division 10, 3rd Corps, the People's Army (1972–1978). HCMC, January 5, 2015.

Nguyễn Thị Kim Huế. Veteran who served as a platoon leader with the Youth Volunteer Corps (1966–1967), and Heroine of the People's Armed Forces. Route 12A, December 12, 2014.

Nguyễn Thị Nguyệt. Veteran who served with the Youth Volunteer Corps, and former Deputy Head of Đông Hà's Women's Union. Đông Hà, December 17, 2014.

Nguyễn Toàn Thi (1946–2016). Artist, Director of the HCMC Fine Arts Museum, and veteran who served with the NLF in the former South Vietnam. HCMC, January 3, 2015.

Nguyễn Văn Hồ. Coffee plantation owner. Near Paksong, December 21, 2014.

Nguyễn Văn Hoàng. Artist, former Director of the HCMC Fine Arts University (1992–2004), and veteran who served with the NLF in the former South Vietnam. HCMC, January 5, 2015.

Nguyễn Văn Trúc. Artist and veteran who served with the NLF in the former South Vietnam. HCMC, January 17, 2002.

Nguyễn Viết Minh. Deputy Director of the Tà Cơn Airstrip Relic. Khe Sanh, December 14, 2014.

Mr. Noukone. Interpreter for the Norwegian People's Aid (NPA) in Salavan, Laos. Salavan and Laongam, December 21, 2014.

Colonel Phạm Thanh Tâm (1933–2019). Artist, author, and veteran of the French and American Wars who served with the People's Army. HCMC, interviews between 2002 and 2019.

Phạm Thị Kim Oanh. Veteran who served with the Youth Volunteer Corps as Senior Sergeant, Head of the Communication Unit, Brigade 559 Command. Đông Hà, December 17, 2014.

Phan Cẩm Thượng. Artist, scholar, author, and former professor of the Hanoi College of Fine Arts. Hòa Bình, December 9, 2014.

Phan Hoài Phi. Artist and veteran who served with the People's Army. HCMC, January 5, 2015.

Bob Phongsavai. Director of the NPA, Salavan, Laos. Salavan, December 20, 2014.

Phùng Chí Thu. Sculptor and broadcaster for Radio Hanoi during the Vietnam War (1966–1973). HCMC, January 13, 2015.

Quách Phong. Artist, former General Secretary of the Fine Arts Association in HCMC, and veteran who served with the NLF in the former South Vietnam. HCMC, January 9, 2015.

Chuck Searcy. Veteran who served with the 519th Military Intelligence Battalion, US Army (1967–1968). He is co-founder of Project RENEW in Quảng Trị Province, co-chair of the Agent Orange Working Group, Vietnam, and co-founder of Chapter 160 of Veterans For Peace. Đông Hà, December 15, 2014.

Don Stille. Engineer and veteran who served as ground radio operator with the US Air Force (1967–1968). Kon Tum, December 27, 2014.

Trần Huy Oánh. Artist, Deputy General Secretary of the Vietnam

Fine Arts Association, Vice Rector of the Hanoi College of Fine Arts, and veteran who served in Cambodia. Hanoi, December 8, 2014.

Trần Trung Tín (1933–2008). Artist and veteran who served with the Việt Minh in Cambodia during the French War (1946–1954). HCMC, interviews between 1995 and 2008.

Mr. Vannaseng. Veteran who served with the People's Army in Laos. Near Xepon, December 18, 2014.

General Võ Nguyên Giáp (1911–2013). Commander-in-Chief of the People's Army during the French and American Wars, Minister of Defense (1948–1980), and the recipient of numerous military awards, including Hero of the People's Armed Forces. Hanoi, March 31, 2006.

Vũ Đức Hiếu. Artist, ceramist, and founder of Mường Studio. Hòa Bình, December 9, 2014.

## *NOTES*

### A BRIEF HISTORY OF THE TRAILS, 1946–1975

1. Michael Clodfelter, *Vietnam in Military Statistics: A History of the Indochina Wars, 1772–1991* (Jefferson, NC: McFarland, 1995), 225: "By the time the United States ended its Southeast Asian bombing campaigns, the total tonnage of ordnance dropped approximately tripled the totals for World War II. The Indochinese bombings amounted to 7,662,000 tons of explosives, compared to 2,150,000 tons in the world conflict."
   Spencer C. Tucker, *Encyclopedia of the Vietnam War* (Oxford University Press, 2011), 48: "By the end of the conflict, seven million tons of bombs had been dropped on the Democratic Republic of Vietnam (North Vietnam), South Vietnam, Laos, and Cambodia."
   James P. Harrison, "History's Heaviest Bombing," in Mark Bradley, Jayne Susan Werner, and Luu Doan Huynh, eds., *The Vietnam War: Vietnamese and American Perspectives* (Armonk, NY: M.E. Sharpe, 1993), 131–32: "... from 1961 to 1972, American aircraft dropped approximately one million tons of bombs on North Vietnam, and much more on rural areas of South Vietnam—approximately four million tons of bombs, four hundred thousand tons of napalm, and nineteen million gallons of herbicides."
2. United Nations Archives, "Article 14, *Agreement on the Cessation of Hostilities in Vietnam,* July 20, 1954," S-0901-0001-01-00001, 755, https://search.archives.un.org/uploads/r/united-nations-archives/b/b/2/.pdf
3. Christian G. Appy, University of Chicago Press Peer Review, August 5, 2019.
4. "Resolution of the 15th Central Conference [of the Vietnamese Communist Party] on strengthening solidarity, resolutely struggling to maintain peace, to implement national unity, January 12–22, 1959," *Vietnam Communist Party Online Newspaper (Báo Điện Tử Đảng Cộng Sản Viet Nam),*

October 11, 2020, http://tulieuvankien.dangcongsan.vn/van-kien-tu-lieu-ve-dang/hoi-nghi-bch-trung-uong/khoa-ii/nghi-quyet-hoi-nghi-trung-uong-lan-thu-15-mo-rong-ve-tang-cuong-doan-ket-kien-quyet-dau-tranh-giu-vung-hoa-binh-thuc-805

5. Nguyễn Bắc Sơn, Vũ Tiến Lộc, Nguyễn Duy Hùng, and Nguyễn Thế Kỷ, eds., *Trường Sơn Road Aspirations (Trường Sơn Đường khát vọng)* (Hanoi: National Political Publishing House, 2009), 2–3, http://www.nxbctqg.org.vn/trng-sn-ng-khat-vng.html
6. US Congress, *Joint resolution to promote the maintenance of international peace and security in Southeast Asia,* Public Law 88–408, *US Statutes at Large* 78 (August 10, 1964): 384, https://www.govinfo.gov/content/pkg/STATUTE-78/pdf/STATUTE-78-Pg384.pdf
7. Errol Morris, *The Fog of War: Eleven Lessons from the Life of Robert S. McNamara,* directed by Errol Morris and starring Robert McNamara (Cannes: Sony Picture Classics), May 21, 2003.
8. Lieutenant Commander Pat Patterson, "The Truth about Tonkin," *Naval History Magazine,* Volume 22, Number 1, February 2008, https://www.usni.org/magazines/naval-history-magazine/2008/february/truth-about-tonkin
Adam Wernick, "What really happened in the Gulf of Tonkin in 1964?" LBJ's War, *The World,* PRI.org, September 14, 2017, para 16, https://www.pri.org/stories/2017-09-14/what-really-happened-gulf-tonkin-1964
9. Lê Duẩn, "Speech Given to the 12th Plenum of the Party Central Committee," *The Vietnamese Communist Party Documents (Văn Kiện Đảng Toàn Tập Đảng Cộng Sản Việt Nam),* Vol. 26, 1965, ed. Phạm Thị Vịnh, trans. Merle Pribbenow for CWIHP (Hanoi: National Political Publishing House, 2003), http://digitalarchive.wilsoncenter.org/document/113970
10. Lyndon B. Johnson, "The President's Address to the Nation Announcing Steps to Limit the War in Vietnam and Reporting His Decision Not to Seek Reelection," March 31, 1968, LBJ Presidential Library, October 11, 2020, http://www.lbjlibrary.org/exhibits/announcing-steps-to-limit-the-war-in-vietnam
11. General Võ Nguyên Giáp, *Điện Biên Phủ: Rendez-vous with History* (Hanoi: Thế Giới, 2004), 459.
12. Agence France-Presse (AFP), "Hanoi gives official count of three million dead in Vietnam War," April 4, 1995, para 2: "more than one million North Vietnamese and Việt Cộng soldiers ... were killed between 1954 and 1975," www.afp.com/
13. Jeffrey J. Clarke, *Advice and Support: The Final Years, 1965–1973 (United States Army in Vietnam)*(Washington, DC: Center of Military History, United States Army, 1988), 275.
14. *Vietnam War US Military Fatal Casualty Statistics,* National Archives, October 11, 2020, https://www.archives.gov/

research/military/vietnam-war/casualty-statistics

15. Agence France-Presse (AFP), "Hanoi gives official count of three million dead in Vietnam War," April 4, 1995, para 2, www.afp.com/
Ronald H. Spector, "Vietnam War," *Encyclopaedia Britannica,* September 10, 2020, para 3: "Not until 1995 did Vietnam release its official estimate of war dead: as many as two million civilians on both sides." https://www.britannica.com/event/Vietnam-War

**CHAPTER 1**

16. Nguyễn Bắc Sơn, Vũ Tiến Lộc, Nguyễn Duy Hùng, and Nguyễn Thế Kỷ, eds., *Trường Sơn Road Aspirations (Trường Sơn Đường khát vọng)* (Hanoi: National Political Publishing House, 2009), 2–3, http://www.nxbctqg.org.vn/trng-sn-ng-khat-vng.html
17. "There is a Road that Bears the Name of Uncle Hồ: The Ho Chi Minh Trail Crosses Trường Sơn," April 7, 2016, Document Publication Online, National Archives Center II, last para, http://luutruvn.com/index.php/2016/04/07/there-is-a-road-bearing-the-name-of-uncle-ho-the-ho-chi-minh-trail-crosses-truong-son/

**CHAPTER 2**

18. Lt. General Đồng Sĩ Nguyên, *The Trans-Trường Sơn Route: A Memoir (Đường xuyên Trường Sơn)* (Hanoi: Thế Giới, 2005), chap. 1.
19. Hồ Chí Minh, "Appeal Made on the Founding of the Indochinese Communist Party, 1930," *Selected Works* (New York: Prism Key Press, 2011), 83.
20. Hồ Chí Minh, "Annamese Women and French Domination, 1922," *ibid.*, 19–20.
21. Walter J. Boyne, "Breaking the Dragon's Jaw," *Air Force Magazine,* August 1, 2011, https://www.airforcemag.com/article/0811jaw/
22. Gary W. Foster, *Phantom in the River: The Flight of Linfield Two Zero One* (Ashland, Oregon: Hellgate Press, 2010), 193.

**CHAPTER 3**

23. Lt. General Đồng Sĩ Nguyên, *The Trans-Trường Sơn Route: A Memoir,* chap. 2.
24. Lt. General Đồng Sĩ Nguyên, *ibid.*, chap 2.
25. William J. Duiker, *Ho Chi Minh: A Life* (New York: Hyperion, 2001), 15–22.
26. Hồ Chí Minh, "The Path Which Led Me To Leninism, 1960," *Selected Works*, 141.
27. Hồ Chí Minh, "Appeal Made on the Founding of the Indochinese Communist Party, 1930," *ibid.*, 83.
28. Hồ Chí Minh, "Letter from Hồ Chí Minh to President Harry S. Truman," January 18, 1946, Indochina 1946; General Records, 1946–1948; Records of the Foreign Service Posts of the Department of State, Record Group 84; National Archives at College Park, College Park, MD, October 11, 2020, https://catalog.archives.gov/id/28469393
----. "Telegram from Hồ Chí Minh

to President Harry S. Truman," February 28, 1946, Washington and Pacific Coast Field Station Files, 1942–1945; Records of the Office of Strategic Services, Record Group 226; National Archives at College Park, College Park, MD, October 11, 2020, https://catalog.archives.gov/id/305263

29. Duy Cường, "Uncle Hồ's Joy to Visit His Home Twice," *Saigon Giai Phong Online*, May 19, 2009, paras 7–8, http://www.sggp.org.vn/nhung-chuyen-cam-dong-trong-hai-lan-bac-ve-tham-que-224261.html
30. Nam Giang, "Promoting the Cultural Value of the National Monument at the Đồng Lộc T-Junction," *Báo Hà Tĩnh Online*, July 18, 2014, paras 2–3, https://baohatinh.vn/khac/phat-huy-gia-tri-van-hoa-di-tich-quoc-gia-dac-biet-nga-ba-dong-loc/83790.htm
31. François Guillemot, "Death and Suffering at First Hand: Youth Shock Brigades During the Vietnam War, 1950–1975," *Journal of Vietnamese Studies*, Vol. 4, no. 3, Fall 2009, 36, https://www.jstor.org/stable/10.1525/
32. Jacob Van Staaveren, *Interdiction in Southern Laos, 1960–1968* (Washington, DC: Center for Air Force History, 1993), 136.
33. Trương Như Tảng, *A Vietcong Memoir* (London: Vintage Books, 1986), 167.
34. John Prados, *The Blood Road: The Ho Chi Minh Trail and the Vietnam War* (New York: John Wiley and Sons, 2000), 313.

**CHAPTER 4**

35. Lt. General Đồng Sĩ Nguyên, *The Trans-Trường Sơn Route: A Memoir*, chap. 3.
36. Xuân Đinh, "One Man Who Opened the Blood Road," *cadn.com.vn (Police News Online)*, April 22, 2011, http://cadn.com.vn/news/64_6796_gap-nguoi-mo-con-duong-mau-.aspx

**CHAPTER 5**

37. Đặng Tài and Ngô Long, "Route 20, The Legendary Way: Determined to Win!" *Báo Dân Trí Online*, August 10, 2015, para 3, http://dantri.com.vn/chinh-tri/duong-20-quyet-thang-con-duong-huyen-thoai-2015081010364844.htm
38. Yên Khương, "Poet Lâm Thị Mỹ Dạ: Real Life is Like a Legend," *Báo Gia đình Online*, October 13, 2009, paras 6 and 7, http://giadinh.net.vn/giai-tri/nha-tho-lam-thi-my-da-cuoc-doi-that-ma-nhu-huyen-thoai-2009101204077441.htm
39. Lâm Thị Mĩ Dạ, *Green Rice: Poems*, trans. Martha Collins and Thúy Đinh (Willimantic CT: Curbstone Press, 2005), 9.
40. Lt. General Đồng Sĩ Nguyên, *The Trans-Trường Sơn Route: A Memoir*, chap. 3.
41. Huỳnh Phương Đông, "Poem to My Wife, 1963," in Sherry Buchanan, *Mekong Diaries: Viet Cong Drawings & Stories 1964–1975* (Chicago: University of Chicago Press, 2008), 180.
42. Sol Sanders, email to the author, March 10, 2016.
43. PSYOP (Psychological Operations), *Operation Wandering Soul (Vietnam War "Ghost Tape" Campaign)*,

audiotape, https://www.youtube.com/watch?v=1ZjZkdkv_is

44. Anthony J. Tambini, *Wiring Vietnam: The Electronic Wall* (Lanham, Maryland: Rowman & Littlefield, 2007), xii and 11.

**CHAPTER 6**

45. Lt. General Đồng Sĩ Nguyên, *The Trans-Trường Sơn Route: A Memoir*, chap. 3.
46. Peter Brush, "Recounting the Casualties at the Deadly Battle of Khe Sanh," *Vietnam Magazine,* June 2007, para 7, https://www.historynet.com/recounting-the-casualties-at-the-deadly-battle-of-khe-sanh.htm
47. Spencer C. Tucker, *Encyclopedia of the Vietnam War*, 1104.
48. David Douglas Duncan, *I Protest!* (New York: The New American Library, 1968), Preface.
49. Chi Phan, "Eighty-One Fierce Days and Nights in the Ancient Quảng Trị Citadel in 1972," *The People's Army Newspaper Online,* July 9, 2012, para 6, https://en.qdnd.vn/military/war-files/81-fierce-days-and-nights-in-quang-tri-ancient-citadel-in-1972-part-1-431967
50. Craig R. Whitney, "Quảng Trị in Ruins after Battles," *The New York Times,* October 8, 1972, https://www.nytimes.com/1972/10/08/archives/quangtri-in-ruins-after-battles-quangtri-city-after-battles-is.html
51. Jonathan Schell, *The Military Half: An Account of Destruction in Quang Nai and Quang Tin* (New York: Alfred A. Knopf, 1968), 20.
52. Christian G. Appy, *American Reckoning: The Vietnam War and Our National Identity* (New York: Penguin Books USA, 2015), 167.
53. Agence France-Presse (AFP), "Hanoi gives official count of three million dead in Vietnam War," April 4, 1995, para 2, www.afp.com/
54. Spencer C. Tucker, *Encyclopedia of the Vietnam War*, 176.
55. Nick Turse, *Kill Anything That Moves: The Real American War in Vietnam* (New York: Henry Holt and Company, 2013); "Anything That Moves," *Author Interviews*, National Public Radio (NPR), January 28, 2013, para 2, https://www.npr.org/2013/01/28/169076259/anything-that-moves-civilians-and-the-vietnam-war
56. Benjamin A. Valentino, *Final Solutions: Mass Killing and Genocide in the 20th Century* (Ithaca, NY: Cornell University Press, 2005), 84 and 88.

**CHAPTER 7**

57. Lt. General Đồng Sĩ Nguyên, *The Trans-Trường Sơn Route: A Memoir*, chap. 3.
58. General Soutchay Vongsavanh, *RLG Military Operations and Activities in the Laotian Panhandle* (Washington DC: US Army Center of Military History, 1981), 9.

**CHAPTER 8**

59. Lt. General Đồng Sĩ Nguyên, *The Trans-Trường Sơn Route: A Memoir,* chap. 4.
60. Lt. General Đồng Sĩ Nguyên, *ibid.,* chap. 4.
61. Nguyễn Bắc Sơn, Vũ Tiến Lộc, Nguyễn Duy Hùng, and Nguyễn

Thế Kỷ, eds., *Trường Sơn Road Aspirations*, chap. 1.

62. General Soutchay Vongsavanh, *RLG Military Operations and Activities in the Laotian Panhandle*, 91.
63. Hồ Chí Minh, "Letter from Nguyễn Ái Quốc to US Secretary of State Robert Lansing," June 18, 1919, General Records, 1918–1931; Records of the American Commission to Negotiate Peace, Record Group 256; National Archives at College Park, College Park, MD, October 11, 2020, https://catalog.archives.gov/id/5049414

----. "Letter from Hồ Chí Minh to President Harry S. Truman," January 18, 1946, National Archives, https://catalog.archives.gov/id/28469393

----. "Telegram from Hồ Chí Minh to President Harry S. Truman," February 28, 1946, National Archives, https://catalog.archives.gov/id/305263

## CHAPTER 9

64. General Soutchay Vongsavanh, *RLG Military Operations and Activities in the Laotian Panhandle*, 59–60 and 67.
65. Theap Vongpakay, "The Storm of Life," *Celebrating Humanity Through Words*, The Southeast Asian Writers' Awards 25th Anniversary, 2003–2004, https://thaiwais.wordpress.com/tw76/
66. Lt. General Đồng Sĩ Nguyên, *The Trans-Trường Sơn Route: A Memoir*, chap. 5.

## CHAPTER 10

67. Lt. General Đồng Sĩ Nguyên, *ibid.*, chap. 6.
68. Spencer C. Tucker, *Encyclopedia of the Vietnam War*, 1304; Jeffrey J. Clarke, *United States Army in Vietnam: Advice and Support*, 275; "Vietnam War US Military Fatal Casualty Statistics," National Archives, https://www.archives.gov/research/military/vietnam-war/casualty-statistics#date
69. Thomas P. McKenna, *Kon Tum: The Battle to Save South Vietnam* (Lexington: University Press of Kentucky, 2015), 192.
70. "Major Describes Move," *New York Times Archive*, February 8, 1968, 14, https://www.nytimes.com/1968/02/08/archives/major-describes-move.html
71. Lt. General Đồng Sĩ Nguyên, *The Trans-Trường Sơn Route: A Memoir*, chap. 6.
72. Lt. General Đồng Sĩ Nguyên, *ibid.*, chap. 6.
73. Spencer C. Tucker, *Encyclopedia of the Vietnam War*, 770.

## CHAPTER 11

74. Gerald R. Ford, "Vietnam: A Television History; End of the Tunnel (1973–1975)," Interview with Gerald R. Ford, April 29, 1982, WGBH Media Library & Archives, http://openvault.wgbh.org/catalog/V_28856C3736014745B1A911AB8B69F4C0
75. Lt. General Đồng Sĩ Nguyên, *The Trans-Trường Sơn Route: A Memoir*, chap. 6.
76. Richard M. Nixon, "Address to the Nation on the Situation in

Southeast Asia," April 30, 1970, The American Presidency Project, Gerhard Peters and John T. Woolley, https://www.presidency.ucsb.edu/node/239701

77. Charles Darwent, "Pieces from a Confessional," *The Independent*, October 18, 1998, https://www.independent.co.uk/arts-entertainment/pieces-from-a-confessional-1179187.html
78. Herman Wouk, *War and Remembrance* (Boston: Little Brown, and Company, 1978), Preface to the First Edition.

## BIBLIOGRAPHY

*READINGS AND REFERENCES*

Agence France-Presse (AFP). "Hanoi gives official count of three million dead in Vietnam War." April 4, 1995. www.afp.com/

Anderson, David L. and John Ernst, eds. *The War That Never Ends: New Perspectives on the Vietnam War.* University Press of Kentucky, 2007.

Appy, Christian G. *American Reckoning: The Vietnam War and Our National Identity.* New York: Penguin Books USA, 2015.

----. *Patriots: The Vietnam War Remembered by All Sides.* New York: Penguin Books USA, 2003.

Arnett, Peter. "Major Describes Move." *New York Times,* February 8, 1968. https://www.nytimes.com/1968/02/08/archives/major-describes-move.html

Boyne, Walter J. "Breaking the Dragon's Jaw." *Air Force Magazine,* August 1, 2011. https://www.airforcemag.com/article/0811jaw/

Bradley, Mark, Jayne Susan Werner, and Luu Doan Huynh, eds. *The Vietnam War: Vietnamese and American Perspectives.* Armonk, NY: M. E. Sharpe, 1993.

Brush, Peter. "Recounting the Casualties at the Deadly Battle of Khe Sanh." *Vietnam Magazine,* June 2007. https://www.historynet.com/recounting-the-casualties-at-the-deadly-battle-of-khe-sanh.htm

----. "The Withdrawal from Khe Sanh." *Vietnam Magazine,* June 2006. https://www.historynet.com/the-withdrawal-from-khe-sanh.htm

Buchanan, Sherry. *Mekong Diaries: Việt Cộng Drawings & Stories 1964–1975.* Chicago: University of Chicago Press, 2008.

----. *Trần Trung Tín: Paintings and Poems from Vietnam.* London: Asia Ink, 2002.

Cao Văn Viên (General). *The Final Collapse.* Washington, DC: United States Army Center of Military History, 1985.

Clarke, Jeffrey J. *Advice and Support: The Final Years, 1965–1973. (United States Army in Vietnam).* Washington, DC: Center of Military History, United States Army, 1988.

Clodfelter, Michael. *Vietnam in Military Statistics: A History of the Indochina Wars, 1772–1991.* Jefferson, NC: McFarland, 1995.

Đặng Tài and Ngô Long. "Route 20: The Legendary Road: Determined to Win!" *Báo Dân Trí Online,* August 10, 2015. http://dantri.com.vn/chinh-tri/duong-20-quyet-thang-con-duong-huyen-thoai-2015081010364844.htm

Darwent, Charles. "Pieces from a Confessional." *The Independent,* October 18, 1998. www.independent.

co.uk/arts-entertainment/pieces-from-a-confessional-1179187.html

Defense POW/MIA Accounting Agency, "Vietnam War POW/MIA List." August 2, 2020. https://www.dpaa.mil/Our-Missing/Vietnam-War/Vietnam-War-POW-MIA-List/

Đồng Sĩ Nguyên (Lt. General). *The Trans-Trường Sơn Route: A Memoir (Đường xuyên Trường Sơn).* Hanoi: Thế Giới, 2005.

Duiker, William J. *Ho Chi Minh: A Life.* New York: Hyperion, 2001.

Duncan, David Douglas. *I Protest!* New York: The New American Library, 1968.

Duy Cường. "Uncle Hồ's Joy to Visit His Home Twice." *SGGP Saigon Giai Phong Online,* May 19, 2009. http://www.sggp.org.vn/nhung-chuyen-cam-dong-trong-hai-lan-bac-ve-tham-que-224261.html

Ford, Gerald R. "Vietnam: A Television History; End of the Tunnel (1973–1975)." Interview with Gerald R. Ford, April 29, 1982, WGBH Media Library & Archives. http://openvault.wgbh.org/catalog/V_28856C3736014745B1A911AB8B69F4C0

Foster, Gary W. *Phantom in the River: The Flight of Linfield Two Zero One.* Ashland, Oregon: Hellgate Press, 2010.

Guillemot, François. "Death and Suffering at First Hand: Youth Shock Brigades During the Vietnam War (1950–1975)." *Journal of Vietnamese Studies,* Vol. 4, No.3, Fall 2009, 17–60. https://www.jstor.org/stable/10.1525/

Hồ Chí Minh. *The Selected Works.* New York: Prism Key Press, 2011.

––––. "Letter from Nguyễn Ái Quốc (Hồ Chí Minh) *to US Secretary of State Robert Lansing.*" June 18, 1919. General Records, 1918–1931; Records of the American Commission to Negotiate Peace, Record Group 256; National Archives at College Park, College Park, MD. https://catalog.archives.gov/id/5049414

––––. "Letter from Hồ Chí Minh to President Harry S. Truman." January 18, 1946. Indochina 1946; General Records, 1946–1948; Records of the Foreign Service Posts of the Department of State, Record Group 84; National Archives at College Park, College Park, MD. https://catalog.archives.gov/id/28469393

––––. "Telegram from Hồ Chí Minh to President Harry S. Truman." February 28, 1946. Washington and Pacific Coast Field Station Files, 1942–1945; Records of the Office of Strategic Services, Record Group 226; National Archives at College Park, College Park, MD. https://catalog.archives.gov/id/305263

Johnson, Lyndon B. "The President's Address to the Nation Announcing Steps to Limit the War in Vietnam and Reporting His Decision Not to Seek Reelection." March 31, 1968. LBJ Presidential Library. http://www.lbjlibrary.org/exhibits/announcing-steps-to-limit-the-war-in-vietnam

Lâm Thị Mỹ Dạ. *Green Rice: Poems.* Translated by Martha Collins and Thúy Đinh. Willimantic CT: Curbstone Press, 2005.

Lê Duẩn. "Speech Given to the 12th Plenum of the Party Central Committee." *The Vietnamese Communist Party Documents (Văn Kiện Đảng Toàn Tập Đảng Cộng Sản*

*Việt Nam*), Vol. 26, 1965, edited by Phạm Thị Vịnh and translated for CWIHP by Merle Pribbenow. Hanoi: National Political Publishing House, 2003. http://digitalarchive.wilsoncenter.org/document/113970

McKenna, Thomas P. *Kon Tum: The Battle to Save South Vietnam*. Lexington: University Press of Kentucky, 2015.

Morris, Virginia and Clive A. Hills. *A History of the Ho Chi Minh Trail: The Road to Freedom*. Bangkok: Orchid Press, 2006.

Nam Giang. "Promoting the Cultural Value of the National Monument at the Đồng Lộc T-Junction." *Báo Hà Tĩnh Online*, July 18, 2014. https://baohatinh.vn/khac/phat-huy-gia-tri-van-hoa-di-tich-quoc-gia-dac-biet-nga-ba-dong-loc/83790.htm

National Archives Center II. "There is a Road that Bears the Name of Uncle Hồ: The Ho Chi Minh Trail Crosses Trường Sơn." *Document Publication Online*, Hanoi, April 7, 2016. http://luutruvn.com/index.php/2016/04/07/there-is-a-road-bearing-the-name-of-uncle-ho-the-ho-chi-minh-trail-crosses-truong-son/

Nguyễn Bắc Sơn, Vũ Tiến Lộc, Nguyễn Duy Hùng, and Nguyễn Thế Kỷ, eds. *Trường Sơn Road Aspirations (Trường Sơn Đường khát vọng)*. Hanoi: National Political Publishing House, 2009. http://www.nxbctqg.org.vn/trng-sn-ng-khat-vng.html

Nixon, Richard M. "Address to the Nation on the Situation in Southeast Asia." April 30, 1970. The American Presidency Project. Gerhard Peters and John T. Woolley. https://www.presidency.ucsb.edu/node/239701

Patterson, Pat (Lt. Commander). "The Truth about Tonkin." *Naval History Magazine*, Volume 22, Number 1, February 2008. https://www.usni.org/magazines/naval-history-magazine/2008/february/truth-about-tonkin

Phạm Thanh Tâm, *Drawing Under Fire: War diary of a young Vietnamese artist*. Edited by Sherry Buchanan. London: Asia Ink, 2005.

Phan Cẩm Thượng. *Tô Ngọc Vân: Tấm Gương Phản Chiếu Xã Hội Việt Nam 1906–1954 (Tô Ngọc Vân: Reflections of Vietnam 1906–1954).* Hanoi: Nhà xuất bản Tri thức (Knowledge Publishing), 2014.

Phan Chi, "Eighty-One Fierce Days and Nights in Quảng Trị's Ancient Citadel in 1972." *The People's Army Newspaper Online,* July 9, 2012. https://en.qdnd.vn/military/war-files/81-fierce-days-and-nights-in-quang-tri-ancient-citadel-in-1972-part-1-431967

Prados, John. *The Blood Road: The Ho Chi Minh Trail and the Vietnam War*. New York: John Wiley and Sons, 2000.

PSYOP (Psychological Operations). *Operation Wandering Soul (Vietnam War "Ghost Tape" Campaign)*, audiotape. https://www.youtube.com/watch?v=1ZjZkdkv_is

Russell, Bertrand. *War Crimes in Vietnam*. London: George Allen & Unwin, 2009.

Schell, Jonathan. *The Military Half: An Account of Destruction in Quang Nai and Quang Tin*. New York: Alfred A. Knopf, 1968.

Spector, Ronald H. "Vietnam War." *Encyclopaedia Britannica*, October 11, 2020. https://www.britannica.

com/event/Vietnam-War

Tambini, Anthony J. *Wiring Vietnam: The Electronic Wall.* Lanham, Maryland: Rowman & Littlefield, 2007.

Trường Chinh. *Marxism and Vietnamese Culture (Chủ nghĩa Mác và vấn đề văn hóa Việt Nam).* Hanoi: Sự thật (Truth) Publishing House, 1974.

Trương Như Tảng. *A Vietcong Memoir.* London: Vintage Books, 1986.

Tucker, Spencer C. *Encyclopedia of the Vietnam War.* Oxford: Oxford University Press, 2011.

Turner, Karen Gottschang with Phan Thanh Hao. *Even the Women Must Fight: Memories of War from North Vietnam.* John Wiley & Sons, 1998.

Turse, Nick. *Kill Anything That Moves: The Real American War in Vietnam.* New York: Henry Holt and Company, 2013.

Valentino, Benjamin A. *Final Solutions: Mass Killing and Genocide in the 20th Century.* Ithaca, NY: Cornell University Press, 2005.

Van Staaveren, Jacob. *Interdiction in Southern Laos, 1960–1968.* Washington DC: Center for Air Force History, 1993.

Vietnam Veterans against the War. *The Winter Soldier Investigation: An Inquiry into American War Crimes.* Boston: Beacon Press, 1972.

Võ Nguyên Giáp (General). *People's War, People's Army.* Hanoi: Thế Giới, 2005.

----. *Điện Biên Phủ: Rendez-vous with History.* Hanoi: Thế Giới, 2004.

Vongpakay, Theap. *The Storm of Life (Pha Nou Xivit).* Vientiane: 2003.

Vongsavanh, Soutchay (General). *RLG Military Operations and Activities in the Laotian Panhandle.* Washington, DC: US Army Center of Military History, 1981.

Wernick, Adam. "What really happened in the Gulf of Tonkin in 1964?" LBJ's War, *The World*, PRI.org, September 14, 2017. https://www.pri.org/stories/2017-09-14/what-really-happened-gulf-tonkin-1964

Whitcomb, Darrel D. "Tonnage and Technology: Air Power on the Ho Chi Minh Trail." *Air Power History*, Vol.44, No.1, Spring 1997. https://www.jstor.org/stable/i26287781

Whitney, Craig R. "Quảng Trị in Ruins After Battles." *The New York Times*, October 8, 1972. https://www.nytimes.com/1972/10/08/archives/quangtri-in-ruins-after-battles-quangtri-city-after-battles-is.html

Wikipedia. *Vietnam War Casualties.* https://en.wikipedia.org/wiki/Vietnam_War_casualties

Wouk, Herman. *War and Remembrance.* Boston: Little Brown, and Company, 1978.

Xuân Đinh. "One Man Who Opened the Blood Road." *cadn.com.vn (Police News Online),* April 22, 2011. http://cadn.com.vn/news/64_6796_gap-nguoi-mo-con-duong-mau-.aspx

Yên Khương. "Poet Lâm Thị Mỹ Dạ: Real Life is Like a Legend." *Báo Gia đình Online.* October 13, 2009. http://giadinh.net.vn/giai-tri/nha-tho-lam-thi-my-da-cuoc-doi-that-ma-nhu-huyen-thoai-2009101204077441.htm

*TELEVISION AND FILM*

Burns, Ken and Lynn Novick, directors. Script by Geoffrey Ward and narration by Peter Coyote.

*The Vietnam War*. A ten-part series. PBS, September 17, 2017.

Morris, Errol. *The Fog of War: Eleven Lessons from the Life of Robert S. McNamara*. Directed by Errol Morris and starring Robert McNamara. Cannes: Sony Picture Classics. May 21, 2003.

### *GOVERNMENT DOCUMENTS AND WEBSITES*

International Committee of the Red Cross (IRC). "United States of America: Practice Related to Rule 76. Herbicides. National Case-law." Customary IHL Database, 2017. https://ihl-databases.icrc.org/customary-ihl/eng/docs/v2_cou_us_rule76

The People's Army. www.qdnd.vn

The Trường Sơn Association. hoitruongson.vn

The Vietnamese Communist Party. dangcongsan.vn

The Vietnamese Communist Party Documents (*Văn kiện Đảng Toàn tập Đảng cộng sản Việt Nam*). Vols. 1–69. Hanoi: National Political Publishing House,1997–2016. http://tulieuvankien.dangcongsan.vn/van-kien-tu-lieu-ve-dang/van-kien-dang-toan-tap

The Vietnamese National Archives II. http://luutruvn.com/

United Nations Archives. "Article 14, Agreement on the Cessation of Hostilities in Vietnam, July 20, 1954." S-0901-0001-01-00001. https://search.archives.un.org/uploads/r/united-nations-archives/b/b/2/.pdf

United Nations Treaty Collection. "Declaration 1 on the Neutrality of Laos." No. 6564, July 23, 1962. https://treaties.un.org/doc/Publication/UNTS/Volume%20456/volume-456-I-6564-English.pdf

US Congress. *Joint resolution to promote the maintenance of international peace and security in Southeast Asia*. Public Law 88–408. US Statutes at Large 78 (August 10, 1964): 384. https://www.govinfo.gov/content/pkg/STATUTE-78/pdf/STATUTE-78-Pg384.pdf

## FURTHER READING

### *WAR ART, CULTURE, AND HERITAGE*

Buchanan, Sherry. "Socialist Republic of Vietnam 1945–." *A History of Communist Posters*. London: Reaktion, 2017.

––––. *Vietnam Posters*. Collection of David Heather. London: Prestel, 2009.

––––. *Vietnam Zippos: American Soldiers' Engravings & Stories, 1965–1973*. Contributions by Bradford Edwards. Chicago: University of Chicago Press, 2007.

Colani, Madeleine. "L'âge de la pierre dans la province de Hòa Bình." *Mémoires du Service Géologique de l'Indochine* 13, 1927.

Harrison-Hall, Jessica. *Vietnam Behind the Lines: Images from the War, 1965–1975*. Contributions by Sherry Buchanan and Thu Stern. London: British Museum Press, 2002.

Howard, Michael C. *Transnationalism in Ancient and Medieval Societies: The Role of Cross-Border Trade and Travel*. Jefferson, North Carolina: McFarland, 2012.

Jamieson, Neil L. *Understanding*

*Vietnam*. Berkeley, California: University of California Press, 1993.

Kiernan, Ben. *Việt Nam: A History from Earliest Times to the Present*. Oxford: Oxford University Press, 2017.

Ngọc, Hữu. *Wandering Through Vietnamese Culture*. Hanoi: Thế Giới, 2004.

Nguyễn Thị Điều. "A mythographical journey to modernity: The textual and symbolic transformations of the Hùng Kings founding myths." *Journal of Southeast Asian Studies*, National University of Singapore, Volume 44, Issue 2, June 2013: 315–337. https://doi.org/10.1017/S002246341300009X

Ninh, Kim N. B. *A World Transformed: Politics of Culture in Revolutionary Vietnam, 1945–1965*. Ann Arbor, Michigan: The University of Michigan Press, 2005.

Pelley, Patricia M. *Postcolonial Vietnam: New Histories of the National Past*. Durham, North Carolina: Duke University Press, 2002.

Quang Phòng. *Vietnamese Painting from 1925 up to Now*. Hanoi: 1995.

Schwenkel, Christina. *The American War in Contemporary Vietnam: Transnational Remembrance and Representation*. Bloomington, Indiana: Indiana University Press, 2009.

*GENERAL*

Bao Ninh. *The Sorrow of War*. London: Vintage Classic, 1994.

Bodard, Lucien. *La guerre d'Indochine*. Paris: Grasset, 1997.

Ellsberg, Daniel. *Secrets: A Memoir of Vietnam and the Pentagon Papers*. Penguin Books, 2003.

Fall, Bernard B. *Street without Joy: The French Debacle in Indochina*. Mechanicsburg, PA: Stackpole Books, 1994.

Hastings, Max. *Vietnam: An Epic Tragedy 1945–1975*. London: William Collins, 2018.

Karnow, Stanley. *Vietnam: A History*. London: Penguin Books, 1997.

Logevall, Fredrik. *Embers of War: The Fall of an Empire and the Making of America's Vietnam*. New York: Random House, 2014.

Sheehan, Neil. *A Bright Shining Lie*. London: Picador, 1990.

## IMAGE CREDITS

COVER IMAGE Dramatic landscape with lonely fisherman and tree reflection on the fog lake. Dalat, Lâm Đồng, Vietnam. Photo monochrome version by Khanh Bui.

BACK COVER FLAP IMAGE The author at the entrance of an escape tunnel at the Việt Cộng headquarters at the end of the Trail, Tây Ninh Province. Photo by Trần Thị Huỳnh Nga.

PAGES 006–007 Phan Hoài Phi, *On the Ho Chi Minh Trail*, oil on canvas, 1995, 120 x 90 cm. Collection of the artist. Photo by Sherry Buchanan.

PAGE 008 On the Trail through southern Laos. Photo by Sherry Buchanan.

PAGES 010–011 On the Trail through the north of Vietnam. Photo by Sherry Buchanan.

PAGE 012 Nguyễn Văn Trúc, *Carrying Ammunition*, watercolor, 1971, 14.5 x 20.5 cm. Private collection. Photo by Hans Kemp.

PAGE 048 War artist's hammock. Collection of the Ho Chi Minh City (HCMC) Fine Arts Museum. Photo by Hans Kemp.

PAGE 048 Huỳnh Phương Đông, *Peace (Hòa Bình)*, pastel, 1975. Collection of the estate of the artist. Photo by Hans Kemp.

PAGE 049 Lê Lam, *Untitled,* watercolor, no date, 25 x 32 cm. Collection of the HCMC Fine Arts Museum. Photo by Hans Kemp.

PAGE 049 War artist's watercolor set and paintbrushes. Collection of the HCMC Fine Arts Museum. Photo by Hans Kemp.

PAGES 072–073 On Route 1A, at the Temple of Lady Triệu, Thanh Hóa Province. Photo by Sherry Buchanan.

PAGE 101 Off Route 15, in the Phong Nha-Kẻ Bàng National Park, Quảng Bình Province. Photo by Sam D. Cruz.

PAGE 108 On Route 15, the author in the Phong Nha Caves, Quảng Bình Province. Photo by Nam Nguyen.

PAGE 114 On Route 12A, Nguyễn Thị Kim Huế, the defender of the Mụ Giạ Pass. Photo by Sherry Buchanan.

PAGE 115 Photograph of Nguyễn Thị Kim Huế holding a bouquet of flowers with President Hồ Chí Minh at the National Congress of the Youth Volunteer Corps, Hanoi, July 1967. Photo by Sherry Buchanan.

PAGE 124 Nguyễn Văn Trực, *Untitled,* watercolor, 1967, 20 x 29.5 cm. Private collection. Photo by Hans Kemp.

PAGE 125 On Route 15, sunset in the Phong Nha-Kẻ Bàng National Park, Quảng Bình Province. Photo by Saigon85.

PAGE 131 On Route 20, in the Cave of the Eight Youth Volunteers *(Di tích lịch Hang 8 Cô TNXP),* Quảng Bình Province. Photo by Sherry Buchanan.

PAGES 142–143 Near the junction of Routes 15 and 9, a tank relic on the airfield of the US Marine Combat Base, Khe Sanh, Quảng Trị Province. Photo by Sherry Buchanan.

PAGE 158 Artist unknown, *Sniper*, ink on paper, 1968. Collection of the HCMC Fine Arts Museum. Photo by Hans Kemp.

PAGE 159 Heroine Hoàng Thị Mai who served with the Youth Volunteer Corps. At Project RENEW, Đông Hà,

Quảng Trị Province. Photo by Sherry Buchanan.

PAGES 174–175 On the Laotian Trail, at a river near Xepon. Photo by Sherry Buchanan.

PAGE 188 On Route 23, between Xepon and Salavan, Laos. Car video screenshots.

PAGE 189 On Route 23, a watchman oversees the crossing of a bridge. Photo by Sherry Buchanan.

PAGE 199 On Route 23, tabletop mountain at sunset between Xepon and Salavan. Photo by Sherry Buchanan.

PAGE 206 On the Laotian Trail, at the Tad Lo Falls, Bolaven Plateau. Photo by Sherry Buchanan.

PAGE 207 Nguyễn Văn Hoàng, *Early Morning River Crossing (Hành quân vượt sông sớm)*, watercolor, February 28, 1972, 24 x 40 cm. Collection of the HCMC Fine Arts Museum. Photo by Hans Kemp.

PAGE 207 Nguyễn Văn Hoàng, *Crossing the River (Vượt thác trên sông)*, watercolor, December 2, 1971, 22 x 42 cm. Collection of the HCMC Fine Arts Museum. Photo by Hans Kemp.

PAGE 215 Sunrise on the Mekong River near Champasak, the westernmost point of the Trail. Photo by Sherry Buchanan.

PAGE 223 On Route 14, the 1975 victory monument in Buôn Ma Thuột, Đắk Lắk Province. Photo by Sherry Buchanan.

PAGE 230 The twenty-first-century skyline of Ho Chi Minh City at night, 2017. Photo by Long Bao.

PAGE 240 Huỳnh Thị Kim Tiến, *In the Forest*, oil on canvas, 2000, 90 x 110 cm.

PAGE 240 Oil lamp at the NLF headquarters. Photo by Sherry Buchanan.

PAGE 241 Reconstructed lodge at the NLF headquarters, Tây Ninh Province. Photo by Sherry Buchanan.

PAGE 248 Trần Trung Tín, *She Couldn't Study*, oil on photographic paper, Saigon 1981, 25 x 20 cm. Private Collection. Photo by Hans Kemp.

PAGE 252 The author with General Võ Nguyên Giáp (1911–2013), at his residence in Hanoi, March 31, 2006. Photo by Susan Hammond.

PAGE 279 On Route 15, the Trường Sơn National Martyrs' Cemetery, Quảng Trị Province. Photo by Loner Nguyen.

I would like to thank all those who, by sharing their stories, made this book possible.

Despite all the help I received, I must take full responsibility for the interpretations in this book.

On Route 15, the Trường Sơn National Martyrs' Cemetery, Quảng Trị Province.